D1360380

WRITER'S JOURNAL
experiments

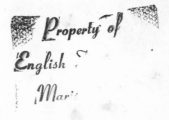

Property of
English
Mari

Property of
English Department
Marist School

domains
in language and composition

WRITER'S JOURNAL

experiments

Dalton H. McBee

HARCOURT BRACE JOVANOVICH, INC.

New York Chicago San Francisco Atlanta Dallas

DALTON H. McBEE has taught in secondary schools in New Hampshire and Florida. For the past sixteen years he has been an instructor in English at Phillips Academy, Andover, Massachusetts, where he currently serves as Admissions Officer and Director of Financial Aid.

Copyright © 1972 by Harcourt Brace Jovanovich, Inc.

All rights reserved. No part of this publication may be reproduced or transmitted in any form or by any means, electronic or mechanical, including photocopy, recording, or any information storage and retrieval system, without permission in writing from the publisher.

PRINTED IN THE UNITED STATES OF AMERICA
ISBN 0-15-312336-2

ACKNOWLEDGMENTS: For permission to reprint copyrighted material, grateful acknowledgment is made to the following publishers, authors, and agents:

THE AMERICAN-SCANDINAVIAN FOUNDATION: "The Father" by Björnstjerne Björnson.
APPLETON-CENTURY-CROFTS: From *Understanding Fiction* by Brooks & Warren, copyright 1943, 1959.
ARNO PRESS INC.: From "Notes on Sculpture" by Henry Moore from *The Painter's Object* by Myfanwy Evans.
ATLANTIC-LITTLE, BROWN AND COMPANY: From *Reading and Writing* by Robert M. Gay, copyright 1935 by Robert M. Gay. From *The Theatre of Revolt* by Robert Brustein, copyright © 1962, 1963, 1964 by Robert Brustein.
ATLANTIC-LITTLE, BROWN AND COMPANY and THE BODLEY HEAD: From "An Old Man on the River Bank" from *Poems* by George Seferis, translated by Rex Warner, English translation © Rex Warner 1960.
THE ATLANTIC MONTHLY PRESS: From "The Peripatetic Reviewer" by Edward Weeks from *The Atlantic Monthly*.
ERIC P. BEST: "The Silers" by Eric Best, copyright © 1972 by Eric Best.
THE BOBBS-MERRILL COMPANY, INC.: From *The Delight of Great Books* by John Erskine, copyright 1928 by The Bobbs-Merrill Company, Inc.
THE BOSTON GLOBE: From the article on Edwin Lahey by Louis Lyons from *The Boston Globe*, July 18, 1969.
BRANDT & BRANDT, MISS SONIA BROWNELL and SECKER & WARBURG, LTD.: From *Nineteen Eighty Four* by George Orwell, copyright, 1949 by Harcourt Brace Jovanovich, Inc.
CECILE S. CLARK: From *Eugene O'Neill, The Man and His Plays* by Barrett H. Clark, Dover Publications, 1960.
B. MARIE DELL: "The Blanket" by Floyd Dell.
DELL PUBLISHING CO., INC.: From *Poetry: A Modern Guide to Its Understanding and Enjoyment* by Elizabeth Drew, copyright © 1959 by Elizabeth Drew.
J. M. DENT & SONS LTD. and the TRUSTEES OF THE JOSEPH CONRAD ESTATE: From *Youth* by Joseph Conrad.
DOUBLEDAY & CO., INC.: From "Writing About Science," by David O. Woodbury and "The Matter of Poetry" by Robert P. Tristram Coffin, both selections from *Writers on Writing*, edited by Herschel Brickell, copyright 1949 by Doubleday & Co., Inc., 1949 by Saturday Review Associates, Inc. From "Simplicity in Art" from *The Responsibilities of the Novelist* by Frank Norris.
DOUBLEDAY & CO., INC. and VICTOR GOLLANCZ, LTD.: from *Lucky Jim* by Kingsley Amis, copyright 1953 by Kingsley Amis.
DOUBLEDAY & CO., INC., the LITERARY EXECUTOR OF W. SOMERSET MAUGHAM, and WM. HEINEMANN LTD.: From "The Summing Up" by W. Somerset Maugham, copyright 1938 by W. Somerset Maugham, from the book, *The Maugham Reader*. From "The Lotus-Eater" by W. Somerset Maugham, copyright 1935 by W. Somerset Maugham, from the book, *The Maugham Reader*.

DUKE UNIVERSITY PRESS and CLINTON S. BURHANS, JR.: From *The Old Man and the Sea: Hemingway's Tragic Vision of Man*" by Clinton S. Burhans, Jr., from *American Literature*, Vol. XXXI, January 1960.

E. P. DUTTON & CO., INC.: From *Supergrow: Essays and Reports on Imagination in America* by Benjamin DeMott, copyright, ©, 1969 by Benjamin DeMott. The essay from which this excerpt is taken first appeared in somewhat different form in *The New York Times Magazine*. From *We* by Eugene Zamiatin, translated by Gregory Zilboorg with an introduction by Peter Rudy, copyright, 1924, by E. P. Dutton & Co., Inc.; copyright renewal, 1952, by Gregory Zilboorg. A Dutton Paperback.

ESQUIRE MAGAZINE: From "Catch Her in the Oatmeal" by Dan Greenberg from *Esquire Magazine*, February 1958, © 1958 by Esquire, Inc.

FARRAR, STRAUS & GIROUX, INC.: From *Imitations* by Robert Lowell, copyright © 1958, 1959, 1960, 1961 by Robert Lowell. From *Complete Poems* by Randall Jarrell, copyright © 1945, 1969 by Mrs. Randall Jarrell.

HARCOURT BRACE JOVANOVICH, INC.: From *The Playwright as Thinker* by Eric Bentley, © 1946, 1967 by Eric Bentley. "Pity This Busy Monster, Manunkind" by E. E. Cummings from *One Times One* by E. E. Cummings, copyright 1944 by E. E. Cummings from his volume *Poems 1923-1954*. "A Hole in the Floor" by Richard Wilbur, copyright 1961 by Richard Wilbur from *Advice to a Prophet and Other Poems* by Richard Wilbur. From "The Waste Land" from *Collected Poems 1909-1962* by T. S. Eliot.

HARCOURT BRACE JOVANOVICH, INC., MISS SONIA BROWNELL and SECKER & WARBURG, LTD.: From "Politics and the English Language" in *Shooting an Elephant and Other Essays* by George Orwell, copyright, 1945, 1946, 1949, 1950 by Sonia Brownell Orwell.

HARPER & ROW, PUBLISHERS, INCORPORATED: From "Calamophobia, or Hints Toward a Writer's Discipline" by Jacques Barzun in *The Writer's Book*, edited by Helen Hull, copyright 1950 by Author's League of America, Inc. From "Security"—September, 1938—in *One Man's Meat* by E. B. White, copyright 1938, 1966 by E. B. White. From *Life on the Mississippi* by Mark Twain. From "Fiction: Some Personal Beliefs" by Christopher LaFarge in *The Writer's Book*, edited by Helen Hull, copyright 1950 by Author's League of America, Inc.

HOLT, RINEHART AND WINSTON, INC.: From *Preface to Critical Reading*, Revised Edition, by Richard D. Altick. From *Steppenwolf* by Hermann Hesse, translated by Basil Creighton, copyright 1929, © 1957 by Holt, Rinehart and Winston, Inc. " 'Out, Out—' " from *The Poetry of Robert Frost* edited by Edward Connery Lathem, copyright 1916, © 1969 by Holt, Rinehart and Winston, Inc.; copyright 1944 by Robert Frost. From "Education by Poetry" from *Selected Prose of Robert Frost* edited by Hyde Cox and Edward Connery Lathem, copyright © 1966 by Holt, Rinehart and Winston, Inc.

HOUGHTON MIFFLIN COMPANY: From *Poetry and Poets* by Amy Lowell, copyright 1958 by Harvey H. Bundy and G. d'andelot Belin. "Patterns" from *The Complete Poetical Works of Amy Lowell*, copyright 1952 by Houghton Mifflin Company. From *The Nature of Drama* by Hubert Heffner, copyright © 1959 by Hubert Heffner.

INDIANA UNIVERSITY PRESS, CANADIAN BROADCASTING CORPORATION and NORTHROP FRYE: From *The Educated Imagination* by Northrop Frye, The Massey Lectures, copyright © Canadian Broadcasting Corporation, 1963, CBC Publications, Toronto; copyright © 1964 by Indiana University Press.

THE JOHNS HOPKINS PRESS and the BALTIMORE SUN: "Gamalielese" from *On Politics: A Carnival of Buncombe* by H L. Mencken. Originally appeared in the *Baltimore Sun*, March 7, 1921.

MARGOT JOHNSON AGENCY: From "The Snow Globe" by Howard Nemerov from *The Salt Garden* by Howard Nemerov, copyright by Howard Nemerov, 1955.

ROBERT P. KNAPP, JR.: From "A Letter" by Robert P. Knapp, Jr.

ALFRED A. KNOPF, INC.: "The Emperor of Ice Cream," copyright 1923 and renewed 1951 by Wallace Stevens, from *The Collected Poems of Wallace Stevens*. From *Life With Father* by Clarence Day, copyright 1933, 1935 and renewed 1962 by Katherine B. Day. From *By Land and by Sea* by Samuel E. Morison.

ALFRED A. KNOPF, INC. and CURTIS BROWN LTD.: From "Out of a Book" from *Collected Impressions* by Elizabeth Bowen. Published 1950 by Alfred A. Knopf, Inc.

LITTLE, BROWN AND COMPANY: "After Great Pain" from *The Complete Poems of Emily Dickinson* edited by Thomas H. Johnson, copyright 1929, © 1957 by Mary L. Hampson. From *The Night the Old Nostalgia Burned Down* by Frank Sullivan, copyright 1948 by The Curtis Publishing Company; copyright 1946, 1948, 1949, 1950, 1951, 1952, 1953 by Frank Sullivan.

THE MACMILLAN COMPANY: From *The Elements of Style* by E. B. White & William Strunk, Jr., copyright © 1959 by the Macmillan Company.

BRANDER MATTHEWS DRAMATIC MUSEUM: From *Papers on Playmaking*, edited by Brander Matthews.

THE NATION: From an essay by Joseph Wood Krutch from *The Nation*, April 17, 1937.

NATIONAL COUNCIL OF TEACHERS OF ENGLISH: From "Writers on Learning to Write" by Lee Frank Howe from *The English Journal*, October 1964.

NEW DIRECTIONS PUBLISHING CORPORATION: "Portrait of a Girl in Glass" from *One Arm and Other Stories* by Tennessee Williams, copyright 1948 by Tennessee Williams.

NEW DIRECTIONS PUBLISHING CORPORATION, CHATTO AND WINDUS LTD., and MR. HAROLD OWEN: "Futility" from *The Collected Poems of Wilfred Owen,* copyright © Chatto & Windus Ltd. 1963.

NEW DIRECTIONS PUBLISHING CORPORATION, J. M. DENT & SONS LTD., and the TRUSTEES FOR THE COPYRIGHTS OF THE LATE DYLAN THOMAS: From "Patricia, Edith and Arnold" from *Portrait of the Artist as a Young Dog,* copyright 1940 by New Directions Publishing Corporation.

THE NEW LEADER: From "A Literary Conversation with Milovan Djilas" from *The New Leader,* December 16, 1968, copyright © The American Labor Conference on International Affairs, Inc.

THE PARIS REVIEW: From the Graham Greene Interview first published in issue no. 3 (Autumn 1953) of *The Paris Review.*

G. P. PUTNAM'S SONS: An excerpt by Anton Chekhov from *Letters on the Short Story, the Drama and Other Literary Topics,* edited by Louis S. Friedland.

RAND McNALLY & COMPANY: From *Counterpoint* by Roy Newquist, copyright 1964 by Rand McNally & Co.

RANDOM HOUSE, INC.: "As you say (not without sadness)" from *The Bourgeois Poet* by Karl Shapiro, copyright © 1964 by Karl Shapiro. From *The Glass Menagerie* by Tennessee Williams, copyright 1945 by Tennessee Williams and Edwina D. Williams. "The Art of Poetry" from *The Complete Works of Horace,* edited by Casper J. Kraemer, Jr. From "Must the Novelist Crusade?" copyright © 1965 by Eudora Welty. This will appear in a collection of literary essays by Eudora Welty to be published by Random House, Inc.

THE REGENTS OF THE UNIVERSITY OF CALIFORNIA: From *Benjamin Franklin: The Autobiography of Benjamin Franklin,* edited by Leonard Labaree and revised by Farrand.

THE BEN ROTH AGENCY, INC.: "Lucky Goldilocks" by Anthony Brode from *Punch,* November 1954, © Punch, London.

SATURDAY REVIEW, INC. and ROBERT FRIEND: "In the Orchard" by Robert Friend, from the *Saturday Review,* September 18, 1957, copyright 1957 by Saturday Review, Inc.

SATURDAY REVIEW, INC. and WILLIAM SAROYAN: From "Why Does a Writer Write" by William Saroyan from *Saturday Review,* February 15, 1961, copyright 1961 by Saturday Review, Inc.

SARAH FISHER SCOTT: From "Theme Writing" by Dorothy Canfield Fisher reprinted in *Essays in Modern Thought,* edited by Thomas R. Cook.

SCOTT, FORESMAN AND COMPANY: From *Reflections on a Gift of Watermelon Pickle and Other Modern Verse* by Stephen Dunning et al., copyright © 1968 by Scott, Foresman and Company. Adapted from "A Summary of All the Ways of Varying" from *Sentence and Theme,* 3rd edition, by C. H. Ward, copyright 1929, 1935 by Scott, Foresman and Company.

CHARLES SCRIBNER'S SONS: From *The Story of a Novel,* pages 8–9 by Thomas Wolfe, copyright 1936 Charles Scribner's Sons; renewal copyright © 1964 Paul Gitlin, Administrator C.T.A. From *A Farewell to Arms* by Ernest Hemingway, copyright 1929 Charles Scribner's Sons; renewal copyright © 1957 Ernest Hemingway. From *The Principles of Playwriting* by Brander Matthews, copyright 1919 Brander Matthews; renewal copyright 1947. From "How I Write My Short Stories" by Jesse Stuart from *Short Stories for Discussion* by Albert K. Ridout and Jesse Stuart, copyright © 1965 Charles Scribner's Sons.

SIMON & SCHUSTER, INC.: From *Enjoyment of Laughter* by Max Eastman, copyright © 1936 by Simon and Schuster, Inc. From *Television Plays* by Paddy Chayefsky, copyright © 1955 by Paddy Chayefsky. From *How to Read a Book* by Mortimer J. Adler, copyright © 1940, 1966 by Mortimer J. Adler.

TIME, THE WEEKLY NEWSMAGAZINE: From *Time,* April 11, 1969, copyright Time Inc., 1969. Time Review of *The Dorp* by Frieda Arkin from *Time,* August 29, 1969, copyright Time Inc., 1969.

TUDOR PUBLISHING COMPANY: From *Keys to Art* by John Canaday.

UNIVERSITY OF TEXAS PRESS: From *Other Inquisitions* by Jorge Luis Borges, translated by Ruth Simms, 1964.

THE UNIVERSITY PRESS OF VIRGINIA: From *Faulkner in the University,* edited by Frederick Gwynn and Joseph Blotner, University of Virginia Press, 1959, Charlottesville.

THE VIKING PRESS, INC.: From *Death of a Salesman* by Arthur Miller, copyright 1949 by Arthur Miller. From *The Grapes of Wrath* by John Steinbeck. From *Once There Was a War* by John Steinbeck, copyright 1943 by John Steinbeck.

WESLEYAN UNIVERSITY PRESS: "The Lifeguard" from *Drowning with Others* by James Dickey, copyright © 1961 by James Dickey.

MASON WILLIAMS: From "ode to the network censor" from *The Mason Williams Reading Matter* by Mason Williams, copyright © 1964, 1966, 1967, 1969 by Mason Williams, published by Doubleday & Company, Inc.

WORLD PUBLISHING COMPANY: From *Webster's New World Dictionary of the American Language,* College Edition, copyright 1968 by The World Publishing Company, Cleveland and New York.

YALE UNIVERSITY PRESS: From *Nathaniel Hawthorne: A Biography* by Randall Stewart.

For Lee and Alice,
Coles and Joel

Contents

Unit 4
Reading for Writing

Unit 5
Fiction

UNIT 1

Learn from Models

Education should involve an
exposure to greatness.
—ALFRED NORTH WHITEHEAD

1|1

IMITATION

In a certain sense all literature begins with imitation.

STEPHEN LEACOCK

. . . it was so, if we could trace it out, that all men have learned; and that is why a revival of letters is always accompanied or heralded by a cast back to earlier and fresher models.

ROBERT LOUIS STEVENSON

It is best to study the worn technique of Ibsen or the wonderful preciseness of Lillian Hellman, after whom I carefully modeled my first dramas.

PADDY CHAYEFSKY

After that Sunday afternoon (in 1896) I read many poets (Chaucer, Keats, Shelley, Milton, and Shakespeare, more than others) and wrote my imitations of them.

JOHN MASEFIELD

All through my boyhood and youth I was known and pointed out for the pattern of an idler; and yet I was always busy on my own private end, which was to learn to write. I kept always two books in my pocket, one to read, one to write in. As I walked, my mind was busy fitting what I saw with appropriate words; when I sat by the roadside I would either read, or a pencil and a penny version book would be in my hand to note down the features of the scene, or commemorate some halting stanzas. Thus I lived with words. And what I thus wrote was for no ulterior use; it was written consciously for practice. It was not so much that I wished to be an author (though I wished that too) as that I vowed

I would learn to write. That was a proficiency that tempted me; and I practiced to acquire it, as men learn to whittle, in a wager with myself. Description was the principal field of my exercise; for to anyone with senses there is always something worth describing, and town and country are but one continuous subject. But I worked in other ways also. . . .

Whenever I read a book or a passage that particularly pleased me, in which a thing was said or an effect rendered with propriety, in which there was either some conspicuous force or some happy distinction in the style, I must sit down at once and set myself to ape that quality. I was unsuccessful and I knew it, and tried again, and was again unsuccessful, and always unsuccessful; but at least, in these vain bouts, I got some practice in rhythm, in construction and the coordination of parts. I have thus played the sedulous ape to Hazlitt, to Lamb, to Wordsworth, to Sir Thomas Browne, to Defoe, to Hawthorne, to Montaigne, to Baudelaire, and to Obermann.

That, like it or not, is the way to learn to write; whether I have profited or not, that is the way. It was so Keats learned, and there was never a finer temperament for literature than Keats's; it was so, if we could trace it out, that all men have learned; and that is why a revival of letters is always accompanied or heralded by a cast back to earlier and fresher models. Perhaps I hear someone cry out: but this is not the way to be original! It is not; nor is there any way but to be born so. Nor yet, if you are born original, is there anything here that should astonish the considerate. Before he can tell what cadences he truly prefers, the student should have tried all that are possible; before he can choose and preserve a fitting key to words, he should long have practiced the literary scales; and it is only after years of such gymnastics that he can sit down at last, legions of words swarming to his call, dozens of turns of phrase simultaneously bidding for his choice, and he himself knowing what he wants to do and (within the narrow limit of a man's ability) able to do it.

ROBERT LOUIS STEVENSON
from *How I Learned to Write*

Stevenson speaks of two books—one to read, one to write in. Here, and elsewhere in this book, the interrelation of reading and writing is made explicit. At the same time, we are supplied with a method. We, too, must be both readers and writers and in both occupations ever concerned with the value of words.

"I practiced to acquire it, . . . in a wager with myself."

Stevenson is sensitive to diction and style. Unabashedly, he sets out to imitate admirable qualities. But note, he does not talk about mindless imitation, or a universal success formula; rather he is pointing to specific cases and saying that these, properly studied, offer the best instruction. His method is one of practice rather than of precept. The practice that he points to is careful, even more than careful! His word is "sedulous": sincere, diligent imitation.

The reader-writer is not enjoined to make a monkey of himself but rather to study every nuance of the original so thoroughly that he can meticulously reproduce the finest shading of detail. Stevenson, himself, thus played "the sedulous ape" (the diligent imitator) in order to realize the ultimate goal, the ultimate possibility, which is to be the writer who "can sit down at last, legions of words swarming to his call, dozens of turns of phrase simultaneously bidding for his choice, and he himself knowing what he wants to do and (within the narrow limits of a man's ability) able to do it."

imitation: A literary work . . . designed to reproduce the style or manner of another author.
from *Webster's Third New International Dictionary*

Imitation differs from paraphrase; the paraphrase seeks to make meaning clear and, consequently, often uses two or three words where one appears in the original. Paraphrase puts a premium on translation; imitation places emphasis on reproducing style.

In starting your own work in imitation, be patient. Resist the temptation to range beyond your model—that will come with emulation after you have had firsthand experience with close imitation. At that point you will be better able to manage assignments that demand originality. The point now is to be aware of all that happens in the model itself and to reproduce the form and devices of the model with such skill as to make your work and the model appear as from the same pen. Were your motives dishonest, your work might be called a forgery, but because what you do is done "for no ulterior use; it [is] written consciously for practice," you are not on your way to fail but on your way to learn to write.

Here is a model paragraph, taken from Joseph Conrad's "Youth." As you read it, note the degree to which Conrad succeeds in realizing his stated ambition: "My task which I am trying to achieve is, by the power of the written word, to make you hear, to make you feel—it is, before all, to make you *see*. That—and no more, and it is, everything."

And this is how I see the East. I have seen its secret places and have looked into its very soul; but now I see it always from a small boat, a high outline of mountains, blue and afar in the morning; like faint mist at noon; a jagged wall of purple at sunset. I have the feel of the oar in my hand, the vision of a scorching blue sea in my eyes. And I see a bay, a wide bay, smooth as glass and polished like ice, shimmering in the dark. A red light burns far off upon the gloom of the land, and the night is soft and warm. We drag at the oars with aching arms, and suddenly a puff of wind, a puff faint and tepid and laden with strange odors of blossoms, of aromatic wood, comes out of the still night—the first sigh of the East on my face. That I can never forget. It was impalpable and enslaving, like a charm, like a whispered promise of mysterious delight.

JOSEPH CONRAD
from "Youth"

Here are two examples of student imitation. They vary in quality; consider each before undertaking your own work.

And this is how I see Hawaii. I have seen its mountains and shores and have lived in its very heart: but now I see it from a road, its vast expanses spread before me in the morning, engulfing me at noon, and bidding me good-by at dusk. And I see a bay, where the balmy breezes gently toss the waves 'til the entire bay is laced with whitecaps.

ANONYMOUS

And this is the sea. I have come to know its secrets and have made them my own: but now I see it from my tiny island, a dazzling dance of fiery specks of gold at sunrise; a smooth blue-green carpet at noon; an ominous gray wall at sunset. I hear the lonely call of a gull in my ear, but cannot find it in the vast expanse of blue both above and below. And I see a spray, a fine white spray darting into the air—an impossible child of the great black sea. A flashing light warns of a plodding tramp steamer; the night wind is strong and free. The dirt-smoke of the tramp loses itself in the fresh, ocean air, the night air freshens, bringing with it that old salt-smell. That, I can never forget. It is the restless call of the unknown.

JOHN F. SEEGAL

But I still long for the West. Not the history or the glory or the newness of it—those things are for people who haven't been there. I long for a lake, high up in the mountains that surround it and guard it from intrusion with their sheer might. I dream of dozing on a boulder, flat, but not smooth, and warmed from the sun, which is dazzling even for closed eyes. The lake is green, deep, bottomless, luscious—liquid emeralds. Chipmunks run about in the sun's white haze. The only sounds are birds and somewhere a brook, cold and alive. We are resting our tired legs for a while. There is a breeze that sweeps through the pines, bearing their green smell and the smell of glaciers and pristine mountain air and pungent odors of moss and living things. And that breeze is my West. I have dreamed of it ever since. It was distinct, there. Yet it was indefinable, unattainable, like the passage of a ghost from paradise.

JOHN K. CRAFORD

In writing your own imitations, follow Robert Gay's advice: "Have faith in the great and natural principle of unconscious imitation, believing that what you learn in your practice will eventually affect profoundly your original writing."

At the moment, the aim is not originality but practice with techniques. How, for example, would your favorite writer have presented the East? How well can you present a scene with which you are familiar? How close can you come to doing the job after the manner of Conrad?

Guides to Imitation

1. Read the passage aloud until you get its rhythm running in your mind.
2. Follow the tone and diction of the original.
3. Reproduce sentence pattern faithfully. Your clauses and phrases should duplicate those of the model in *kind, order,* and *number.* Sentence length may be approximated. (How closely you wish to seek word-for-word correspondence is a matter of individual choice.)
4. Write on a topic that parallels the subject of the model. In order to promote individual thought, do not use the subject of the model itself.
5. Have your model before you as you work; refer to it unhesitatingly.

Here is one example of imitation:

Model: Better to wear out than to rust out.
ROBERT LOUIS STEVENSON

Imitation: Wiser to spend all than to save all.
A STUDENT

Assignment 1

1. Read the chapter up to this point.
2. In your journal do *one* of the following:
   a. Write your own imitation of the Conrad paragraph.
   b. Select a model you particularly like and imitate it.
   c. Imitate a professional writer whose work appears in this text.

Assignment 2

> Write quickly and you will never write well; write well and you will soon write quickly.
>
> QUINTILIAN

> Some ignorant, unlearned, and idle student, or some busy looker upon this poor little book, that hath neither will to do good himself, nor skill to judge right of others, but can lustily contemn, by pride and ignorance, all painful diligence and right order in study, will perchance say that I am too precise, too curious, in marking and piddling thus about the imitation of others, and that the old worthy authors did never busy their heads and wits, in following precisely what other men wrote, or else the manner how other men wrote.
>
> ROGER ASCHAM
> from *The Schoolmaster*

The old schoolmaster's statement carries truth to our day, and it expresses the position of this book. "Right order in study" does require painful diligence in imitation of what worthy authors have written. There is reward and need for precisely noting the matter and manner of the experts.

This method of study and imitation has a continuing tradition. Paddy Chayefsky says,

> The point is that each story demands its own kind of construction, and each writer must construct his stories as best suits his ways. I wouldn't

recommend that people just starting out as writers take this extravagant attitude, at least not at first. It is best to study the worn technique of Ibsen or the wonderful preciseness of Lillian Hellman, after whom I carefully modeled my first dramas. *The Front Page* by Hecht and MacArthur is another fine piece of orthodox structure. And the television drama is really not too different in structure from the stage play. They differ in weight and approach and substance, but they are both in the three-act form and follow the lines imposed by that form. Eventually, the writer attains a security in his ability and he breaks out here and there from the techniques of other writers and tells his own stories in his own way.

PADDY CHAYEFSKY
from *Television Plays*

As a prelude to the ultimate objective of "telling your own story in your own way" there is first the necessity of studying the tried techniques of orthodox structure.

1. Read the three excerpts in this assignment.
2. In your journal do *one* of the following:
   a. Use the Hemingway paragraph that follows as a model for a paragraph of your own.

In the late summer of that year we lived in a house in a village that looked across the river and the plain to the mountains. In the bed of the river there were pebbles and boulders, dry and white in the sun, and the water was clear and swiftly moving and blue in the channels. Troops went by the house and down the road and the dust they raised powdered the leaves of the trees. The trunks of the trees too were dusty and the leaves fell early that year and we saw the troops marching along the road and the dust rising and leaves, stirred by the breeze, falling and the soldiers marching and afterward the road bare and white except for the leaves.

ERNEST HEMINGWAY
from *A Farewell to Arms*

b. Imitate a model of your own choice. (Copy or paste the model into your journal.)

c. Try to write an imitation of a poem that you like.

Assignment 3

Edwin Lahey is a distinguished writer and reporter whose formal education terminated with grammar school but who, at thirty-six, was chosen one of Harvard's first Nieman fellows. Lahey was asked by Louis M. Lyons how he taught himself to write. Here is the answer as reported by Lyons.

> Mr. Lahey had grown up on the sidewalks of Chicago and his vocabulary was enriched with the argot of the streets. His sentences crackled with freshness and excitement. I once asked him how he taught himself to write. He said he had worked in a railroad freight shed and in the long spaces between trains he used to read Dickens and took to trying to write "sentences as long as Dickens'."
>
> LOUIS M. LYONS
> from *The Boston Globe*

1. Read the excerpt for this assignment.
2. In your journal do *one* of the following:
   a. Write an imitation of the model given below.

> It was Miss Murdstone who was arrived, and a gloomy-looking lady she was; dark, like her brother, whom she greatly resembled in face and voice; and with very heavy eyebrows, nearly meeting over her large nose, as if, being disabled by the wrongs of her sex from wearing whiskers, she had carried them to that account. She brought with her two uncompromising hard black boxes, with her initials on the lids in hard brass nails. When she paid the coachman she took her money out of a hard steel purse, and she kept the purse in a very jail of a bag which hung upon her arm by a heavy chain, and

shut up like a bite. I had never, at that time, seen such a metallic lady altogether as Miss Murdstone was.

CHARLES DICKENS
from *David Copperfield*

b. Write from a model of your own choice. (Copy or paste the model into your journal.)

c. Study the opening of a short story that you like. Then set about making a close imitation of it.

1|2

FURTHER IMITATION

The writer who knows the rules has a choice. He can follow the rules or break them. Whereas the writer who does not know or understand them has no choice. He can only break them.

JOAN RANSOM

At first there is a natural tendency to resist practice that calls for the continued use of models. After an attempt or two, one is apt to become impatient and say, "I want to get on with my own writing." And human nature being what it is, teachers and students press on in order to get at more important things, ultimately to discover that a good deal of time has been lost in making haste. True, one need not imitate forever, but a considerable experience with the method will bring its own rewards.

At this point you may ask, "But what is the goal? What is to be gained by following so closely the work of another?" The answer is practice—practice in essentials. The imitation of models requires you to:

1. practice close reading
2. practice seeing the shape and hearing the ring of sentences
3. practice recognizing what constitutes good writing, hence practice setting a standard for yourself
4. practice managing tone, diction, and sentence pattern

As an aid to your work with sentence pattern, here is a summary of the ways to vary a sentence, adapted from *Sentence and Theme* by C. H. Ward:

1. *Ask a question.*
    Do I dare?
2. *Use a form of command.*
    Go feasting elsewhere.

3. *Begin with an adverb.*
   Often have I been there.
4. *Begin with a preposition.*
   By this time you get the point.
5. *Use an appositive.*
   Muse, daughter of Zeus, tell us in our time.
6. *Begin with an object.*
   Her story the gods themselves will sing.
7. *Put something between the subject and verb.*
   His daughter, upon an island in the running sea, would not let Odysseus go.
8. *Begin with a verb.*
   Enter the butler.
9. *Use an active participle and have it modify some definite word.*
   A blinding flash was seen across the sky.
10. *Use passive and perfect participles.*
    The beaten gold lay shining in the sun.
    Having slept long hours, she arose.
11. *Use a direct quotation.*
    He said, "I shall go to my own house."
12. *Use a compound verb.*
    He turned and looked again.
13. *Use a gerund.*
    After traveling all these days, I am home.
14. *Use an infinitive.*
    To see the dawn in your own land is to be blessed.
15. *Combine simple sentences.*
    He lay down. He slept in peace.
    He lay down and slept in peace.
16. *Use a relative clause.*
    A man who is brave may journey far.
17. *Use a noun clause.*
    We were told that you had been given gifts.
18. *Use an adverb clause.*
    Odysseus looked just as he used to.
19. *Combine independent statements in complex sentences.*
    He leapt up. He picked a discus. He set it whirling.
    He leapt up that he might set the mighty discus whirling.

20. *Use compound sentences.*

   The roll of the sea waves wearied me, and the victuals in my ship ran low.

21. *Use indirect quotation and indirect question.*

   He asked if I had known the man and I was forced to say that I was not certain.

22. *Begin with a conjunction.*

   And the earth was without form, and void; . . .

23. *Use an expletive.*

   There is no excuse for what he did.

Assignment 4

1. Read the chapter up to this point.
2. In your journal do *one* of the following:
   a. Imitate the Hawthorne model that follows. Do as much as time permits.

   There, beside the fireplace, the brave old General used to sit; while the Surveyor—though seldom, when it could be avoided, taking upon himself the difficult task of engaging him in conversation—was fond of standing at a distance, and watching his quiet and almost slumberous countenance. He seemed away from us, although we saw him but a few yards off; remote, though we passed close beside his chair; unattainable, though we might have stretched forth our hands and touched his own. It might be that he lived a more real life within his thoughts than amid the unappropriate environment of the Collector's office. The evolutions of the parade; the tumult of the battle; the flourish of old heroic music, heard thirty years before;—such scenes and sounds, perhaps, were all alive before his intellectual sense. Meanwhile, the merchants and shipmasters, the spruce clerks and uncouth sailors, entered and departed; the bustle of this commercial and Custom House life kept up its little murmur round about him; and neither with the men nor their affairs did the General appear to sustain the most distant relation. He was as much out of place as an old sword—now rusty, but which had flashed once in the battle's front, and showed still a bright gleam along its blade—would have been, among the inkstands, paper-folders, and mahogany rulers, on the Deputy Collector's desk.

NATHANIEL HAWTHORNE
from *The Scarlet Letter*

b. Identify the variety of sentence forms used in the Hawthorne paragraph.

c. Work from a model of your own choice. (Copy or paste the model into your journal.)

Assignment 5

The two paragraphs by John Steinbeck that follow provide models for further imitation and close study.

The great troopship sneaks past the city and the tugs leave her, a dark thing steaming into the dark. On the decks and in the passages and in the bunks the thousands of men are collapsed in sleep. Only their faces show under the dim blue blackout lights —faces and an impression of tangled hands and feet and equipment. Officers and military police stand guard over this great sleep, a sleep multiplied, the sleep of thousands. An odor rises from the men, the characteristic odor of an army. It is the smell of wool and the bitter smell of fatigue and the smell of gun oil and leather. Troops always have this odor. The men lie sprawled, some with their mouths open, but they do not snore. Perhaps they are too tired to snore, but their breathing is a pulsing, audible thing.

JOHN STEINBECK
from *Once There Was a War*

And over the grass at the roadside a land turtle crawled, turning aside for nothing, dragging his high-domed shell over the grass. His hard legs and yellow-nailed feet threshed slowly through the grass, not really walking, but boosting and dragging his shell along. The barley beards slid off his shell, and the clover burrs fell on him and rolled to the ground. His horny beak was partly open, and his fierce, humorous eyes, under brows like fingernails, stared straight ahead. He came over the grass leaving a beaten trail behind him, and the hill, which was the highway embankment, reared up ahead of him. For a moment he stopped, his head held high. He blinked and looked up and down. At last he started to climb the embankment. Front clawed feet reached forward but did not touch. The hind feet kicked his shell along, and it scraped on the grass, and on the gravel. As the embankment grew steeper and steeper, the more frantic were the efforts of the land turtle.

JOHN STEINBECK
from "The Turtle"
in *The Grapes of Wrath*

1. Read the two Steinbeck excerpts.
2. In your journal do *one* of the following:
   a. Write a close imitation of either of the models presented here.
   b. Work from a model of your own choice. (Copy or paste the model into your journal.)
   c. Make a study of the sentence pattern used with regularity by a writer you admire. Report your findings in your journal. Include a model paragraph by the author and draw your illustrations from it.

Assignment 6

Before I start writing a novel I read *Candide* over again so that I may have in the back of my mind the touchstone of that lucidity, grace and wit. . . .

W. SOMERSET MAUGHAM
from *The Summing Up*

The following excerpt is from *Candide:*

Candide listened attentively to these remarks and conceived a great idea of the speaker; and, as the marchioness had been careful to place him beside her, he leaned over to her ear and took the liberty of asking her who was the man who talked so well. "He is a man of letters," said the lady, "who does not play cards and is sometimes brought here to supper by the abbé; he has a perfect knowledge of tragedies and books and he has written a tragedy which was hissed and a book of which only one copy has ever been seen outside his bookseller's shop and that was one he gave me." "The great man!" said Candide. "He is another Pangloss." Then, turning to him, Candide said: "Sir, no doubt you think that all is for the best in the physical world and in the moral, and that nothing could be otherwise than as it is?" "Sir," replied the man of letters, "I do not think anything of the sort. I think everything goes awry with us, that nobody knows his rank or his office, nor what he is doing, nor what he ought to do, and that except at supper, which is quite gay and where there appears to be a certain amount of sociability, all the rest of their time is passed in senseless quarrels: Jansenists with Molinists, lawyers with churchmen, men of letters with men of letters, courtiers with courtiers, financiers with the people, wives with husbands, relatives with relatives—'tis an eternal war." Candide replied: "I have seen worse things; but a wise man, who has since had the misfortune to be hanged, taught me that it is all for the best; these are only the shadows in a fair picture." "Your wise man who was hanged was poking fun at the world," said Martin; "and your shadows are horrible stains." "The stains are made by men," said Candide, "and they cannot avoid them." "Then it is not their fault," said Martin. Most of the gamblers, who had not the slightest understanding of this kind of talk, were drinking;

Martin argued with the man of letters and Candide told the hostess some of his adventures.

VOLTAIRE

This you will recognize as Jonathan Swift:

That we often put this powder into large hollow balls of iron, and discharged them by an engine into some city we were besieging, which would rip up the pavements, tear the houses to pieces, burst and throw splinters on every side, dashing out the brains of all who came near. That I knew the ingredients very well, which were cheap, and common; I understood the manner of compounding them, and could direct his workmen how to make those tubes of a size proportionable to all other things in his Majesty's kingdom, and the largest need not be above an hundred foot long; twenty or thirty of which tubes, charged with the proper quantity of powder and balls, would batter down the walls of the strongest town in his dominions in a few hours, or destroy the whole metropolis, if ever it should pretend to dispute his absolute commands. This I humbly offered to his Majesty, as a small tribute of acknowledgment in return of so many marks that I had received of his royal favor and protection.

The King was struck with horror at the description I had given of those terrible engines, and the proposal I had made. He was amazed how so impotent and groveling an insect as I (these were his expressions) could entertain such inhuman ideas, and in so familiar a manner as to appear wholly unmoved at all the scenes of blood and desolation, which I had painted as the common effects of those destructive machines, whereof he said some evil genius, enemy to mankind, must have been the first contriver. As for himself, he protested that although few things delighted him so much as new discoveries in art or in nature, yet he would rather lose half his kingdom than be privy to such a secret, which he commanded me, as I valued my life, never to mention any more.

A strange effect of narrow principles and short views! that a prince possessed of every quality which procures veneration, love, and esteem; of strong parts, great wisdom, and profound learning, endued with admirable talents for government, and almost adored by his subjects, should from a nice unnecessary scruple, whereof in Europe we can have no conception, let slip an opportunity put into his hands, that would have made him absolute master of the lives, the liberties, and the fortunes of his people.

from *Gulliver's Travels*

The paragraph that appears here may serve you as a useful model:

We picked up one excellent word—a word worth traveling to New Orleans to get; a nice limber, expressive, handy word—"Lagniappe." They pronounce it lanny-*yap*. It is Spanish—so they said. We discovered it at the head of a column of odds and ends in the *Picayune* the first day; heard twenty people use it the second; inquired what it meant the third; adopted it and got facility in swinging it the fourth. It has a restricted meaning, but I think the people spread it out a little when they choose. It is the equivalent of the thirteenth roll in a "baker's dozen." It is something thrown in, gratis, for good measure. The custom originated in the Spanish quarter of the city. When a child or a servant buys something in a shop—or even the mayor or the governor, for aught I know—he finishes the operation by saying . . .

MARK TWAIN
from *Life on the Mississippi*

1. Read the preceding excerpts.
2. In your journal do *one* of the following:

a. Use the Twain paragraph on definition to explain a term that has recently come into your ken.
b. Imitate the model from *Candide* or the one by Swift.
c. Imitate a paragraph of your own choice. (Copy or paste the model into your journal.)

1|3

EMULATION

In emulation you seek to equal or excel the worth of your model. You are not limited or bound by it as you were when working with close imitation. Here you are free to say your own things in your own way. You have simply determined that in saying them you will reach a standard of expression and a clarity of thought equal to or even better than that of the model which served you as inspiration or point of departure.

The method is very old and many men have taught themselves to write in just this way, for they were prompted always by the excellence of the example in front of them. It was so that Benjamin Franklin taught himself. His account, which follows, may be of service to any serious student.

About this time I met with an odd Volume of *The Spectator.** It was the third. I had never before seen any of them. I bought it, read it over and over, and was much delighted with it. I thought the Writing excellent, and wish'd if possible to imitate it. With that View, I took some of the Papers, and making short Hints of the Sentiment in each Sentence, laid them by a few Days, and then without looking at the Book, try'd to compleat the Papers again, by expressing each hinted Sentiment at length and as fully as it had been express'd before,

* *The Spectator* was a paper issued daily between March 1, 1711, and December 6, 1712, containing essays of which Joseph Addison wrote nearly half and Richard Steele most of the rest. They dealt with many topics, including literary criticism, esthetics, and the satirical treatment of society and manners. The style, which Samuel Johnson called "familiar, but not coarse, and elegant, but not ostentatious," greatly influenced English prose writing. A set of bound volumes of the papers was kept in James Franklin's printing office.

in any suitable Words, that should come to hand.

Then I compar'd my Spectator with the Original, discover'd some of my Faults and corrected them. But I found I wanted a Stock of Words or a Readiness in recollecting and using them, which I thought I should have acquir'd before that time, if I had gone on making Verses, since the continual Occasion for words of the same Import but of different Length, to suit the Measure, or of different Sound for the Rhyme, would have laid me under a constant Necessity of searching for Variety, and also have tended to fix that Variety in my Mind, and make me Master of it. Therefore I took some tales and turn'd them into Verse: And after a time, when I had pretty well forgotten the Prose, turn'd them back again. I also sometimes jumbled my Collections of Hints into Confusion, and after some Weeks, endeavor'd to reduce them into the best Order, before I began to form the full Sentences, and compleat the Paper. This was to teach me Method in the Arrangement of Thoughts. By comparing my work afterward with the original, I discover'd many faults and amended them; but I sometimes had the Pleasure of Fancying that in certain Particulars of small Import, I had been lucky enough to improve the Method or the Language and this encourag'd me to think I might possibly in time come to be a tolerable English Writer, of which I was extremely ambitious.

from *The Autobiography of Benjamin Franklin*

Franklin understood the value of imitation. But you'll also notice that he went beyond sheer imitation. On occasion his practice led him to improve on the model itself. And when he thought he had managed to "improve the Method or the Language," he was clearly pleased. As he said, ". . . this encourag'd me to think I might possibly in time come to be a tolerable English Writer, of which I was extremely ambitious."

In Chapters 3 and 4 of this unit you will be seeking to equal or excel a model. You will try to improve on its method or language—that is, to emulate it. In these chapters the model is no longer used as a strict measure but rather as a starting place, a springboard for your own thought and expression. At the same time, the model you use for emulation provides guidelines, suggests techniques, and provides a standard of excellence against which you may judge your own work.

Perhaps the best way to see how the method works is to look at an example. Here is the model:

> Alas! what is bloodshed but murder; what are the pretenses of war but words; what its dire effects but cold-blooded, purchased butchery. For deeds of true valor, done without brutal excitement, but in the honest and lawful pursuit of the means of livelihood, we may safely point to the life of a whaleman, and dare the whole world to produce a parallel.
>
> **OBED MACY**
> from *The History of Nantucket*

Here is an emulation of the model:

> Butchers we are, that is true. But butchers, also, and butchers of the bloodiest badge, have been all Martial Commanders whom the world invariably delights to honor. And as for the matter of the alleged uncleanliness of our business, ye shall soon be initiated into certain facts hitherto pretty generally unknown, and which, upon the whole, will triumphantly plant the sperm whale-ship at least among the cleanliest things of this tidy earth. But even granting the charge in question to be true; what disordered slippery decks of a whale-ship are comparable to the unspeakable carrion of those battlefields from which so many soldiers return to drink in all ladies' plaudits? And if the idea of peril so much enhances the popular conceit of the soldier's profession; let me assure ye that many a veteran who has freely marched up to a battery,

would quickly recoil at the apparition of the sperm whale's vast tail, fanning into eddies the air over his head. For what are the comprehensible terrors of man compared with the interlinked terrors and wonders of God!

HERMAN MELVILLE
from *Moby Dick*

Here Melville takes his hint from Obed Macy and succeeds in shaping the original material to his own purpose by making it more interesting, more imaginative, more in harmony with his particular work.

Suggestions for Emulation

1. Work with the model at hand, but remember you are not seeking to reproduce it; you are to use it as a springboard for your own invention.
2. Write on a parallel but not an identical topic.
3. Establish a controlling purpose for your own work and let it influence the tone of your writing.
4. Bring personal vision to your topic. See your subject in your own way and show keen regard for its individuality.
5. Use anecdote, analogy, and wit.
6. Employ imagination to expand and vivify hints provided by the model.

The Distinction Between Imitation and Emulation

1. In imitation the starting and ending points are predetermined by the model. In emulation there is no such limitation.
2. Imitation approximates the original and follows sentence pattern in *kind, number,* and *order* of phrases and clauses. Emulation is free; the writer simply seeks to equal or better his model.
3. The model in imitation provides sentence pattern. In emulation it provides perhaps no more than tone.

Plagiarism

In doing the exercises in this book and in undertaking similar work on your own, it is imperative that you understand the meaning of plagiarism. In imitation, the work done is not intended as original. Rather it is a deliberate attempt to copy and approximate the salient features of the model. In moving from imitation to emulation there may on occasion arise some ambiguity about plagiarism. In emulation, the student seeks to find his own voice and to be himself, although he is doing it within the conscious confines and tutelage of another. Acknowledgment of the models from which one departs is usually a safe way of avoiding confusion. Experience will ultimately teach the thoughtful student how to make use of emulation in an independent and creative way, and encourage the fuller and more independent expression of self.

Perhaps it will be helpful in understanding how this method works if you again look at the excerpt from Conrad's "Youth" and then read the student's emulation of it that follows.

> And this is how I see the East. I have seen its secret places and have looked into its very soul; but now I see it always from a small boat, a high outline of mountains, blue and afar in the morning; like a faint mist at noon; a jagged wall of purple at sunset. I have the feel of the oar in my hand, the vision of a scorching blue sea in my eyes. And I see a bay, a wide bay, smooth as glass and polished like ice, shimmering in the dark. A red light burns far off upon the gloom of the land, and the night is soft and warm. We drag at the oars with aching arms, and suddenly a puff of wind, a puff faint and tepid and laden with strange odors of blossoms, of aromatic wood, comes out of the still night—the first sigh of the East on my face. That I can never forget. It was impalpable and enslaving, like a charm, like a whispered promise of mysterious delight.
>
> JOSEPH CONRAD
> from "Youth"

The following passage, an emulation of Conrad's paragraph, describes the way a student sees his school.

And this is how I see Andover—through red, brown, and yellow leaves, her old brick buildings contrasting with the new. The stillness of an autumn evening after the bells have stopped. As they pass the headmaster's house on the way to Brothers Field, a football band playing "Brave Old Army Team." Around the bell tower, great soft dunes of snow piled up against the north side and on the street large flakes pass slowly in front of the electric lights. The smell of a spring morning while walking to class in a madras jacket, trying to study when you know you can't. Then standing in a great circle waiting for your name to be called.

JACK MC LEAN

Assignment 7

1. Read the chapter up to this point.
2. In your journal define "plagiarism" and then do *one* of the following:
   a. Pick a passage from the Gettysburg Address (see below) and show how a plagiarist might use the material.
   b. Take a passage from the Gettysburg Address and show how it might serve an independent and original mind for purposes of emulation.

Fourscore and seven years ago our fathers brought forth on this continent a new nation, conceived in liberty and dedicated to the proposition that all men are created equal. Now we are engaged in a great civil war, testing whether that nation, or any nation so conceived and so dedicated, can long endure. We are met on a great battlefield of that war. We have come to dedicate a portion of that field as a final resting place for those who here gave their lives that that nation might live. It is altogether fitting and proper that we should do this.

But, in a larger sense, we cannot dedicate—we cannot consecrate—we cannot hallow—this ground. The brave men, living and dead, who struggled here have consecrated it far above our poor power to add or to detract. The world will little note nor long remember what we say here, but it can never forget what they did here. It is for us, the living, rather to be dedicated here to the unfinished work which they who fought here have thus far so nobly advanced. It is rather for us to be here dedicated to the great task remaining before us—that from these honored dead we take increased devotion to that cause for which they gave the last full measure of devotion; that we here highly resolve that these dead shall not have died in vain; that this nation, under God, shall have a new birth of freedom; and that government of the people, by the people, for the people, shall not perish from the earth.

ABRAHAM LINCOLN

c. Write a full journal entry that might serve as a graduation speech before your entire school.

Assignment 8

As I had done before, I copied passages and then tried to write them out again from memory. I tried altering words or the order in which they were set. I found that the only possible words were those Swift had used and that the order in which he had placed them was the only possible order. It is an impeccable prose.

But perfection has one grave defect: it is apt to be dull. Swift's prose is like a French canal, bordered with poplars, that runs through a gracious and undulating country. Its tranquil charm fills you with satisfaction, but it neither excites the emotions nor stimulates the imagination. You go on and on and presently you are a trifle bored. So, much as you may admire Swift's wonderful lucid-

ity, his terseness, his naturalness, his lack of affectation, you find your attention wandering after a
while unless his matter peculiarly interests you. I
think if I had my time over again I would give to
the prose of Dryden the close study I gave to that of
Swift. I did not come across it till I had lost the
inclination to take so much pains. The prose of
Dryden is delicious.

W. SOMERSET MAUGHAM
from *The Summing Up*

What follows is a paragraph by John Steinbeck and a student's emulation of it. You will see that the work here has
been done with much the same attention Maugham gave to
his models.

The man's clothes were new—all of them, cheap
and new. His gray cap was so new that the visor was
still stiff and the button still on, not shapeless and
bulged as it would be when it had served for a while
all the various purposes of a cap—carrying sack, towel,
handkerchief. His suit was of cheap gray hardcloth
and so new that there were creases in the trousers.
His blue chambray shirt was stiff and smooth with
filler. The coat was too big, the trousers too short, for
he was a tall man. The coat shoulder peaks hung down
on his arms, and even then the sleeves were too short
and the front of the coat flapped loosely over his
stomach. He wore a pair of new tan shoes of the kind
called "army last," hobnailed and with half-circles
like horseshoes to protect the edges of the heels from
wear. This man sat on the running board and took off
his cap and mopped his face with it. Then he put on
the cap, and by pulling started the future ruin of the
visor. His feet caught his attention. He leaned down
and loosened the shoelaces, and did not tie the ends
again. Over his head the exhaust of the Diesel engine
whispered in quick puffs of blue smoke.

JOHN STEINBECK
from *The Grapes of Wrath*

In emulation, the goal is to rival or surpass the model. Using the model as a point of departure, one seeks to make an original and personal statement. Latitude is wide, although the general tone and direction is suggested by the model. Here is an example of emulation which was prompted by the Steinbeck paragraph you have just read.

> As the general's car drove in through the gate, the sentry then on duty snapped to attention as abruptly and rigidly as a penknife clips together when being closed. The soldier was a little shorter than a door and just a little narrower at the shoulders, with his torso tapering neatly to the solid, narrow hips which rested upon legs so rippling with muscles that they looked as if a child had molded them out of toy modeling clay. He wore a G.I. helmet with the shining whiteness of a new billiard ball. It was secured by a thin leather strap under his chin. He wore a stiff, clean khaki shirt, with freshly pressed creases running through the centers of his breast pockets. Here and there on the soldier's chest were various metal insignia, finely polished. The soldier's baggy but immaculate knickers were held up by a bleached, stiff white belt, buckled by a large, rectangular, glistening plate which, from a distance, might be mistaken for a cowboy's belt buckle which had been shined to a high gloss. The knickers were bordered at the opposite end by fresh, milk-white spats, held onto brilliantly spit-shined combat boots by a row of tiny, white cloth-covered buttons which ran up the outside of each of the soldier's ankles. After the car had passed through the gate, the oversized boots parted and the soldier stood at ease.
>
> STEPHEN MARSHALL

The student writer, like Steinbeck, has made description his business. Both have detailed the dress of their subjects and both have by indirection said much about the wearer of the clothes. The student writer has caught the clarity and vigor of Steinbeck's first sentence and in his own way improved upon it for his own purposes.

The student is moving freely. He has found his own subject and his own voice. One sees that he has been prompted by the model but not limited by it.

1. Read the preceding material.
2. In your journal do *one* of the following:
   a. Select a passage by Swift. Give it close study, then write your emulation.
   b. Select a passage by Dryden. Give it close study, then write your own emulation of it.
   c. Select a passage by an author you admire. Give it close study, then write your own emulation of it.

Assignment 9

Johnson observes that no writer likes to owe something to his contemporaries; Hawthorne was as unaware of them as possible. Perhaps he did the right thing; perhaps our contemporaries . . . always seem too much like us, and if we are looking for new things we shall find them more easily in the ancients.

JORGE LUIS BORGES
from *Other Inquisitions*

1. Consider the statement by Borges.
2. In your journal do *one* of the following:
   a. Turn to the ancients and find a model. Then write a passage in emulation. (Copy or paste the model itself into your journal.)
   b. Stevenson said, " . . . a revival of letters is always accompanied or heralded by a cast back to earlier or fresher models." Write a full journal entry in which you examine and document this point.
   c. Choose a character from "The General Prologue" to *The Canterbury Tales*. Use the character you have chosen as the basis for a character sketch of your own.

1|4

FURTHER EMULATION

There are all kinds of humor. Some is derisive, some sympathetic, and some merely whimsical. That is just what makes comedy so much harder to create than serious drama; people laugh in many different ways, and they cry only in one.

GROUCHO MARX
from *Enjoyment of Laughter*
by Max Eastman

To create humor, what you need most is a sense of the ridiculous. If you don't have that, then follow Will Rogers's example: "I don't make jokes," he said; "I just watch the government and report the facts."

But when you do feel the ridiculous coming on, and want to let it out by writing humor, here are ten commandments, to be transgressed at your own peril. These commandments are taken from Max Eastman's *Enjoyment of Laughter*.

1. Be interesting.
2. Be unimpassioned.
3. Be effortless.
4. Remember the difference between cracking practical jokes and conveying ludicrous impressions.
5. Be plausible.
6. Be sudden.
7. Be neat.
8. Be right with your timing.
9. Give a good measure of serious satisfaction.
10. Redeem all serious disappointments.

As you read the humor of other writers, consider how they use these points or how they neglect them and at what cost.

With the exception of writing poetry the most difficult

thing to do with words is make them funny. Still the effort is always rewarding—if not always to the audience, at least to the writer himself; for creating humor demands a control of diction and an awareness of tone and timing that can put a lasting edge on the dullest prose. If you decide to sharpen your own writing in this way, you may find help by first reviewing the principles that seem to govern fun—and the funny:

The first law of humor is that things can be funny only when we are in fun. There may be a serious thought or motive lurking underneath our humor. We may be only "half in fun" and still funny. But when we are not in fun at all, when we are "in dead earnest," humor is the thing that is dead.

The second law is that when we are in fun, a peculiar shift of values takes place. Pleasant things are still pleasant, but disagreeable things, so long as they are not disagreeable enough to "spoil the fun," tend to acquire a pleasant emotional flavor and provoke a laugh.

The third law is that "being in fun" is a condition most natural to childhood, and that children at play reveal the humorous life in its simplest and omnivorous form. To them every untoward, unprepared for, unmanageable, inauspicious, ugly, disgusting, puzzling, startling, deceiving, shaking, blinding, jolting, deafening, banging, bumping, or otherwise shocking and disturbing thing, unless it be calamitous enough to force them out of the mood of play, is enjoyable as fun.

The fourth law is that grown-up people retain in varying degrees this aptitude of being in fun, and thus enjoying unpleasant things as funny. But those not richly endowed with humor manage to feel a very comic feeling only when within, or behind, or beyond, or suggested by the playfully unpleasant thing, there is a pleasant one. Only then do they laugh uproariously like playing children. And they call this complicated thing or combination of things at which they laugh, a joke. That is about all there is to the science of humor as seen from a distance.

MAX EASTMAN
from *Enjoyment of Laughter*

We all know how easy it is to spoil a good joke by putting a word in the wrong place. We also know how words properly placed can detonate laughter. But funny or not, you'll learn a lot about writing by working with humor.

Humor comes in a number of packages. Without bogging down in a morass of definitions, you will nonetheless do well to review the concept of "irony" before you go on to the next assignment.

In this chapter the focus is on irony. Irony is a form (sometimes a grim form) of humor. Irony is the discrepancy between what is anticipated and what is received. Irony is created by having words or events go in one direction while meaning or situation moves in the opposite. For example, on seeing a lawn strewn with papers you might say, "How pretty." Irony may be as trite as the preceding example or as subtle as a poet's mind.

Ozymandias

I met a traveler from an antique land
Who said: "Two vast and trunkless legs of stone
Stand in the desert. . . . Near them, on the sand,
Half sunk, a shattered visage lies, whose frown,
And wrinkled lip, and sneer of cold command
Tell that its sculptor well those passions read
Which yet survive, stamped on these lifeless things,
The hand that mocked them, and the heart that fed;
And on the pedestal these words appear;
'My name is Ozymandias, king of kings;
Look on my works, ye Mighty, and despair!'
Nothing beside remains. Round the decay
Of that colossal wreck, boundless and bare
The lone and level sands stretch far away."

PERCY BYSSHE SHELLEY

Irony may be obvious or so subtle that the ordinary reader will take it as a literal statement. Indeed, the sophistication of a reader may be measured by his ability to detect irony. The mob in *Julius Caesar,* for example, at first believed Mark Antony when he said, "For Brutus is an honorable man." An alert reader makes no such mistake.

Irony is a situation created by the difference between appearance (that which seems to be the case) and reality (that which is the case).

Irony involves opposites. Two favorite ways of exposing the nature of these opposites is through overstatement and understatement. Yet all ironic devices are but different ways of revealing where truth is to be found, and as all thoughtful readers know, truth is seldom nesting with appearance on the literal or obvious branch.

Irony in its simplest terms is the difference between what is literally said and what is intended or implied by the maker of the statement. Irony in its more complex forms presents a statement that carries a different meaning for the hearer than for the speaker. The meaning for the speaker is usually understood in a limited way; whereas the hearer, including the audience, understands the statement in a more complex way. Statements by Oedipus and Hamlet illustrate this point. Irony may be used for a variety of purposes and produced in a number of ways, but in every case an element of humor is intended. This humor is in part concealed, but the reader or knowing audience is flattered by discovering it and realizing that the jibe is not directed at them but at the unknowing or uninitiated. Skillfully used, irony is a valuable device for making a point because it combines humor with flattery.

The discrepancy between the expected and the received is the hallmark of the ironic. The six types of irony identified below are each provided with a convenient label. Here are the six types and guidelines for identifying them:

1. Behind all irony there is a real or pretended ignorance. But if the actual intention is to hurt another, that form of irony is called *sarcasm.*
2. Sometimes irony is employed in the guise of praise. The intention here is to hold the subject up to laughter. This form of irony is called *ridicule.*

3. In argument when the speaker, like Socrates, pretends to ignorance in order to expose his opponent's error, we have a situation that is termed *Socratic irony*.
4. In theater the ironic paradox is called *dramatic irony*. (paradox: an apparent contradiction that nonetheless is somehow true)
5. In ordinary living, the outcome of events that reverses reasonable expectancy is termed the *irony of life*.
6. We may even laugh at ourselves. The disparity created by our acts or inabilities to act, as against our own expectancy or that of the world, produces a form of irony called the *sardonic*. James Thurber's "Walter Mitty" is an example of this form of humor.

The quality of humor permitted by irony is wide-ranging and each type has its brute and blessed practitioners. As you read, look for irony. Some aspect of it exists in every major literary work. In evaluating a work, consider whether irony has been added as decoration or whether it is an integral part of the work itself.

Assignment 10

1. Read the chapter up to this point.
2. In your journal do *one* of the following:
   a. Find examples in your reading of each of the six forms of irony outlined in this lesson.
   b. Write an amusing and ironic entry of your own based on the "Ozymandias" idea.
   c. Choose a model that makes successful use of the ironic. Then write an emulation of it.

Assignment 11

The form of humor that best combines the skills of imitation and emulation is parody. The intention of parody is to amuse. This is usually done by exaggerating some false note struck by the writer being parodied. The desired result is often achieved by the close imitation of words but with a shift of motive that moves from the lofty to the low. Another device for achieving the desired absurd effect is through imitation of form with special emphasis on the affectation or mannerism of the writer. Sense itself may be parodied by duplication of diction and style and the treatment of a special premise through caricature. The following none-too-serious treatment of J. D. Salinger's *Catcher in the Rye* may suggest a way of learning from models.

CATCH HER IN THE OATMEAL

DAN GREENBERG

If you actually want to hear about it, what I'd better do is I'd better warn you right now that you aren't going to believe it. I mean it's a true *story* and all, but it still sounds sort of phony.

Anyway, my name is Goldie Lox. It's sort of a boring name, but my parents said that when I was born I had this very blonde hair and all. Actually, I was born bald. I mean how many babies get born with blonde hair? None. I mean I've *seen* them and they're all wrinkled and red and slimy and everything. And bald. And then all the phonies have to come around and tell you he's as cute as a bug's ear. A bug's ear, boy, that really kills me. You ever *seen* a bug's ear? What's cute about a bug's *ear,* for Pete's sake! Nothing, that's what.

So, like I was saying, I always seem to be getting into these very stupid situations. Like this time I was telling you about. Anyway, I was walking through the forest and all when I see this very interesting house. A *house.* You wouldn't think anybody would be living way the hell out in the damn *forest,* but they were. No one was home or anything and the door was open, so I walked in. I figured what I'd do is I'd probably horse around until the guys that lived there came home and maybe asked me to stay for dinner or something. Some people think they *have* to ask you to stay for dinner even if they *hate* you. Also I didn't exactly feel like going home and getting asked a lot of lousy questions. I mean that's *all* I ever seem to do.

Anyway, while I was waiting I sort of sampled some of this stuff they had on the table that tasted like oatmeal. *Oatmeal.* It would have made you puke, I mean it. Then something very spooky started happening. I started getting dizzier than hell. I figured I'd feel better if I could just rest for a while. Sometimes if you eat something like lousy oatmeal you can feel better if you just rest for a while, so I sat down. That's when the damn *chair* breaks in half. No kidding, you start feeling lousy and some stupid *chair* is going to break on you every time. I'm not kidding. Anyway I finally found the crummy bedroom and I lay down on this very tiny bed. I was really depressed.

I don't know how long I was asleep or anything, but all of a sudden I hear this very strange voice say, "Someone's been sleeping in *my* sack, for Pete's sake, and there she is!" So I open my eyes and here at the foot of the bed are these three crummy *bears. Bears!* I swear to God. By that time I was *really* feeling depressed. There's nothing more depressing than waking up and finding three *bears* talking about you, I mean.

So I didn't stay around and shoot the breeze with them or anything. If you want to know the truth, I sort of ran out of there like a madman or something. I do that quite a little when I'm depressed like that.

On the way home, though, I got to figuring. What probably happened is these bears wandered in when they smelled this oatmeal and all. Probably bears *like* oatmeal, *I* don't know. And the voice I heard when I woke up was probably something I dreamt.

So that's the story.

I wrote it all up once as a theme in school, but

my crummy teacher said it was too *whimsical.*
Whimsical. That killed me. You got to meet her
sometime, boy. She's a real queen.

The excerpt below, from Kingsley Amis's novel *Lucky
Jim,* presents a confrontation between the hero, Jim Dixon,
and his employer, Professor Welch, who is the chairman of
a college history department. Jim is trying to learn whether
he will be rehired for the next school year.

Dixon waited, planning faces. He looked round
the small, cosy room with its fitted carpet, its rows
of superseded books, its filing cabinets full of antique examination papers and of dossiers relating
to past generations of students, its view from closed
windows on to the sunlit wall of the physics laboratory. Behind Welch's head hung the departmental
timetable, drawn up by Welch himself in five differ-
ent-colored inks corresponding to the five teaching
members of the department. The sight of this
seemed to undam Dixon's mind; for the first time
since arriving at the college he thought he felt real,
overmastering, orgiastic boredom, and its compan-
ion, real hatred. If Welch didn't speak in the next
five seconds, he'd do something which would get
himself flung out without possible question—not
the things he'd often dreamed of when sitting next
door pretending to work. He no longer wanted, for
example, to inscribe on the departmental timetable
a short account, well tricked out with obscenities,
of his views on the professor of history, the Department of History, medieval history, history, and
Margaret and hang it out of the window for the
information of passing students and lecturers, nor
did he, on the whole, now intend to tie Welch up
in his chair and beat him about the head and
shoulders with a bottle until he disclosed why, without being French himself, he'd given his sons
French names. . . .
"Well, these things aren't as easy as you might
imagine, you know," Welch said suddenly. "This

is a very difficult matter, Dixon, you see. There's a great deal, a lot of things you've got to keep in mind."

"I see that, of course, Professor. I just wanted to ask when the decision will be taken that's all. If I'm to go, it's only fair I should be told soon." He felt his head trembling slightly with rage as he said this.

Welch's glance, which had flicked two or three times at Dixon's face, now dropped to a half-curled-up letter on the desk. He muttered: "Yes . . . well . . . I . . ."

Dixon said in a still louder voice: "Because I shall have to start looking for another job, you see. And most of the schools will have made their appointments for September before they break up in July. So I shall want to know in good time."

An expression of unhappiness was beginning to settle on Welch's small-eyed face. Dixon was at first pleased to see this evidence that Welch's mind could still be reached from the outside; next he felt a momentary compunction at the spectacle of one man disliking to reveal something that would cause pain to another; finally panic engulfed him. What was Welch's reluctance concealing? He, Dixon, was done for. . . .

"Let you know as soon as anything's decided," Welch said with incredible speed. "Nothing as yet. . . ."

Now, as Dixon had been half expecting all along, Welch produced his handkerchief. It was clear that he was about to blow his nose. This was usually horrible, if only because it drew unwilling attention to Welch's nose itself, a large, open-pored tetrahedron. But when the familiar miraculously sustained blares beat against the walls and windows, Dixon hardly minded at all; the noise had the effect of changing his mood. Any statement that could be battered out of Welch was invariably trustworthy, so that Dixon was back where he was. But how lovely to be back where he was, instead of out in front where he didn't want to be. How wrong people always were when they said: "It's better to know the worst than go on not knowing either way." No; they had it exactly the wrong way round. Tell me the truth, Doctor, I'd sooner know. But only if the truth is what I want to hear.

KINGSLEY AMIS
from *Lucky Jim*

The following piece parodies the style of *Lucky Jim* as well as the attitudes of Jim Dixon.

LUCKY GOLDILOCKS

ANTHONY BRODE

The three bears lived in a maddeningly neat house in a pimply suburb which straggled depressingly along the former by-pass of a small industrial town in the provinces. When Goldilocks found that the house was called "Garmisch" she made her Lawrence of Arabia face and walked in without knocking; the bears had gone to a fiendish concert of clever-clever Bach concertos (which they called *concerti*) given by a group of nauseatingly highbrow little gnomes at the other end of town.

Goldilocks was hungry as usual and made straight for the dining room, which was furnished in Tottenham Court Road Jacobean with a horror suite of sticky-looking chairs and a table with twisted legs like varnished barley sugar. There were three plastic plates on the table, each containing a different type of American breakfast cereal.

Did she like the first sort? No in italics. Did she like the second? Far from it in capitals. Did she like the third? Not at all in 72-point Gill sanserif heavy upper and lower case.

Goldilocks made her outraged cannibal face, which involved sticking out her lower lip and tongue as far as possible and showing the whites of her eyes, and ran to the bedroom in her Groucho Marx manner. This was difficult to do going up the stairs, but she did it.

The bedroom, Goldilocks felt instinctively, was known to the Three Bears as the Boudoir. Everything was pink and frilly, and entering the room was like waking up inside a raspberry fondant. She bounced up and down on the three beds in turn, and they gave out three different but equally depressing kinds of rachety groan.

At that moment there was a confused waffle of voices downstairs. They sorted themselves out into a bass voice which said, "Somebody's been eating my Crunchimunch," a contralto voice which said ("fluted" was the word of which Goldilocks instantly thought), "Somebody's been eating my Flaxibix!" and a nasty piping lisp which said, "Thomebody'th been eating my Toathtieripth!" Goldilocks made her Shirley Temple face and jumped under the biggest bed.

An uneven clumping noise grew louder and the bedroom door opened. Goldilocks realized that she could stand anything except the three-part expostulation which seemed the Three Bears' favorite method of conversing, and jumped out into the middle of the room.

"I'm sorry, Three Bears," she said earnestly, "but I was hungry and tired, so I came here. Please don't ask me any questions. . . ." Her voice faltered as she noticed that the Three Bears were wearing precisely the kind of clothes which irritated her most. One wore a nylon shirt and gaberdine trousers, the second a yellow satin dress and "sensible" shoes, and the third (or smallest and most repulsive) a frilly short skirt and white ankle-socks.

"Why weren't you at the concert?" said the nylon bear after a short pause.

"I . . . I wasn't invited," said Goldilocks wildly.

"You don't have to be invited," said the satin bear. "People just pop in."

Yes, it would be that sort of place, thought Goldilocks, and I'll bet when it was over they had meat-paste sandwiches and coffee made from something out of a bottle. "I'll bet when it was over you had meat-paste sandwiches and coffee made from something out of a bottle," she said.

"You mutht have been there," said the frilly bear in an accusing manner.

The nylon bear now spoke again. He was large and obviously accustomed to being listened to, and pitched his voice so that it carried right to the back of the hall. As the bedroom was very small, the effect was much the same as holding a competition for town-criers in an airing cupboard.

"I feel it would be for the best," he boomed in a fruity central office manner, "if you came heah to live with us and, ah, looked after the house. After all, you do appear to be somewhat at a larss."

Goldilocks made her Clement Atlee face and said nothing.

"We would allow you three nights off a week to do folk dancing," said the satin bear, "or, of course, pottery or woodwork classes if you prefer it."

"And you could take me to ballet thchool in the afternoonth," piped the frilly bear.

Goldilocks gave a controlled but vibrant scream like an impatient locomotive and rushed away to the nearest public house for a game of darts and the double Scotch to which, according to a recently initiated economy campaign, she was not entitled until the following Tuesday week.

1. Read the material for this assignment.
2. In your journal do *one* of the following:
   a. Write your own parody of *Catcher in the Rye* or *Lucky Jim.*

b. Write your own version of a fairy tale or children's story, parodying the style of a famous author.

c. Take a subject that has been given serious treatment. Write on the same topic, but from a humorous point of view.

Assignment 12

Your models need not be examples of serious or stately prose. Here a student has taken a paragraph from H. L. Mencken and used it for his own purposes. He has, you will note, taken the trouble to consider closely how Mencken got his effects. In your own work, you will find it useful to give close consideration to what makes the model effective. Then in your own writing you can imitate or emulate that quality.

Here is the Mencken model together with a student's analysis and imitation of it.

> But when it comes to the style of a great man's discourse, I can speak with a great deal less prejudice, and maybe with somewhat more competence, for I have earned most of my livelihood for twenty years past by translating the bad English of a multitude of authors into measurably better English. Thus qualified professionally, I rise to pay my small tribute to Dr. Harding. Setting aside a college professor or two and half a dozen dipsomaniacal newspaper reporters, he takes first place in my Valhalla of literati. That is to say, he writes the worst English that I have ever encountered. It reminds me of a string of wet sponges; it reminds me of tattered washing on the line; it reminds me of stale bean soup, of college yells, of dogs barking idiotically through endless nights. It is so bad that a sort of grandeur creeps into it. It drags itself out of the dark abysm (I was about to write abscess!) of pish, and crawls insanely up the topmost pinnacle of posh. It is rumble and bumble. It is flap and doodle. It is balder and dash.
>
> H. L. MENCKEN
from "Gamalielese"

The author has used irony and exaggeration as his primary tools in the shaping of his satire, but he also has employed parallel structure, repetition, new words, comparison (whether metaphors or similes), and emotionally charged language to build his paragraph. Even in the first sentence, Mencken is ironical when he calls Harding "a great man"— exactly what he is attempting to disprove. Again in the second sentence he ironically "rises to pay tribute" to a doctor who he feels is neither worthy of the tribute nor the title. In the next sentence he is again ironical when he states that the worst grammarians are those whom we usually consider the best; he further heightens his effect by employing two rare and emotionally charged terms— "dipsomaniacal" (drunk) and "Valhalla of literati." Next he exaggerates, for surely someone has written worse English than Harding. In the following sentence he makes a series of parallel comparisons (metaphors) to related images—those of dampness and staleness. In the final sentences he gains added effect by the use of parallel constructions (here verbs of undignified motion), by the use of rare— and probably recent invented—connotative words such as abysm, pish, posh, balder, and dash, and he maintains his ironic tone by speaking of grandeur and the "pinnacle of posh."

JOHN SEEGAL

Here is the same student's emulation of Mencken.

Having had the singular honor of meeting the illustrious personage, I feel as qualified as I ever will be to translate the oratory of the good doctor into the English language that most of us are familiar with. And yet, to remove his sonorous nonsense from the audience of small-town yokels, political serfs, and morons at whom it was originally aimed is to denude it of its inherent grandeur. For without this audience the thunder of a stump speech is reduced to a trickle of incomprehensible polysyllables, and the salvos of artillery are as ineffectual as the logic which first created them. That is to say, the speech is nonsense if you, the listener, are not the sort of man whom the good doctor is used to talking to, which is to say that you are not a jackass.

JOHN SEEGAL

1. Read the Mencken excerpt along with its analysis and emulation.
2. In your journal do *one* of the following:
   a. Write an emulation based on the Mencken paragraph.
   b. Write an emulation based on the opening of a short story you like.
   c. Select a model paragraph. Discuss in detail the qualities in it you find worthy of emulation.

15

INFLUENCES

A scrupulous writer, in every sentence that he writes, will ask himself at least four questions, thus: What am I trying to say? What words will express it? What image or idiom will make it clearer? Is the image fresh enough to have an effect? and he will probably ask himself two more: Could I put it more shortly? Have I said anything that is avoidably ugly? But you are not obliged to go to all this trouble. You can shirk it by simply throwing your mind open and letting the ready-made phrases come crowding in.

GEORGE ORWELL
from "Politics and
the English Language"

The work of this chapter will be carried forward in Unit 4, "Reading for Writing." But here you should make yourself familiar with the possibility of responding to influences. Robert Lowell makes interesting and helpful comments in the Introduction to his translations of European poems, *Imitations*. He says,

This book is partly self-sufficient and separate from its sources, and should be first read as a sequence, one voice running through many personalities, contrasts and repetitions. I have hoped somehow for a whole, to make a single volume, a small anthology of European poetry. The dark and against the grain stand out, but there are other modifying strands. I have tried to keep something equivalent to the fire and finish of my originals. This has forced me to do considerable rewriting.

Boris Pasternak has said that the usual reliable translator gets the literal meaning but misses the tone, and that in poetry tone is of course everything. I have been reckless with literal meaning, and labored hard to get the tone. Most often this has been *a* tone, for *the* tone is something that will always more or less escape transference to another language and cultural moment. I have tried to write alive English and to do what my authors might have done if they were writing their poems now and in America.

Most poetic translations come to grief and are less enjoyable than modest photographic prose translations, such as George Kay has offered in his *Penguin Book of Italian Verse*. Strict metrical translators still exist. They seem to live in a pure world untouched by contemporary poetry. Their difficulties are bold and honest, but they are taxidermists, not poets, and their poems are likely to be stuffed birds. A better strategy would seem to be the now fashionable translations into free or irregular verse. Yet this method commonly turns out a sprawl of language, neither faithful nor distinguished, now on stilts, now low, as Dryden would say. It seems self-evident that no professor or amateur poet, or even good poet writing hastily, can by miracle transform himself into a fine metricist. I believe that poetic translation—I would call it an imitation—must be expert and inspired, and needs at least as much technique, luck and rightness of hand as an original poem.

Pasternak has given me special problems. From reading his prose and many translations of his poetry, I have come to feel that he is a very great poet. But I know no Russian. I have rashly tried to improve on other translations, and have been helped by exact prose versions given me by Russian readers. This is an old practice; Pasternak himself, I think, worked this way with his Georgian poets. I hope I caught something worthy of his all-important tone.

ROBERT LOWELL
from the Introduction to *Imitations*

Assignment 13

1. Read the chapter up to this point.
2. In your journal do *one* of the following:
   a. Make a "modest photographic prose translation" of a poem.
   b. Give your voice to a restatement of a passage of prose or poetry. Try to "keep something equivalent to the fire and finish" of your original.
   c. Select a passage from an author of a classic work. Then do with the passage what the author himself might have done were he writing now in America. The following passage from *Uncle Tom's Cabin* may provide a point of departure.

"Well, Sam," said Mrs. Shelby, "as you appear to have a proper sense of your errors, you may go now and tell Aunt Chloe she may get you some of that cold ham that was left of dinner today. You and Andy must be hungry."

"Missis is a heap too good for us," said Sam, making his bow with alacrity, and departing.

It will be perceived, as has been before intimated, that Master Sam had a native talent that might, undoubtedly, have raised him to eminence in political life—a talent of making capital out of everything that turned up, to be invested for his own especial praise and glory; and having done up his piety and humility, as he trusted, to the satisfaction of the parlor, he clapped his palm leaf on his head, with a sort of rakish, free-and-easy air, and proceeded to the dominions of Aunt Chloe, with the intention of flourishing largely in the kitchen.

HARRIET BEECHER STOWE
from *Uncle Tom's Cabin*

Assignment 14

The importance of influences and their proper use are much misunderstood. Perhaps your own understanding will be clarified by a brief consideration of a Russian novel, *We,* and Orwell's *1984*. The opening pages of both books are presented for comparison, but first you may find it helpful to know something more about *We* and its author, Eugene Zamiatin. The statements by Peter Rudy and by the translator, Gregory Zilboorg, that follow are from the Introduction to *We*. You will note that Zamiatin himself was strongly influenced by Dostoevsky and that his own novel, *We*, was a forerunner of works like *Brave New World* and *1984*.

We is, as Zamiatin himself calls it, the most jocular and the most earnest thing he has written thus far. It is a novel that puts before every thoughtful reader with great poignance and earnestness the most difficult problem that exists today in the civilized world—the problem of the preservation of the independent, original, creative personality.

GREGORY ZILBOORG

In the first years of the twenties, *We* was simply another variation on the utopian theme, a clever, stimulating, satirical fantasy that inspired speculation and debate. The ruling principle of the rigidly controlled society in *We* is that freedom and happiness are incompatible: men are congenitally incapable of using their freedom for constructive ends and merely make themselves miserable by their abuse of it; most of them yearn for a materialistic happiness and are eager to surrender their troublesome freedom and to be reduced to the status of lotus-eaters. This was hardly a new theory, except in its application. Zamiatin had obviously become intrigued by the guiding philosophy of the Grand Inquisitor in Dostoevsky's *Brothers Karamazov* and had skillfully adapted it to the needs of a modern technological state.

With respect to the most extreme practices outlined in *We*, the question was not *whether* but *when* they would be realized. It became plain that even if man is born a rebel at heart, his psychological make-up is so plastic that he can usually be effectively intimidated to the point where he will accept a rigidly controlled pattern of life for a long period of time. Since history proved Zamiatin right in this respect, the problems of the people in *We* who dared to think have lost their haze of unreality. In the light of what has been and is still occurring in totalitarian states, such problems have become fresh and compelling.

In this novel, Zamiatin tried to put into practice his belief that in its content a literary work should be heretical, refusing to accept reality at its face value and always posing those two "final, most terrifying, most fearless" questions: Why? And what lies ahead? He also attempted to carry out his conviction that form should keep up with ideas, that only a heretical form could adequately dramatize heretical ideas. Drawing on the techniques of Gogol, Dostoevsky, Andreev, and Blok, Zamiatin had created his own synthesis, and this was now adapted to the special needs of *We*.

The novel uses the notebook format, which is a particularly flexible medium for reflecting the varying moods of the narrator. A dynamic pace as well as a multidimensional characterization is obtained by techniques that are grounded in the principles of human psychology. As the narrator's emotional state changes, his perception moves between the extreme limits of objectivity and subjectivity. There is a dramatic running duel between the rational and irrational forces within him, a shifting between his conscious and unconscious powers of perception, and a constant association of ideas that forms elaborate networks. Accompanying this psychological method is a laconic language that frequently lapses into the provocatively elliptical and imparts a sensation of breathlessness. Compressed and startlingly strange similes and metaphors are used in a variety of sophisticated roles: they not only serve the conventional purpose of intensifying the description of a person or object, but they also

sharply characterize the narrator and his environment; they are frequently linked to an individual
through so much repetition that they attain an im-
pressionistic force; and sometimes they are employed as a triggering mechanism to flood the
reader's mind with impressions that were associated
with these figures earlier in the narrative. The total
effect of this imagery is to provide the novel with a
strong inner unity.

Zamiatin once gave an apt metaphorical definition of good books, and this definition could well
apply to *We*: "There are books of the same chemical composition as dynamite. The difference lies
only in the fact that one stick of dynamite explodes once, but one book explodes thousands of
times." . . .

PETER RUDY

The novel *We* is presented in the form of a journal. Here
are the opening entries:

RECORD ONE

An Announcement
The Wisest of Lines
A Poem

This is merely a copy, word for word, of what
was published this morning in the State newspaper:
"In another hundred and twenty days the building of the *Integral* will be completed. The great
historic hour is near, when the first *Integral* will
rise into the limitless space of the universe. One
thousand years ago your heroic ancestors subjected
the whole earth to the power of the United State.
A still more glorious task is before you: the integra-
tion of the indefinite equation of the Cosmos by
the use of the glass, electric, fire-breathing *Integral*.
Your mission is to subjugate to the grateful yoke of
reason the unknown beings who live on other
planets, and who are perhaps still in the primitive

state of freedom. If they will not understand that we are bringing them a mathematically faultless happiness, our duty will be to force them to be happy. But before we take up arms, we shall try the power of words.

"In the name of the Well-Doer, the following is announced herewith to all Numbers of the United State:

"Whoever feels capable must consider it his duty to write treatises, poems, manifestoes, odes, and other compositions on the greatness and the beauty of the United State.

"This will be the first cargo which the *Integral* will carry.

"Long live the United State! Long live the Numbers!! Long live the Well-Doer!!!"

I feel my cheeks burn as I write this. To integrate the colossal, universal equation! To unbend the wild curve, to straighten it out to a tangent— to a straight line! For the United State is a straight line, a great, divine, precise, wise line, the wisest of lines!

I, D-503, the builder of the *Integral,* I am only one of the many mathematicians of the United State. My pen, which is accustomed to figures, is unable to express the march and rhythm of consonance; therefore I shall try to record only the things I see, the things I think, or, to be more exact, the things *we* think. Yes, "we"; that is exactly what I mean, and *We,* therefore, shall be the title of my records. But this will only be a derivative of our life, of our mathematical, perfect life in the United State. If this be so, will not this derivative be a poem in itself, despite my limitations? It will. I believe it, I know it.

My cheeks still burn as I write this. I feel something similar to what a woman probably feels when for the first time she senses within herself the pulse of a tiny, blind, human being. It is I, and at the same time it is not I. And for many long months it will be necessary to feed it with my life, with my blood, and then with a pain at my heart, to tear it from myself and lay it at the feet of the United State.

Yet I am ready, as everyone, or nearly everyone of us, is. I am ready.

RECORD TWO

Ballet
Square Harmony
X

SPRING. From behind the Green Wall, from some unknown plains the wind brings to us the yellow honeyed pollen of flowers. One's lips are dry from this sweet dust. Every moment one passes one's tongue over them. Probably all women whom I meet in the street (and certainly men also) have sweet lips today. This somewhat disturbs my logical thinking. But the sky! The sky is blue. Its limpidness is not marred by a single cloud. (How primitive was the taste of the ancients, since their poets were always inspired by these senseless, formless, stupidly rushing accumulations of vapor!) I love, I am sure it will not be an error if I say *we* love, only such a sky—a sterile, faultless sky. On such days the whole universe seems to be molded of the same eternal glass, like the Green Wall, and like all our buildings. On such days one sees their wonderful equations, hitherto unknown. One sees these equations in everything, even in the most ordinary, everyday things.

Here is an example: this morning I was on the dock where the *Integral* is being built, and I saw the lathes; blindly, with abandon, the balls of the regulators were rotating; the cranks were swinging from side to side with a glimmer; the working beam proudly swung its shoulder; and the mechanical chisels were dancing to the melody of unheard tarantellas. I suddenly perceived all the music, all the

beauty, of this colossal, this mechanical ballet, il-
lumined by light blue rays of sunshine. Then the
thought came: why beautiful? Why is the dance
beautiful? Answer: because it is an *unfree* movement. Because the deep meaning of the dance is
contained in its absolute, ecstatic submission, in the
ideal *nonfreedom*. If it is true that our ancestors
would abandon themselves in dancing at the most
inspired moments of their lives (religious mysteries, military parades), then it means only one
thing: the instinct of nonfreedom has been characteristic of human nature from ancient times, and
we in our life of today, we are only consciously——

I was interrupted. The switchboard clicked. I
raised my eyes—O-90, of course! In half a minute
she will be here to take me for the walk.

Dear O-! She always seems to me to look like her
name, O-. She is approximately ten centimeters
shorter than the required Maternal Norm. Therefore she appears round all over; the rose-colored O
of her lips is open to meet every word of mine. She
has a round soft dimple on her wrist. Children have
such dimples. As she came in, the logical flywheel
was still buzzing in my head, and following its inertia, I began to tell her about my new formula which
embraced the machines and the dancers and all of
us.

"Wonderful, isn't it?" I asked.

"Yes, wonderful . . . Spring!" she replied, with
a rosy smile.

You see? Spring! She talks about Spring! Fe-
males! . . . I became silent.

We were down in the street. The avenue was
crowded. On days when the weather is so beautiful,
the afternoon personal hour is usually the hour of
the supplementary walk. As always, the big Musical
Tower was playing the March of the United State
with all its pipes. The Numbers, hundreds, thousands of Numbers in light blue unifs (probably a
derivative of the ancient uniform) with golden
badges on the chest—the State number of each one,

male or female—the Numbers were walking slowly, four abreast, exaltedly keeping step. I, we four, were but one of the innumerable waves of a powerful torrent: to my left, O-90 (if one of my long-haired ancestors were writing this a thousand years ago he would probably call her by that funny word, *mine*); to my right, two unknown Numbers, a she-Number and a he-Number.

Blue sky, tiny baby suns in each one of our badges; our faces are unclouded by the insanity of thoughts. Rays. . . . Do you picture it? Everything seems to be made of a kind of smiling, a raylike matter. And the brass measures: Tra-ta-ta-tam . . . Tra-ta-ta-tam . . . Stamping on the brassy steps that sparkle in the sun, with every step you rise higher and higher into the dizzy blue heights. . . . Then, as this morning on the dock, again I saw, as if for the first time in my life, the impeccably straight streets, the glistening glass of the pavement, the divine parallelepipeds of the transparent dwellings, the square harmony of the grayish-blue rows of Numbers. And it seemed to me that not past generations, but I myself, had won a victory over the old god and the old life, that I myself had created all this. I felt like a tower: I was afraid to move my elbow, lest the walls, the cupola, and the machines should fall to pieces.

Then without warning—a jump through centuries: I remembered (apparently through an association by contrast) a picture in the museum, a picture of an avenue of the twentieth century, a thundering, many-colored confusion of men, wheels, animals, billboards, trees, colors, and birds. . . . They say all this once actually existed!

It seemed to me so incredible, so absurd, that I lost control of myself and laughed aloud. A laugh, as if an echo of mine, reached my ear from the right. I turned. I saw white, very white, sharp teeth, and an unfamiliar female face.

"I beg your pardon," she said, "but you looked about you like an inspired mythological god on the seventh day of creation. You look as though you are sure that I, too, was created by you, by no one but you. It is very flattering."

All this without a smile, even with a certain degree of respect (she may know that I am the builder of the *Integral*). In her eyes, nevertheless, and on her brows, there was a strange irritating X, and I was unable to grasp it, to find an arithmetical expression for it. Somehow I was confused; with a somewhat hazy mind, I tried logically to explain my laughter.

"It was absolutely clear that this contrast, this impassable abyss, between the things of today and of years ago——"

"But why impassable?" (What bright, sharp teeth!) "One might throw a bridge over that abyss. Please imagine: a drum battalion, rows—all this existed before and consequently——"

"Oh, yes, it is clear," I exclaimed.

It was a remarkable intersection of thoughts. She said almost in the same words the things I had written down before the walk! Do you understand? Even the thoughts! It is because nobody is *one,* but *one of.* We are all so much alike——

"Are you sure?" I noticed her brows that rose to the temples in an acute angle—like the sharp corners of an X. Again I was confused, casting a glance to the right, then to the left. To my right—she, slender, abrupt, resistantly flexible like a whip, I-330 (I saw her number now). To my left, O-, totally different, all made of circles with a childlike dimple on her wrist; and at the very end of our row, an unknown he-Number, double-curved like the letter S. We were all so different from one another. . . .

The one to my right, I-330, apparently caught the confusion in my eye, for she said with a sigh, "Yes, alas!"

I don't deny that this exclamation was quite in place, but again there was something in her face or in her voice . . .

With an abruptness unusual for me, I said,

"Why, 'alas'? Science is developing and if not now, then within fifty or one hundred years——"

"Even the noses will——"

"Yes, noses!" This time I almost shouted, "Since there is still a reason, no matter what, for envy. . . . Since my nose is buttonlike and someone else's is——"

"Well, your nose is rather classic, as they would have said in ancient days, although your hands—— No, no, show me your hands!"

I hate to have anyone look at my hands; they are covered with long hair—a stupid atavism. I stretched out my hand and said as indifferently as I could, "Apelike."

She glanced at my hand, then at my face.

"No, a very curious harmony."

She weighed me with her eyes as though with scales. The little horns again appeared at the corners of her brows.

"He is registered in my name," exclaimed O-90 with a rosy smile.

I made a grimace. Strictly speaking, she was out of order. This dear O-, how shall I say it? The speed of her tongue is not correctly calculated; the speed per second of her tongue should be slightly less than the speed per second of her thoughts—at any rate not the reverse.

At the end of the avenue the big bell of the Accumulating Tower resounded seventeen. The personal hour was at an end. I-330 was leaving us with that S-like he-Number. He has such a respectable, and I noticed then, such a familiar, face. I must have met him somewhere, but where I could not remember. Upon leaving me I-330 said with the same X-like smile:

"Drop in day after tomorrow at auditorium 112."

I shrugged my shoulders: "If I am assigned to the auditorium you just named——"

She, with a peculiar, incomprehensible certainty: "You will be."

The woman had a disagreeable effect upon me,

like an irrational component of an equation which you cannot eliminate. I was glad to remain alone with dear O-, at least for a short while. Hand in hand with her, I passed four lines of avenues; at the next corner she went to the right, I to the left. O- timidly raised her round blue crystalline eyes.

"I would like so much to come to you today and pull down the curtains, especially today, right now. . . ."

How funny she is. But what could I say to her? She was with me only yesterday and she knows as well as I that our next sexual day is day after to-morrow. It is merely another case in which her thoughts are too far ahead. It sometimes happens that the spark comes too early to the motor.

At parting I kissed her twice—no, I shall be exact, three times, on her wonderful blue eyes, such clear, unclouded eyes.

EUGENE ZAMIATIN
from *We*

What follows is the opening of *1984*.

It was a bright cold day in April, and the clocks were striking thirteen. Winston Smith, his chin nuzzled into his breast in an effort to escape the vile wind, slipped quickly through the glass doors of Victory Mansions, though not quickly enough to prevent a swirl of gritty dust from entering along with him.

The hallway smelt of boiled cabbage and old rag mats. At one end of it a colored poster, too large for indoor display, had been tacked to the wall. It depicted simply an enormous face, more than a meter wide: the face of a man of about forty-five, with a heavy black mustache and ruggedly handsome features. Winston made for the stairs. It was no use trying the lift. Even at the best of times it was seldom working, and at present the electric current was cut off during daylight hours. It was part of the economy drive in preparation for Hate

Week. The flat was seven flights up, and Winston, who was thirty-nine and had a varicose ulcer above his right ankle, went slowly, resting several times on the way. On each landing, opposite the lift shaft, the poster with the enormous face gazed from the wall. It was one of those pictures which are so contrived that the eyes follow you about when you move. BIG BROTHER IS WATCHING YOU, the caption beneath it ran.

Inside the flat a fruity voice was reading out a list of figures which had something to do with the production of pig iron. The voice came from an oblong metal plaque like a dulled mirror which formed part of the surface of the right-hand wall. Winston turned a switch and the voice sank somewhat, though the words were still distinguishable. The instrument (the telescreen, it was called) could be dimmed, but there was no way of shutting it off completely. He moved over to the window: a smallish, frail figure, the meagerness of his body merely emphasized by the blue overalls which were the uniform of the Party. His hair was very fair, his face naturally sanguine, his skin roughened by coarse soap and blunt razor blades and the cold of the winter that had just ended.

Outside, even through the shut windowpane, the world looked cold. Down in the street little eddies of wind were whirling dust and torn paper into spirals, and though the sun was shining and the sky a harsh blue, there seemed to be no color in anything except the posters that were plastered everywhere. The black-mustachio'd face gazed down from every commanding corner. There was one on the house front immediately opposite. BIG BROTHER IS WATCHING YOU, the caption said, while the dark eyes looked deep into Winston's own. Down at street level another poster, torn at one corner, flapped fitfully in the wind, alternately covering and uncovering the single word INGSOC. In the far distance a helicopter skimmed down between the roofs, hovered for an instant like a bluebottle, and darted away again with a curving flight. It was the Police Patrol, snooping into people's windows. The patrols did not matter, however. Only the Thought Police mattered.

Behind Winston's back the voice from the telescreen was still babbling away about pig iron and the overfulfillment of the Ninth Three-Year Plan. The telescreen received and transmitted simultaneously. Any sound that Winston made, above the level of a very low whisper, would be picked up by it; moreover, so long as he remained within the field of vision which the metal plaque commanded, he could be seen as well as heard. There was of course no way of knowing whether you were being watched at any given moment. How often, or on what system, the Thought Police plugged in on any individual wire was guesswork. It was even conceivable that they watched everybody all the time. But at any rate they could plug in your wire whenever they wanted to. You had to live—did live, from habit that became instinct—in the assumption that every sound you made was overheard, and, except in darkness, every movement scrutinized.

Winston kept his back turned to the telescreen. It was safer; though, as he well knew, even a back can be revealing. A kilometer away the Ministry of Truth, his place of work, towered vast and white above the grimy landscape. This, he thought with a sort of vague distaste—this was London, chief city of Airstrip One, itself the third most populous of the provinces of Oceania. He tried to squeeze out some childhood memory that should tell him whether London had always been quite like this. Were there always these vistas of rotting nineteenth-century houses, their sides shored up with balks of timber, their windows patched with cardboard and their roofs with corrugated iron, their crazy garden walls sagging in all directions? And the bombed sites where the plaster dust swirled in the air and the willow herb straggled over the heaps of rubble; and the places where the bombs had cleared a larger patch and there had sprung up sordid colonies of wooden dwellings like chicken houses? But it was no use, he could not remember: nothing remained of his childhood except a series of bright-lit tableaux, occurring against no background and mostly unintelligible.

The Ministry of Truth—Minitrue, in Newspeak*—was startlingly different from any other object in sight. It was an enormous pyramidal structure of glittering white concrete, soaring up, terrace after terrace, three hundred meters into the air. From where Winston stood it was just possible to read, picked out on its white face in elegant lettering, the three slogans of the Party:

WAR IS PEACE
FREEDOM IS SLAVERY
IGNORANCE IS STRENGTH

The Ministry of Truth contained, it was said, three thousand rooms above ground level, and corresponding ramifications below. Scattered about London there were just three other buildings of similar appearance and size. So completely did they dwarf the surrounding architecture that from the roof of Victory Mansions you could see all four of them simultaneously. They were the homes of the four Ministries between which the entire apparatus of government was divided: the Ministry of Truth, which concerned itself with news, entertainment, education, and the fine arts; the Ministry of Peace, which concerned itself with war; the Ministry of Love, which maintained law and order; and the Ministry of Plenty, which was responsible for economic affairs. Their names, in Newspeak: Minitrue, Minipax, Miniluv, and Miniplenty.

The Ministry of Love was the really frightening one. There were no windows in it at all. Winston

---

* Newspeak was the official language of Oceania. For an account of its structure and etymology, see Appendix [of *1984*].

had never been inside the Ministry of Love, nor within half a kilometer of it. It was a place impossible to enter except on official business, and then only by penetrating through a maze of barbed-wire entanglements, steel doors, and hidden machine-gun nests. Even the streets leading up to its outer barriers were roamed by gorilla-faced guards in black uniforms, armed with jointed truncheons.

Winston turned round abruptly. He had set his features into the expression of quiet optimism which it was advisable to wear when facing the telescreen. He crossed the room into the tiny kitchen. By leaving the Ministry at this time of day he had sacrificed his lunch in the canteen, and he was aware that there was no food in the kitchen except a hunk of dark-colored bread which had got to be saved for tomorrow's breakfast. He took down from the shelf a bottle of colorless liquid with a plain white label marked VICTORY GIN. It gave off a sickly, oily smell, as of Chinese rice-spirit. Winston poured out nearly a teacupful, nerved himself for a shock, and gulped it down like a dose of medicine.

Instantly his face turned scarlet and the water ran out of his eyes. The stuff was like nitric acid and, moreover, in swallowing it one had the sensation of being hit on the back of the head with a rubber club. The next moment, however, the burning in his belly died down and the world began to look more cheerful. He took a cigarette from a crumpled packet marked VICTORY CIGA-RETTES and incautiously held it upright, whereupon the tobacco fell out onto the floor. With the next he was more successful. He went back to the living room and sat down at a small table that stood to the left of the telescreen. From the table drawer he took out a penholder, a bottle of ink, and a thick, quarto-sized blank book with a red back and a marbled cover.

For some reason the telescreen in the living room was in an unusual position. Instead of being placed, as was normal, in the end wall, where it could command the whole room, it was in the longer wall, opposite the window. To one side of it there was a shallow alcove in which Winston was now sitting, and which, when the flats were built, had probably been intended to hold bookshelves. By sitting in the alcove, and keeping well back, Winston was able to remain outside the range of the telescreen, so far as sight went. He could be heard, of course, but so long as he stayed in his present position he could not be seen. It was partly the unusual geography of the room that had suggested to him the thing that he was now about to do.

But it had also been suggested by the book that he had just taken out of the drawer. It was a peculiarly beautiful book. Its smooth creamy paper, a little yellowed by age, was of a kind that had not been manufactured for at least forty years past. He could guess, however, that the book was much older than that. He had seen it lying in the window of a frowsy little junk shop in a slummy quarter of the town (just what quarter he did not now remember) and had been stricken immediately by an overwhelming desire to possess it. Party members were supposed not to go into ordinary shops ("dealing on the free market," it was called), but the rule was not strictly kept, because there were various things such as shoelaces and razor blades which it was impossible to get hold of in any other way. He had given a quick glance up and down the street and then had slipped inside and bought the book for two dollars fifty. At the time he was not conscious of wanting it for any particular purpose. He had carried it guiltily home in his briefcase. Even with nothing written in it, it was a compromising possession.

The thing that he was about to do was to open a diary. This was not illegal (nothing was illegal, since there were no longer any laws), but if detected it was reasonably certain that it would be punished by death, or at least by twenty-five years in a forced-labor camp. Winston fitted a nib into the penholder and sucked it to get the grease off. The pen was an archaic instrument, seldom used even for signatures, and he had procured one, furtively and with some difficulty, simply because of a feeling that the beautiful creamy paper deserved to be written on with a real nib instead of being scratched with an ink pencil. Actually he was not used to writing by hand. Apart from very short notes, it was usual to dictate everything into the speak-write, which was of course impossible for his present purpose. He dipped the pen into the ink and then faltered for just a second. A tremor had gone through his bowels. To mark the paper was the decisive act. In small clumsy letters he wrote:

April 4th, 1984.

He sat back. A sense of complete helplessness had descended upon him. To begin with, he did not know with any certainty that this *was* 1984. It must be round about that date, since he was fairly sure that his age was thirty-nine, and he believed that he had been born in 1944 or 1945; but it was never possible nowadays to pin down any date within a year or two.

GEORGE ORWELL
from *1984*

1. Read the excerpts from *We* and *1984*.
2. In your journal do *one* of the following:
   a. Write a full journal entry based on the opening of *We* and *1984*. Consider the parallels that you find.
   b. Select an author to act as an influence on your own writing. Then write a page that shows your response to this influence.
   c. Consider the statement by Orwell given at the opening of this chapter. Let it influence your revision of a previous entry.

Assignment 15

HUXLEY: Clarity, first of all. Coherence. Orderliness. Those who take an esthetic interest in language and its uses should be encouraged to study good models and to analyze the means employed for the achievement of the results obtained.

MAYER: Sensitivity to the fact of style—that such a thing exists and creates meaning. For this reason, students should not be asked to develop "their own style" any more than they should be graded simply on the basis of formally correct or incorrect usage. Models should be before them—and before their teachers—at all times.

LEE FRANK HOWE
from "Writers on Learning to Write"

As a further way of responding to the constructive force of influence, do the work of this assignment.

In your journal do *one* of the following:
a. Use "The Red-Headed League" by A. Conan Doyle or any other Sherlock Holmes story as an influence and then start your own piece of detection.
b. Choose a favorite detective writer. Moving from his method and influence, start a story of your own.
c. Write a full journal entry under an influence of your own choice.

1 Review

This review requires a time allowance equivalent to that given to four regular assignments.

Review Assignment

In your journal do *one* of the following:

a. Trace the influence of one writer on another.
   (1) Make a bibliography.
   (2) Summarize your actual reading.
   (3) Make a statement about the nature and extent of the influence. For example, show the influence of H. G. Wells on Zamiatin, or Zamiatin's influence on Orwell.

b. Demonstrate your ability to emulate or otherwise respond to the influence of a major writer. For example, start a sequel to *Great Expectations* that takes up Pip's life ten years after the close of the first book.

c. Copy out an event as presented by one author and then show how you think the same situation might have been treated by another author. Below is a brief example. The model is from Jane Austen's *Pride and Prejudice;* the scene occurs right after Elizabeth has refused Mr. Collins's proposal. In the second excerpt, a student has written Austen's scene in the style of George Eliot's *Adam Bede.*

> Mr. Collins was not left long to the silent contemplation of his successful love; for Mrs. Bennet, having dawdled about in the vestibule to watch for the end of the conference, no sooner saw Elizabeth open the door and with quick step pass her toward the staircase, than she entered the breakfast room, and congratulated both him and herself in warm terms on the happy prospect of their nearer connection. Mr. Collins received and returned these felicitations with equal pleasure, and then proceeded to relate the particulars of their interview, with the result of which he trusted

he had every reason to be satisfied, since the refusal which his cousin had steadfastly given him would naturally flow from her bashful modesty and the genuine delicacy of her character.

As Mr. Collins was of that well-meaning yet stubborn and imperceptive type of man who sacrifices all truth to believe that which he wishes; so we now see him in the process of distorting the previous scene into a fantasy in which Elizabeth coquettishly tantalized him and was soon to accept his proposal. And you will recall that Mrs. Bennet, waiting in the vestibule, was of the same obstinacy as Mr. Collins and was forming an even wilder fantasy; for she had led herself to anticipate an immediate acceptance on the part of Elizabeth, and upon her daughter's exit rushed into the breakfast room for the confirmation of these imaginings. She greeted him enthusiastically and listened to his recounting of the conversation with her daughter— I should say, his recounting of the distorted version which assured the imminence of her acceptance, as he had by that time completely persuaded himself that her refusal was a natural initial reply and stemmed merely from her bashfulness and coquetry.

JONATHAN B. STEVENS

In the excerpt below, the student presents Austen's scene in the manner of James Joyce's *A Portrait of the Artist as a Young Man:*

But Collins let blinding Hope conquer and disrupt and reject and rephrase her words of a minute ago, and she became as a rose budding rather than withering; a climbing, not a falling; a summit, not an abyss. And in popped Mrs. Bennet to aid him in the nurturing of this bud, to water it and drown it with a glimmering smiling seeping unknowing assuring wetness and they then saw not distant graves but gowns, not shrouds but veils; they mistook the tolling for another warmer sound. She would go; but he would not know, and translated politeness for excitement, bluntness for confusion, rejection for enticement.

JONATHAN B. STEVENS

UNIT 2

Learn from Poetry

*One of the most quoted ko-an
of the Zen Buddhists goes as follows:
"There is a live goose in a bottle.
How does one remove the goose without
hurting it or damaging the bottle?"
An admired answer is "Behold,
I have done it!"
There is a definition of poetry
to be found in this.*—JOHN HOLMES

2|1

WORD CHOICE

You may begin this study with the clear understanding that no one is trying to turn you into a poet. The purpose of the unit is to help you find ways to improve your prose. One certain way is to develop skill in selecting words, and there the poets can help.

It seems appropriate to begin with a poem by a writer who is himself a journalizer. Here is Mason Williams's ode to the network censor who:

> Snips out
> The rough talk
> The unpopular opinion
> Or anything with teeth
> And renders
> A pattern of ideas
> Full of holes
> A doily
> For your mind.
> MASON WILLIAMS

Time Magazine reports, "If the poetry seems painfully simple, it is explained in part by the fact that Mason taught himself."

Part of that self-teaching is the result of Mason Williams's keeping a journal in which random thoughts are recorded. He uses 500-page accounting ledgers and by now has filled up some nine books of that size. *The Mason Williams Reading Matter* gives an edited version of some of those entries. His book is amusing proof that poetry can be fun and that journal keeping pays. But our concern here is with the poem, and our first concern is with the word. Poetry depends on words—words used with intensity. For example, consider the word "doily" in the poem you just read. What does it mean? Webster says, in part, "a small napkin, used at table with the fruit, etc." The censor's job is nicely described: he carries out a decorative and protective function for household minds. All is nicely balanced, and the word "doily" carries an absolute rightness that detonates and makes the total statement a success.

Now let's look at another word grouping that talks about simple objects in a dimensional and evocative way. You may not understand the "total meaning," but the poem may prove one of your favorites just the same. In any case, the title is a delight—"The Emperor of Ice-Cream." Here are the words Wallace Stevens has used to express that conception:

The Emperor of Ice-Cream

Call the roller of big cigars,
The muscular one, and bid him whip
In kitchen cups concupiscent curds.
Let the wenches dawdle in such dress
As they are used to wear, and let the boys
Bring flowers in last month's newspapers.
Let be be finale of seem.
The only emperor is the emperor of ice-cream.

Take from the dresser of deal,
Lacking the three glass knobs, that sheet
On which she embroidered fantails once
And spread it so as to cover her face.
If her horny feet protrude, they come
To show how cold she is, and dumb.
Let the lamp affix its beam.
The only emperor is the emperor of ice-cream.

WALLACE STEVENS

There is a poem that neither you, nor *Time* Magazine, nor anyone in his right mind will call simple. Indeed, part of its pleasure rests in its complexity, and the superdimensional meanings that Stevens causes to arise from the words. It's a poem you have to think about, and work over, and live with. The process will increase your vocabulary in the approved "College Board way" even if you go no further than looking up the meaning of "concupiscent," "deal," and "fantails." If you consider the expression "let be be finale of seem," you will have gone even further.

Yes, poetry can act as a first aid to prose if you will let it. But first you, yourself, have to experience a poem. Passive reading won't do. Archibald MacLeish in "Ars Poetica" was right when he said "a poem should not mean but be." Making words *be* is the poet's job in part, but it is also yours. Part of the "be-ness" of a poem depends on its reader. Poets—the real ones—use their words with a tightness that even a miser must admire. One word and bang—the world is made or unmade.

The Death of the Ball Turret Gunner

From my mother's sleep I fell into the State
And I hunched in its belly till my wet fur froze.
Six miles from earth, loosed from its dream of life,
I woke to black flak and the nightmare fighters.
When I died they washed me out of the turret with a hose.

RANDALL JARRELL

Let the poets lend you their power of word choice. The lesson may be learned by example, by practice, or by being a genius. For those who feel that example and practice will help, here is a starting place, a way of getting at the inside of a poem. These four ideas are from the Preface of *Reflections on a Gift of Watermelon Pickle . . . and Other Modern Verse*. See if they don't help.

1. Take your time in judging each poem. Poems don't spring from poets' brains. Poets spend more hours finding right words than you will spend minutes reading them. If a word or a line confuses you at first, try to discover why the poet may have left it just as he did.
2. Read each poem slowly. Give every poem a chance to speak to you. Reread. Read aloud. Make your ears and your eyes work on each poem. Expect to find surprises—then read slowly enough to enjoy them.

3. Read only a few poems at one time. The language of poetry is condensed. You will have to supply words that are missing and puzzle over lines that aren't clear at first reading. Better to read one or two poems well than to read a dozen poems carelessly.
4. Judge poems by their quality, not by their subjects. You may not like cats, but there are good cat poems. . . . Read each poem with the idea that you will "let" the poet write on any subject he chooses and in any way he chooses.

Perhaps the best insight into what poems and poets are all about appears in the following prose poem:

As you say (not without sadness)

As you say (not without sadness), poets don't see, they feel. And that's why people who have turned to feelers seem like poets. Why children seem poetic. Why when the sap rises in the adolescent heart the young write poetry. Why great catastrophes are stated in verse. Why lunatics are named for the moon. Yet poetry isn't feeling with the hands. A poem is not a kiss. Poems are what ideas feel like. Ideas on Sunday, thoughts on vacation.

Poets don't see, they feel. They are conductors of the senses of men, as teachers and preachers are the insulators. The poets go up and feel the insulators. Now and again they feel the wrong thing and are thrown through a wall by a million-volt shock. All insulation makes the poet anxious: clothes, strait jackets, iambic five. He pulls at the seams like a boy whose trousers are cutting him in half. Poets think along the electric currents. The words are constantly not making sense when he reads. He flunks economics, logic, history. Then he describes what it feels like to flunk economics, logic, history. After that he feels better.

People say: it is sad to see a grown man feeling his way, sad to see a man so naked, desireless of any defenses. The people walk back into their boxes and triple-lock the doors. When their children begin to read poetry the parents watch them from the corner of their eye. It's only a phase, they aver. Parents like the word "aver" though they don't use it.

KARL SHAPIRO

Then, too, appreciation for exact expressions will in part grow from your own thinking and scrutiny of words. As you read poems, have confidence in the great and natural principle of unconscious imitation. Don't get encumbered by rules. Study your butterflies while they are alive, not impaled on pins: turn to poems themselves.

Begin by letting the poem make its own sound. *Read the poem out loud.* Don't mumble. *Read;* enunciate; let the sound *be.* Practice this precept now. Read aloud Shakespeare's lines describing Cleopatra's progress down the Nile as she goes to meet her Antony. Enobarbus reports the scene.

> The barge she sat in, like a burnish'd throne,
> Burn'd on the water. The poop was beaten gold;
> Purple the sails, and so perfumèd that
> The winds were lovesick with them. The oars were
>   silver,
> Which to the tune of flutes kept stroke, and made
> The water which they beat to follow faster,
> As amorous of their strokes. For her own person,
> It beggar'd all description: she did lie
> In her pavilion, cloth of gold of tissue,
> O'er-picturing that Venus where we see
> The fancy outwork nature. On each side her
> Stood pretty dimpled boys, like smiling Cupids,
> With divers-color'd fans, whose wind did seem

To glow the delicate cheeks which they did cool,
And what they undid did. . . .
Her gentlewomen, like the Nereides,
So many mermaids, tended her i' the eyes,
And made their bends adornings. At the helm
A seeming mermaid steers; the silken tackle
Swell with the touches of those flower-soft hands,
That yarely frame the office. From the barge
A strange invisible perfume hits the sense
Of the adjacent wharfs. The city cast
Her people out upon her; and Antony,
Enthronèd i' the marketplace, did sit alone,
Whistling to the air, which, but for vacancy,
Had gone to gaze on Cleopatra too,
And made a gap in nature.

WILLIAM SHAKESPEARE
from *Antony and Cleopatra*

Then turn to a piece of student writing. Its author, a member of a dramatic cast of *Antony and Cleopatra,* let the words of that play become so much a part of him that he was prompted to write his own version of the drama. The point is not to write after the manner of Shakespeare—that was this student's self-appointed exercise; the point is that exposure permits words and sentence rhythm to grow within you, to become a part of you, to increase your own verbal resources. Read and absorb; read aloud and listen, and without conscious effort you will find your prose improves. Here is a scene from the student's play. Its diction and humor are reminiscent of Shakespeare and of his treatment of the carter's scene in *Henry IV, Part I.*

ALEXANDER: Can this be so! Does Darius forsake
His one great vantage for such a size,
Which be the open plain—now to find
Himself pinched in the narrow way
Between the mountain and shore?
His numbers, if thus caught, will
Want much skill. Quick! To catch him

Thus were to catch the world while
On its knees.
                    Dispatch Parmenio!
Haste pleads our cause!

                                        (*exeunt omnes*)

SCENE VI
A field near Issus

Enter two village peasants.

1ST PEASANT: Didst thou hear? 'Tis like the two
   armies
Meet upon yon shore.
2ND PEASANT: Ay, which dost thou think will win?
1ST: I do not think, nor do I care;
   What matter but that there be a loser?
2ND: There's the point. 'Tis our chance
   That the fight be here.
1ST: Ay, my hands do wish to leave their toil
   And feed upon the dead.
2ND: True, if we be quick enough,
   A fortune be ours.
1ST: Ay, 'tis better sport to pillage the slain,
   Than rob a wench of her treasure.
2ND: Justly! For that which we find upon the dying
   Will buy the treasure o' full many a maid.
1ST: Indeed! With one to the other
   We'll be kings both, lacking naught!
2ND: I'll to the armor and sword,
   For such abound at time of death.
1ST: For me, 'twill be the rings I take
   From sweaty fingers; though they
   Be not so plentiful, their quality be above,
   And so I'll be the richer.
2ND: How now? The richer thou sayest?
1ST: Such will I be.
2ND: Thou dost o'ercount thyself.
1ST: Indeed then, who will have more?
2ND: Why 'tis I.

1ST: Thou? When dost quality fall second to quantity?

2ND: When quantity be the better.

1ST: But 'tis he that at the head dost spot
The better, the better goods.

2ND: If such is true, then it needs must be I.

1ST: Thou art too sure of thyself. Methinks
The better man be here amongst us.

2ND: What sayest thou? There be here but two.

1ST: Truly sir, thus the better is I.

2ND: How now? 'Tis my honor thou now touchest
upon.

1ST: For its worth, it could not withstand
More than a touch.

2ND: Knave! I'll unhair thy head,
And split thy chaps!

1ST: Thine are so as now, spilling emptiness.

2ND: And dost thou say my words hold no weight?

1ST: Truly so, being but air.

2ND: Villain, avaunt! 'Ere anger o'ersways my judgment!

1ST: Being both the same, thou art
Disjoint 'ere thou speakest.

2ND: Rogue! Thou temptest me too far ——

(strikes and misses; other strikes and kills)

1ST: Art thou dead? 'Tis well thou'rt dead;
For now when I say I'm the richer,
Thou canst say but naught.

(exit)

JAMES DANIEL MOORE, JR.

Assignment 1

Now give yourself a chance to play with words. Attend to
propriety and economy of statement. Have confidence that
your efforts here will later show themselves in improved
prose.

As a start, write a few *cinquains*. In this form of poetry

there is an association of parts rather than a flow of ideas, but the form is easily manageable and will get you started with word choice. These are the rules:

First line: Use a single word to name a topic.

Second line: Use two words to describe or define the topic named.

Third line: Use three words to express action.

Fourth line: Use four words that reflect your own personal attitude.

Fifth line: Use one word that is a synonym for your defined topic.

It is good practice to work a few of these out as a group and then write some on your own. Here is one written by a student:

> Mirrors
> with curves
> make you weird
> laughing world to see
> untruths.
>
> JEFF CLAUS

A poem is quick. Quick, I say, as chain lightning.
ROBERT P. TRISTRAM COFFIN

1. Read the chapter up to this point.
2. In your journal do *one* of the following:
   a. Write several cinquains. Try to make at least one truly satisfying to yourself. Practice in word choice is the point of this exercise.
   b. One way to develop skill in word choice is to increase the words from which you may choose. Turn to the special vocabulary of poetry listed in Unit 2, "Review," and learn the words with which you are unfamiliar. Write out the definitions from Abrams's *Glossary of Literary Terms* or a source of your own choice.
   c. Design your own "word choice through poetry" exercise and do it. (Write out your exact assignment before you start.)

Assignment 2

The advantages which rhyme has over blank verse are so many, that it were lost time to name them. . . . But that benefit which I consider most in it, because I have not seldom found it, is, that it bounds and circumscribes the fancy. For imagination in a poet is a faculty so wild and lawless, that, like an high-ranging spaniel, it must have clogs tied to it, lest it outrun the judgment. The great easiness of blank verse renders the poet too luxuriant; he is tempted to say many things, which might be omitted, or at least shut up in fewer words; but when the difficulty of artful rhyming is interposed, where the poet commonly confines his sense to his couplet, and must contrive that sense into such words, that the rhyme shall naturally follow them, not they the rhyme; the fancy then gives leisure to the judgment to come in, which, seeing so heavy a tax imposed, is ready to cut off all unnecessary expenses. This last consideration has already answered an objection which some have made, that rhyme is only an embroidery of sense, to make that, which is ordinary in itself, pass for excellent with less examination. But certainly, that, which most regulates the fancy, and gives the judgment its busiest employment, is like to bring forth the richest and clearest thoughts.

JOHN DRYDEN
from "Dedication of the Rival-Ladies"

Haiku is an art form that presents the rhythmical flow of an idea within a strict pattern. The rules require that seventeen syllables be distributed over three lines in this way:

First line: Use five syllables.
Second line: Use seven syllables.
Third line: Use five syllables.

The intention of haiku is to capture the spirit of a season or of a single object in nature. Here are two examples, both by the same student. You will be amused to note that the one that defines haiku also violates it by disregarding nature and the seasons. But in word play it is accurate and an achievement. (For a more detailed explanation and examples, see *An Introduction to Haiku,* by Harold G. Henderson.)

The Portent

There is not a stir,
Not even one leaf; awesome
Is the summer gone.

Haiku

A stick man feeling,
Knowing that words must be found
To build skeletons.

JEFF CLAUS

1. Read the material for this assignment.
2. In your journal do *one* of the following:
   a. Write haiku on objects in nature.
   b. Write haiku on the seasons.
   c. Look up additional material on haiku. Copy out the best examples that you find. Give sources.

Assignment 3

I love mankind, but I hate the institutions of the dead unkind. Men execute nothing so faithfully as the wills of the dead, to the last codicil and letter. They rule this world, and the living are but their executors.

HENRY DAVID THOREAU
from *A Week on the Concord and Merrimack Rivers*

pity this busy monster,manunkind

pity this busy monster,manunkind,

not.   Progress is a comfortable disease:
your victim(death and life safely beyond)

plays with the bigness of his littleness
—electrons deify one razorblade
into a mountainrange;lenses extend

unwish through curving wherewhen till unwish
returns on its unself.
                          A world of made
is not a world of born—pity poor flesh

and trees,poor stars and stones,but never this
fine specimen of hypermagical

ultraomnipotence.   We doctors know

a hopeless case if—listen:there's a hell
of a good universe next door;let's go

                                E. E. CUMMINGS

1. Read the material for this assignment.
2. In your journal do *one* of the following:
   a. Write your understanding of the poem. Focus attention
      on Cummings's use of words. How is the first line of the
      poem related to the excerpt by Thoreau?
   b. Copy out a poem whose word choice especially interests
      you. Discuss the poet's language in this poem.
   c. Write your own word-play entry.
      (1) Explain your objective.
      (2) Do your thing.
      (3) State how close you feel you came to accomplishing
          your stated objective.

2|2

SKILL WITH METAPHORS

> I can connect
> Nothing with nothing.
>
> T. S. ELIOT
> from *The Waste Land*

A metaphor is a connector. It is the equals sign in poetic equations. Thought itself is based on likeness and association; metaphor compresses thought—catches correspondences and sketches them with the vividness and economy of Japanese line drawings. Metaphor is how poetry gets said. Here the term is used to embrace all comparisons made in poetry. Your previously taught definitions for simile, image, and symbol are right enough. But here, for economy and convenience, we'll lump them all under the great equals sign of metaphor and go ahead to consider our equations.

A poet is the man who you'll find can help, and poems are poets at their best. But before you get too rarefied, listen to some plain talk by a poet who understood the power of metaphor—Robert Frost. These remarks are among the things he said at a writing conference at the University of New Hampshire.

Education by poetry is education by metaphor.

I do not think anybody ever knows the discreet use of a metaphor, his own and other people's, the discreet handling of metaphor, unless he has been properly educated in poetry.

Poetry begins in trivial metaphors, pretty metaphors, "grace" metaphors, and goes on to the profoundest thinking that we have. Poetry provides the one permissible way of saying one thing and meaning another. People say, "Why don't you say what you mean?" We never do that, do we, being all of us too much poets. We like to talk in parables and in hints and in indirections—whether from diffidence or some other instinct.

What I am pointing out is that unless you are at home in the metaphor, unless you have had your proper poetical education in the metaphor, you are not safe anywhere. Because you are not at ease with figurative values: you don't know the metaphor in its strength and its weakness. You don't know how far you may expect to ride it and when it may break down with you. You are not safe in science; you are not safe in history. In history, for instance—to show that it is the same in history as elsewhere—I heard somebody say yesterday that Aeneas was to be likened unto (those words, "likened unto"!) George Washington. He was that type of national hero, the middle-class man, not thinking of being a hero at all, bent on building the future, bent on his children, his descendants. A good metaphor, as far as it goes, and you must know how far. And then he added that Odysseus should be likened unto Theodore Roosevelt. I don't think that is so good. Someone visiting Gibbon at the point of death, said he was the same Gibbon as of old, still at his parallels.

Let me ask you to watch a metaphor breaking down here before you.

Somebody said to me a little while ago, "It is easy enough for me to think of the universe as a machine, as a mechanism."

I said, "You mean the universe is like a machine?"

He said, "No. I think it is one. . . . Well, it is like. . . ."

"I think you mean the universe is like a machine."

"All right. Let it go at that."

I asked him, "Did you ever see a machine without a pedal for the foot, or a lever for the hand, or a button for the finger?"

He said, "No—no."

I said, "All right. Is the universe like that?"

And he said, "No, I mean it is like a machine, only. . . ."

". . . it is different from a machine," I said.

He wanted to go just that far with that metaphor and no further. And so do we all. All metaphor breaks down somewhere. That is the beauty of it. It is touch and go with the metaphor, and until you have lived with it long enough you don't know when it is going. You don't know how much you can get out of it and when it will cease to yield. It is a very living thing. It is as life itself.

We still ask boys in college to think, as in the nineties, but we seldom tell them what thinking means; we seldom tell them it is just putting this and that together; it is just saying one thing in terms of another. To tell them is to set their feet on the first rung of a ladder the top of which sticks through the sky.

We ask people to think, and we don't show them what thinking is. Somebody says we don't need to show them how to think; by and by they will think. We will give them the forms of sentences and, if they have any ideas, then they will know how to write them. But that is preposterous. All there is to writing is having ideas. To learn to write is to learn to have ideas.

The first little metaphor . . . Take some of the trivial ones. I would rather have trivial ones of my own to live by than the big ones of other people.

I remember a boy saying, "He is the kind of person that wounds with his shield." That may be a slender one, of course. It goes a good way in character description. It has poetic grace. "He is the kind that wounds with his shield."

The shield reminds me—just to linger a minute —the shield reminds me of the inverted shield spoken of in one of the books of the *Odyssey,* the book that tells about the longest swim on record. I forget how long it lasted—several days, was it?—but at last as Odysseus came near the coast of Phoenicia, he saw it on the horizon "like an inverted shield."

There is a better metaphor in the same book. In the end Odysseus comes ashore and crawls up the beach to spend the night under a double olive tree, and it says, as in a lonely farmhouse where it is hard to get fire—I am not quoting exactly—where it is hard to start the fire again if it goes out, they cover the seeds of fire with ashes to preserve it for the night, so Odysseus covered himself with the leaves around him and went to sleep. There you have something that gives you character, something of Odysseus himself. "Seeds of fire." So Odysseus covered the seeds of fire in himself. You get the greatness of his nature.

But these are slighter metaphors than the ones we live by. They have their charm, their passing charm. They are as it were the first steps toward the great thoughts, grave thoughts, thoughts lasting to the end.

The metaphor whose manage we are best taught in poetry—that is all there is of thinking. It may not seem far for the mind to go but it is the mind's furthest. The richest accumulation of the ages is the noble metaphors we have rolled up.

I want to add one thing more that the experience of poetry is to anyone who comes close to poetry. There are two ways of coming close to poetry. One is by writing poetry. And some people think I want people to write poetry, but I don't; that is, I don't necessarily. I only want people to write poetry if they want to write poetry. I have never encouraged anybody to write poetry that did not want to write it, and I have not always encouraged those who did want to write it. That ought to be one's own funeral. It is a hard, hard life, as they say.

But as I say, there is another way to come close to poetry, fortunately, and that is in the reading of it, not as linguistics, not as history, not as anything but poetry. It is one of the hard things for a teacher to know how close a man has come in reading poetry. How do I know whether a man has come close to Keats in reading Keats? It is hard for me to know. . . .

The closeness—everything depends on the closeness with which you come, and you ought to be marked for the closeness, for nothing else. And that will have to be estimated by chance remarks, not by question and answer. It is only by accident that you know some day how near a person has come.

The person who gets close enough to poetry, he is going to know more about the word *belief* than anybody else knows, even in religion nowadays. There are two or three places where we know belief outside of religion. One of them is at the age of fifteen to twenty, in our self-belief. A young man knows more about himself than he is able to prove to anyone. He has no knowledge that anybody else will accept as knowledge. In his foreknowledge he has something that is going to believe itself into fulfillment, into acceptance.

There is another belief like that, the belief in someone else, a relationship of two that is going to be believed into fulfillment. That is what we are talking about in our novels, the belief of love. And the disillusionment that the novels are full of is simply the disillusionment from disappointment in that belief. That belief can fail, of course.

Then there is a literary belief. Every time a poem is written, every time a short story is written, it is written not by cunning, but by belief. The beauty, the something, the little charm of the thing to be, is more felt than known. There is a common jest, one that always annoys me, on the writers, that they write the last end first, and then work up to it; that they lay a train toward one sentence that they think is pretty nice and have all fixed up to set like a trap to close with. No, it should not be that way at all. No one who has ever come close to the arts has failed to see the difference between things written that way, with cunning and device, and the kind that are believed into existence, that begin in something more felt than known. This you can realize quite as well—not quite as well, perhaps, but nearly as well—in reading as you can in writing. I would undertake to separate short stories on that principle; stories that have been believed into existence and stories that have been cunningly devised. And I could separate the poems still more easily.

ROBERT FROST
from *A Book of Prose of Robert Frost*
edited by Edward Lathem and Hyde Cox

Assignment 4

1. Read the chapter up to this point.
2. In your journal do *one* of the following:
   a. Write some "grace" (pretty, decorative) metaphors—perhaps half a dozen. Write your own or use a poet's as a model. Give sources. Then write a few metaphors (again, your own or ones modeled after a poet) that go on "to the profoundest thinking we have."
   b. Write a parable.
   c. Just put this and that together; just say one thing in terms of another and see where a full journal entry puts you on the ladder of ideas.

Assignment 5

The Snow Globe

A long time ago, when I was a child,
They left my light on while I went to sleep,
As though they would have wanted me beguiled
By brightness if at all; dark was too deep.

And they left me one toy, a village white
With the fresh snow and silently in glass
Frozen forever. But if you shook it,
The snow would rise up in the rounded space

And from the limits of the universe
Snow itself down again. O world of white,
First home of dreams! Now that I have my dead,
I want so cold an emblem to rehearse
How many of them have gone from the world's light,
As I have gone, too, from my snowy bed.

HOWARD NEMEROV

1. Read the Nemerov poem.
2. In your journal do *one* of the following:
   a. Discuss the poem. Give special attention to metaphor. Be sure to consider its title and use of words. For example, consider "want," "rehearse," and "snowy."
   b. Choose an image from your own childhood and use it as a symbol to discuss some later discovery.
   c. Choose a subject and write about it, using any form.

Assignment 6

Holy Sonnet XIV

Batter my heart, three-personed God; for, you
As yet but knock, breathe, shine, and seek to mend;
That I may rise and stand, o'erthrow me, and bend
Your force, to break, blow, burn, and make me new.
I, like an usurpèd town, to another due,
Labor to admit you, but oh, to no end,
Reason, your viceroy in me, me should defend,
But is captived, and proves weak or untrue.
Yet dearly I love you, and would be lovèd fain,
But am betrothed unto your enemy:
Divorce me, untie, or break that knot again,
Take me to you, imprison me, for I
Except you enthrall me, never shall be free,
Nor ever chaste, except you ravish me.

JOHN DONNE

In this sonnet dissimilar and paradoxical ideas are held in balance through Donne's extraordinary control of metaphor. The poem is worth your attention not because you, yourself, will want to work in just this way but because it demonstrates the outer limits of the power that can be achieved through skill with metaphor.

1. Read Donne's Sonnet.
2. In your journal do *one* of the following:
   a. Study the Donne poem and then give your interpretation of it. Give special attention to Donne's use of metaphor.
   b. Reprinted below is Elizabeth Drew's comment on this poem of Donne's. Read her commentary and then write a summary of what she has to say about the poem.

When Henry James discussed the fiction of George Eliot he said that in spite of her depth and power in presenting the human condition, her conception of the novelist's task was never in the least as the *game* of art. No one could bring such a criticism against Donne. At the same time no one could feel here that he isn't profoundly moved by his subject, or that the fun he must have had working out his analogies in any way falsifies his faith and fervor. The complexity of the verbal pattern communicates the conflict in his own being: his burning emotional need for religious fulfillment on the one hand, and, on the other, his unsuccessful efforts to achieve it by any rational or impersonal approach.

Violent emotion indeed is at the center of the whole poem. The paradoxical theme is the achievement of final peace only through the violent conflicts and ultimate surrenders of war and of love. "Batter my heart," he starts, combining at once the two metaphorical strands. The address, though, is to "three-personed God," and he is going to weave "trinities" into the formal elements of his design. Though the final unity is that of the sonnet, the structure is divided into three clusters of metaphors, two in the octet and one in the sestet. Beyond that, the first metaphor, the direct prayer to the three-in-one God not to use gentle ways, but to re-create after destruction, presents the argument in two groups of three words each, then summed up in a phrase unifying them. God must not "knock, breathe, shine, and seek to mend," but "break, blow, burn, and make me new." In the thematic scheme, each of the words in the first line suggests a quiet action, while each of the second group intensifies it into a vehement one.

Various words in the first quatrain, *batter, o'erthrow, burn,* make links to the next cluster of metaphors, dominated by that of the captive town. The poet's heart, though true to its rightful owner, has been overpowered and is helpless. Reason, reigning in the place of God, should be an aid, but has no power. It again is not active enough. This quatrain is also colored by the love imagery, which develops as the main strand in the last six lines. The "usurpèd town, to another due" has a suggestion of a betrayed maiden, and the "weak or untrue" reason implies a faithless friend. In the same way when the sexual imagery comes to the fore, suggestions of capture and imprisonment keep the war theme alive. Again the pattern of the need for the violent to invade what is too gentle is played out in the language. The betrothal to another sounds like an inert drifting, and the language is inert too. It comes to life again in the violent, crowded, rushing images of the last four lines and the startling paradox of the consummation.

ELIZABETH DREW
from *Poetry: A Modern Guide to Its Understanding and Enjoyment*

c. Choose a poem whose metaphors you admire. Copy out the poem or insert it in your journal. Then write your own analysis of the way the metaphors work within this particular poem.

2|3

THE DISCOVERY
OF SUBJECT AND THEME

If you find yourself looking for a composition topic or a story idea, or a way to get started, and can't find what you want, try the poets. They have written on every conceivable subject. Their work stands as a reminder of what can be done, and as an invitation to work the same theme with your own variations. Because poems are intense, they tend to evoke idea and emotion. Very often the experience of the poem will itself suggest a direction for writing. Here is an example. Below is a poem, and following it are a student's notes indicating possible writing topics. Clearly, not all the responses will serve as theme subjects, but when it comes time to sit down and write, the variety and range of ideas suggested by even one poem can be helpful.

A Hole in the Floor

FOR RENÉ MAGRITTE

> The carpenter's made a hole
> In the parlor floor, and I'm standing
> Staring down into it now
> At four o'clock in the evening,
> As Schliemann stood when his shovel   5
> Knocked on the crowns of Troy.
>
> A clean-cut sawdust sparkles
> On the gray, shaggy laths,
> And here is a cluster of shavings

From the time when the floor was laid. 10
They are silvery-gold, the color
Of Hesperian apple parings.

Kneeling, I look in under
Where the joists go into hiding.
A pure street, faintly littered 15
With bits and strokes of light,
Enters the long darkness
Where its parallels will meet.

The radiator pipe
Rises in middle distance 20
Like a shuttered kiosk, standing
Where the only news is night.
Here it's not painted green,
As it is in the visible world.

For God's sake, what am I after? 25
Some treasure, or tiny garden?
Or that untrodden place,
The house's very soul,
Where time has stored our footbeats
And the long skein of our voices? 30

Not these, but the buried strangeness
Which nourishes the known:
That spring from which the floor lamp
Drinks now a wilder bloom,
Inflaming the damask love seat 35
And the whole dangerous room.

RICHARD WILBUR

line 5: Schliemann—discovery
lines 7–10: a house was built
line 12: Hesperian apple parings—Greek myth
line 17: long darkness—death
line 21: kiosk—look up
line 24: the visible world—theme
line 26: tiny garden—Alice in Wonderland? Tiny
Alice?

line 27: that untrodden place—time's storehouse
　　　　(see line 29)
line 30: the long skein of our voices
lines 31–32: the buried strangeness which nour-
　　　　　ishes the known—how? why? give ex-
　　　　　amples
line 36: dangerous room

Show the way reality informs imagination. Use this poem as an example.

As you see, no theme is as yet written, but a starting place may have been found. No two people will make an identical set of notes nor should they. Still, each poem stands as an invitation to thought and response.

Another way of using poems to prompt themes is to write a paraphrase. This is more work than the straightaway impulsive response that has been outlined, but it has its advantages. You are forced to consider the poem long enough and clearly enough to grasp its controlling idea and to be explicit rather than vague. This bit of writing and thinking may be just enough to get you started writing on your own.

The business of finding topics and developing them is a mystery. Even the poets have their problems and conflicting theories. Here is a brief essay by Amy Lowell that says as much as can perhaps be said about where poems or, for that matter, themes come from. As you read it, note the poet's dependence on the subconscious—however that works. There is a useful lesson here for the nonpoet but would-be theme writer. The point is really a double one: (1) Respond, keep notes, journalize on ideas that "come to you"; write them up, or if time does not allow, at least write them down. (2) Give yourself time for subconscious thought. This approach means that you can't start Monday's theme on Sunday night. At least if you do, your subconscious is not apt to be of much help to you. But if you start a few days in advance to look at poems and ruminate on topics, there is more than a good chance that you'll find a topic and some subconscious promptings that help.

This is how a poet explains the process. Has anything of the same kind ever been a part of your experience?

In answering the question, How are poems made? my instinctive answer is a flat "I don't know." It makes not the slightest difference that the question as asked me refers solely to my own poems, for I know as little of how they are made as I do of anyone else's. What I do know about them is only a millionth part of what there must be to know. I meet them where they touch consciousness, and that is already a considerable distance along the road of evolution.

Whether poetry is the fusion of contradictory ideas, as Mr. [Robert] Graves believes, or the result and relief of emotional irritation and tension, as Sara Teasdale puts it, or the yielding to a psychical state verging on daydream, as Professor Prescott has written a whole book to prove, it is impossible for anyone to state definitely. All I can confidently assert from my own experience is that it is not daydream, but an entirely different psychic state and one peculiar to itself.

The truth is that there is a little mystery here, and no one is more conscious of it than the poet himself. Let us admit at once that a poet is something like a radio aerial—he is capable of receiving messages on waves of some sort; but he is more than an aerial, for he possesses the capacity of transmuting these messages into those patterns of words we call poems.

It would seem that a scientific definition of a poet might put it something like this: a man of an extraordinarily sensitive and active subconscious personality, fed by, and feeding, a nonresistant consciousness. A common phrase among poets is, "It came to me." So hackneyed has this become that one learns to suppress the expression with care, but really it is the best description I know of the conscious arrival of a poem.

Sometimes the external stimulus which has produced a poem is known or can be traced. It may be a sight, a sound, a thought, or an emotion. Sometimes the consciousness has no record of the initial impulse, which has either been forgotten or springs from a deep, unrealized memory. But whatever it is, emotion, apprehended or hidden, is a part of it, for only emotion can rouse the subconscious into action. How carefully and precisely the subconscious mind functions, I have often been a witness to in my own work. An idea will come into my head for no apparent reason; "The Bronze Horses," for instance. I registered the horses as a good subject for a poem; and, having so registered them, I consciously thought no more about the matter. But what I had really done was to drop my subject into the subconscious, much as one drops a letter into the mailbox. Six months later, the words of the poem began to come into my head, the poem—to use my private vocabulary—was "there."

Some poets speak of hearing a voice speaking to them, and say that they write almost to dictation. I do not know whether my early scientific training is responsible for my using a less picturesque vocabulary, or whether their process really differs from mine. I do not hear a voice, but I do hear words pronounced, only the pronouncing is toneless. The words seem to be pronounced in my head, but with nobody speaking them. This is an effect with which I am familiar, for I always *hear* words even when I am reading to myself, and still more when I am writing. In writing, I frequently stop to read aloud what I have written, although this is really hardly necessary, so clearly do the words sound in my head.

The subconscious is, however, a most temperamental ally. Often he will strike work at some critical point and not another word is to be got out of him. Here is where the conscious training of the poet comes in, for he must fill in what the subconscious has left, and fill it in as much in the key of the rest as possible. Every long poem is sprinkled with these *lacunae;* hence the innumerable rewritings which most poems undergo. Sometimes the sly subconscious partner will take pity on the struggling poet and return to his assistance; sometimes he will have nothing to do with that particular passage again. This is the reason that a poet must be both born and made. He must be born with a subconscious factory always working for him or he never can be a poet at all, and he must have knowledge and talent enough to "putty" up his holes—to use Mr. Graves's expression. Let no one undervalue this process of puttying; it is a condition of good poetry. Of the many first manuscript drafts of great poets that have passed through my hands in the last twenty-five years, I have seen none without its share of putty, and the one of all most worked over is Keats's "The Eve of St. Agnes."

Long poems are apt to take months preparing in the subconscious mind; in the case of short poems, the period of subconscious gestation may be a day or an instant, or any time between. Suddenly words are there, and there with an imperious insistence which brooks no delay. They must be written down immediately or an acute suffering comes on, a distress almost physical, which is not relieved until the poem is given right of way. I never deny poems when they come; whatever I am doing, whatever I am writing, I lay it aside and attend to the arriving poem. I am so constituted that poems seldom come when I am out of doors, or actively engaged in company. But when I am alone, an idea contingent upon something I have seen or done when I am out will announce itself, quite as though it had been biding its time until it had me quiescent and receptive.

I seldom compose in my head. The first thing I do when I am conscious of the coming of a poem is to seek paper and pencil. It seems as though the simple gazing at a piece of blank paper hypnotized me into an awareness of the subconscious. For the same reason, I seldom correct poems while walking or driving; I find that the concentration needed for this is in the nature of trance (although that is too exaggerated a word for it), and must not be broken into by considerations of where I am going or what station I am to get out at.

This state of semitrance is not surprising when we think of short poems; what is curious is that the trancelike state can hold over interruptions in the case of long poems. When a poem is so long that days or weeks are needed to write it, the mere sitting down to continue it produces the requisite frame of mind, which holds (except for the *lacunae* I have spoken of) throughout its correction. On the other hand, no power will induce it if the subconscious is not ready; hence the sterile periods known to all poets.

I do believe that a poet should know all he can. No subject is alien to him, and the profounder his knowledge in any direction, the more depth will there be to his poetry. I believe he should be thoroughly grounded in both the old and the new poetic forms, but I am firmly convinced that he must never respect tradition above his intuitive self. Let him be sure of his own sincerity above all, let him bow to no public acclaim, however alluring, and then let him write with all courage what his subconscious mind suggests to him.

AMY LOWELL
"The Process of Making Poetry"

Assignment 7

1. Read the chapter up to this point.
2. In your journal do *one* of the following:
   a. Write a paraphrase of the poem by Richard Wilbur. List all theme topics that the exercise prompts you to think of. Put an asterisk by the one you think the best.
   b. Select a poem of your own choice. Copy it out or paste it into your journal. Then record the potential theme topics that it suggests to you.
   c. Write your own explanation of ways to discover writable topics.

Assignment 8

Patterns

I walk down the garden-paths,
And all the daffodils
Are blowing, and the bright blue squills.
I walk down the patterned garden-paths
In my stiff, brocaded gown.
With my powdered hair and jeweled fan,
I too am a rare
Pattern. As I wander down
The garden-paths.

My dress is richly figured,
And the train
Makes a pink and silver stain
On the gravel, and the thrift
Of the borders.
Just a plate of current fashion,
Tripping by in high-heeled, ribboned shoes.
Not a softness anywhere about me,
Only whalebone and brocade.
And I sink on a seat in the shade
Of a lime tree. For my passion
Wars against the stiff brocade.
The daffodils and squills
Flutter in the breeze
As they please.
And I weep;
For the lime-tree is in blossom
And one small flower has dropped upon my bosom.

And the plashing of waterdrops
In the marble fountain
Comes down the garden-paths.
The dripping never stops.
Underneath my stiffened gown
Is the softness of a woman bathing in a marble
    basin,
A basin in the midst of hedges grown

So thick, she cannot see her lover hiding,
But she guesses he is near,
And the sliding of the water
Seems the stroking of a dear
Hand upon her.
What is Summer in a fine brocaded gown!
I should like to see it lying in a heap upon the
    ground.
All the pink and silver crumpled up on the ground.

I would be the pink and silver as I ran along the
    paths,
And he would stumble after,
Bewildered by my laughter.
I should see the sun flashing from his sword-hilt and
    the buckles on his shoes.
I would choose
To lead him in a maze along the patterned paths,
A bright and laughing maze for my heavy-booted
    lover.
Till he caught me in the shade,
And the buttons of his waistcoat bruised my body
    as he clasped me,
Aching, melting, unafraid.
With the shadows of the leaves and the sundrops,
And the plopping of the waterdrops,
All about us in the open afternoon—
I am very like to swoon
With the weight of this brocade,
For the sun sifts through the shade.

Underneath the fallen blossom
In my bosom
Is a letter I have hid.
It was brought to me this morning by a rider from
    the Duke.
"Madam, we regret to inform you that Lord Hart-
    well
Died in action Thursday se'nnight."
As I read it in the white, morning sunlight,
The letters squirmed like snakes.

"Any answer, Madam," said my footman.
"No," I told him.
"See that the messenger takes some refreshment.
No, no answer."
And I walked into the garden,
Up and down the patterned paths,
In my stiff, correct brocade.
The blue and yellow flowers stood up proudly in
    the sun,
Each one.
I stood upright too,
Held rigid to the pattern
By the stiffness of my gown;
Up and down I walked,
Up and down.

In a month he would have been my husband.
In a month, here, underneath this lime,
We would have broke the pattern;
He for me, and I for him,
He as Colonel, I as Lady,
On this shady seat.
He had a whim
That sunlight carried blessing.
And I answered, "It shall be as you have said."
Now he is dead.

In Summer and in Winter I shall walk
Up and down
The patterned garden-paths
In my stiff, brocaded gown.
The squills and daffodils
Will give place to pillared roses, and to asters, and
    to snow.
I shall go
Up and down
In my gown.
Gorgeously arrayed,
Boned and stayed.
And the softness of my body will be guarded from
    embrace

By each button, hook, and lace.
For the man who should loose me is dead,
Fighting with the Duke in Flanders,
In a pattern called a war.
Christ! What are patterns for?

AMY LOWELL

1. Read "Patterns."
2. In your journal do *one* of the following:
   a. Write an entry on "Patterns."
   b. Write a list of theme topics suggested by this poem.
   c. Write down some of the narrative possibilities suggested by this poem.

Assignment 9

> Stories is not as simple as is usually believed.
>
> FREDERICK C. CREWS
from The Pooh Perplex

This assignment is intended to help you find themes and topics for stories. The approach is that used in the other lessons.

The particular poem that follows is a difficult one and subject to a variety of interpretations. But its complexity and narrative line make it useful for the purpose of suggesting stories. Don't worry if you aren't sure what it is all about. You may find yourself returning to it many times before you can say definitely. But for now explore its story possibilities.

The Lifeguard

In a stable of boats I lie still,
From all sleeping children hidden.
The leap of a fish from its shadow
Makes the whole lake instantly tremble.
With my foot on the water, I feel
The moon outside

Take on the utmost of its power.
I rise and go out through the boats.
I set my broad sole upon silver,
On the skin of the sky, on the moonlight,
Stepping outward from earth onto water
In quest of the miracle

This village of children believed
That I could perform as I dived
For one who had sunk from my sight.
I saw his cropped haircut go under.
I leapt, and my steep body flashed
Once, in the sun.

Dark drew all the light from my eyes.
Like a man who explores his death
By the pull of his slow-moving shoulders,
I hung head down in the cold,
Wide-eyed, contained, and alone
Among the weeds,

And my fingertips turned into stone
From clutching immovable blackness.
Time after time I leapt upward
Exploding in breath, and fell back
From the change in the children's faces
At my defeat.

Beneath them I swam to the boathouse
With only my life in my arms
To wait for the lake to shine back
At the risen moon with such power
That my steps on the light of the ripples
Might be sustained.

Beneath me is nothing but brightness
Like the ghost of a snowfield in summer.
As I move toward the center of the lake,
Which is also the center of the moon,
I am thinking of how I may be
The savior of one

Who has already died in my care.
The dark trees fade from around me.
The moon's dust hovers together.
I call softly out, and the child's
Voice answers through blinding water.
Patiently, slowly,

He rises, dilating to break
The surface of stone with his forehead.
He is one I do not remember
Having ever seen in his life.
The ground I stand on is trembling
Upon his smile.

I wash the black mud from my hands.
On a light given off by the grave
I kneel in the quick of the moon
At the heart of a distant forest
And hold in my arms a child
Of water, water, water.

JAMES DICKEY

1. Read "The Lifeguard."
2. In your journal do *one* of the following:
   a. Tell the story outlined by the poem from the point of view of a child who was there.
   b. Tell of these events as a resort visitor learns of them in another summer.
   c. Tell your own version of this story.

24

WAYS TO KILL A CLICHÉ

Political language—and with variations this is
true of all political parties, from Conservatives to
Anarchists—is designed to make lies sound truthful
and murder respectable, and to give an appearance
of solidity to pure wind. One cannot change this all
in a moment, but one can at least change one's own
habits, and from time to time one can even, if one
jeers loudly enough, send some worn-out and useless phrase—some *jackboot, Achilles' heel, hotbed,
melting pot, acid test, veritable inferno* or other
lump of verbal refuse—into the dustbin where it
belongs.

GEORGE ORWELL
from "Politics and
the English Language"

Jargon, gobbledygook, and pretentious writing are all very
much the same bad thing. The following anecdote may help
you remember what to avoid.

A foreign-born plumber in New York City wrote
to the Federal Bureau of Standards that he found
hydrochloric acid did a good job of cleaning out
clogged drains.

The bureau wrote: "The efficacy of hydrochloric
acid is indisputable, but the corrosive residue is
incompatible with metallic permanence."

The plumber replied he was glad the bureau
agreed.

Again the bureau wrote: "We cannot assume re-
sponsibility for the production of toxic and noxious
residue with hydrochloric acid and suggest you use
an alternative procedure."

The plumber was happy again at bureau agreement with his idea.

Then the bureau wrote: "Don't use hydrochloric acid. It eats hell out of the pipes."

RICHARD D. ALTICK
from Preface to Critical Reading

Some purists insist that English is in such bad shape that communication is all but impossible. Your own good sense and daily experience will prompt you to balk at such distortion, but it is true that everyone's writing can be improved by deleting the dead wood, circumlocution, paste, and filler that is a part of most first drafts. Few people go as far with the cliché as the next example suggests, but it is a reminder that even the critics may have their "platitudes" done up in clichés.

Q: Mr. Arbuthnot, you are an expert on the clichés of the drama, and in particular of drama criticism?

A: I am a battle-scarred veteran of not a few first nights.

Q: Then, with your permission, I shall test your competence in the field by putting a few questions to you.

A: Please do so.

Q: Where is Gilbert Miller?

A: On his way to London to secure the American rights.

Q: Excellent. And what did you think of *The Gay Mortician,* which opened at the Patricia Collinge Theatre last Monday night under the management of——

A: Please do not say "under the management." The correct phrase is "under the aegis." Well, in this reviewer's opinion *The Gay Mortician* was powerfully wrought, richly rewarding, utterly engaging, eminently satisfactory, wholly convincing, beautifully integrated, admirably played, and fairly obvious.

Q: In what way was it effective?

A: It was pictorially effective.

Q: How beautiful was it?

A: It was breathtakingly beautiful, and it was magnificently mounted.

Q: And how contrived?

A: Poorly contrived.

Q: I think you qualify, Mr. Arbuthnot. Tell me . . .

Q: What kind of plays are there?

A: Oh, their number is legion. There are dramas of frustration and dramas of extramarital love, or the eternal triangle. There are plays that are penetrating studies and plays that are valuable human documents. There are pageants, which ought to be glittering, if possible. Tragedies should, of course, be stark, and melodramas lurid, and spectacles, to be *de rigueur,* should be lavish, colorful, or handsome. But lampoons must be merry, farces must be rollicking, and comedies must be either of ancient vintage or sophisticated.

Q: What does the playwright do in a sophisticated comedy?

A: He pokes fun at our foibles. He dissects our tribal mores.

Q: Using what kind of vein?

A: A rich vein of satire.

Q: The task of the playwright sounds onerous enough, Mr. Arbuthnot.

A: Oh, you have no idea of the angles he must consider. He must, for instance, make sure that his play has compelling moments. He must take care that it is well knit and fast-moving, and that it is brilliant in conception, builds up to an exciting climax, and ends on a happy note. Then, there is the character insight.

Q: What about that?

A: Well, he must provide plenty of it, along with a scope.

Q: Must have a scope, too, eh?
A: Yes, preferably wide.

FRANK SULLIVAN
from "The Cliché Expert
Testifies on the Drama"

George Orwell would have you pay attention to the following rules, presented here with a few of his own prefatory comments:

What is above all needed is to let the meaning choose the word, and not the other way about. In prose, the worst thing one can do with words is to surrender them. When you think of a concrete object, you think wordlessly, and then, if you want to describe the thing you have been visualizing, you probably hunt about till you find the exact words that seem to fit it. When you think of something abstract you are more inclined to use words from the start, and unless you make a conscious effort to prevent it, the existing dialect will come rushing in and do the job for you, at the expense of blurring or even changing your meaning. Probably it is better to put off using words as long as possible and get one's meaning as clear as one can through pictures or sensations. Afterward one can choose—not simply *accept*—the phrases that will best cover the meaning, and then switch around and decide what impressions one's words are likely to make on another person. This last effort of the mind cuts out all stale or mixed images, all prefabricated phrases, needless repetitions, and humbug and vagueness generally. But one can often be in doubt about the effect of a word or a phrase, and one needs rules that one can rely on when instinct fails. I think the following rules will cover most cases:

(i) Never use a metaphor, simile or other figure of speech which you are used to seeing in print.

(ii) Never use a long word where a short one will do.

(iii) If it is possible to cut a word out, always cut it out.

(iv) Never use the passive where you can use the active.

(v) Never use a foreign phrase, a scientific word or a jargon word if you can think of an everyday English equivalent.

(vi) Break any of these rules sooner than say anything barbarous.

These rules sound elementary, and so they are, but they demand a deep change of attitude in anyone who has grown used to writing in the style now fashionable.

GEORGE ORWELL
from "Politics and the English Language"

The rules work, but no one works them better than the poets. If you would improve your prose, turn to the poets for examples of words used with precision. In doing this work, you may find it useful to consider verse versus poetry. The difference is sufficiently dramatic to help you feel the need for avoiding the banal in statements of any kind.

Assignment 10

A cliché is a low-grade verbal dragon. Killing dragons—any grade—is not apt to happen by accident. You have to make an effort. To kill these verbal horrors you don't need magic words. Just use Professor Packard's formula: "If you have a nail to hit, hit it on the head." The words you need most are everyday words—clear, precise, picture-making words that say what you are thinking. That's the real secret. Thinking kills clichés.

1. Read the chapter up to this point.
2. In your journal do *one* of the following:
   a. Review three of your own entries. See if you can find (and delete) any clichés. Then write an entry in which you report and comment on your discoveries.

b. Write a paragraph or two after the manner of "The Cliché Expert."

c. Look up the term "poetic diction." In what sense can such a convention produce clichés? As you discuss this topic, supply specific examples.

Assignment 11

She knelt upon her brother's grave,
  My little girl of six years old—
He used to be so good and brave,
  The sweetest lamb of all our fold;
He used to shout, he used to sing,
Of all our tribe the little king—
And so unto the turf her ear she laid,
To hark if still in that dark place he play'd.
  No sound! no sound!
  Death's silence was profound;
  And horror crept
  Into her aching heart, and Dora wept.
If this is as it ought to be,
My God, I leave it unto thee.

T. E. BROWN

Futility

Move him into the sun—
Gently its touch awoke him once,
At home, whispering of fields unsown.
Always it woke him, even in France,
Until this morning and this snow.
If anything might rouse him now
The kind old sun will know.

Think how it wakes the seeds—
Woke, once, the clays of a cold star.
Are limbs, so dear-achieved, are sides,
Full-nerved—still warm—too hard to stir?
Was it for this the clay grew tall?

—O what made fatuous sunbeams toil
To break earth's sleep at all?

WILFRED OWEN

After Great Pain

After great pain, a formal feeling comes—
The Nerves sit ceremonious, like Tombs—
The stiff Heart questions was it He, that bore,
And Yesterday, or Centuries before?

The Feet, mechanical, go round—
Of Ground, or Air, or Ought—
A Wooden way
Regardless grown,
A Quartz contentment, like a stone—

This is the Hour of Lead—
Remembered, if outlived,
As Freezing persons, recollect the Snow—
First—Chill—then Stupor—then the letting go—

EMILY DICKINSON

1. Read the three poems for this assignment.
2. In your journal do *one* of the following:
   a. Consider the use of language in any one or all three of the poems presented in this assignment.
   b. Review *Hamlet*. Locate some of its clichés. Explain their presence in such a well-known work.
   c. Reread a poem you like. Consider its words and their effectiveness. (Copy out or paste the poem into your journal.)

Assignment 12

The artistic temperament is a disease that afflicts amateurs—its greatest tragedy is that it cannot produce any art.

G. K. CHESTERTON

The comments that follow are by Robert P. Tristram Coffin. Do they apply to prose as well as to poetry?

At the root—and at the fruit—a poem is, first of all, stenography. It represents reality, it does not present it. It leaves it to history and science to do that. Poetry was stenography when it began many thousands of years ago; it is so now when the life intellectual is so much fuller and richer; and it will be so when our books may read themselves, or who knows, write themselves, in the azure tomorrow.

Scarcity is the alpha and omega of the matter. Economy is the first step. The twenty words out of the countless scores there are for this experience, and these words the right ones. The exact, the central ones. The silver needle in the haystack of brittle useless needles of the straw. A poem is the finding of that one particular little robin in all Robin Hood's barn. Being particular—that is the other name for being a poet. Not all the words, only the best. The chosen few. The ones you often work the hardest to find. But you know them, and your friends know them, when you find them.

Almost every beginning poet will discover that his poem grows ten times stronger by being cut in two. Or by saving three stanzas out of the seven. Strength and volume are gained by cutting away the stanzas that extend, apply, or explain. . . . A poem is not an explanation or an application; it is an act. Once and for all. Its singleness is its secret.

As with the poem as a whole, so with its parts. One adjective is better than three. Better still, omit the adjective altogether and find the right sinewy noun. Better yet, lean on athletic verbs. Act words, figure-of-speech words. And even better often are the livest parts of the English verb—those separable prefixes of our Germanic verbs—the prepositions. These are the rocks to strike great sparks out of. These are the words that keep our native sentences alive. Sing in elementals: nouns, verbs, and prepositions. A. E. Housman and Yeats can teach you the use of these exquisite tendons and muscles of speech, verbs, and athletic nouns.

The time you won your town the race
We chaired you through the marketplace;
Man and boy stood cheering by,
And home we brought you shoulder-high.

Today, the road all runners come,
Shoulder-high we bring you home,
And set you at your threshold down,
Townsman of a stiller town.

It will be good for you to take a page, too, out of
the book of rare and spare Ben Jonson. He writes
his verses as if they were going to go on gravestones,
as if he were composing epitaphs to be cut in expensive bronze or marble; every syllable must count.
So you, too, better be brief, quick to get into your
poem, point it up, and quick to get out of it.

Underneath this stone doth lie
As much beauty as could die.

Write as though you were putting gold letters on
marble, with a small stone as your page. Be eco-
nomical. Poetry began long ago with this urgency
for bettering the random and anticlimactic talk of
men, improving on the desultory drift of events
which is history. That ancient urgency of being
better than speech, better than lecture, quicker
than homily, better than man in the act, is on us
and on poetry still. Be the stenographer of life.
That way, and that way only, you will get life down
quick, with its bloom, more delicate than the azure
powder on blueberries that vanishes at a touch,
upon it.

ROBERT P. TRISTRAM COFFIN
from "The Matter of Poetry"

1. Read the excerpt for this assignment.
2. In your journal do *one* of the following:
   a. Turn to a poem by Yeats. Comment on it and on his
      use of verbs and nouns.

b. Turn to Ben Jonson and read a few of his poems. Comment on the poems and his use of language.

c. Study "To an Athlete Dying Young" by A. E. Housman, quoted in part by Coffin. Write a paraphrase of it. Comment on Housman's use of language.

2|5

NARRATIVE TECHNIQUES

Sing in me, Muse, and through me
tell the story. . . .

from the *Odyssey*

The oldest written story that we know is an epic poem, the *Odyssey*. The bard, the poet, has ever been the traditional teller of tales. You may look at the forms of the past and learn useful things about storytelling. You will remember that Geoffrey Chaucer did just that and learned much from Boccaccio, Petrarch, and Dante.

Specifically, what might the poets teach? Scene, character, events, and the focused interest that makes a story. To be sure, not all poems or poets are storytellers. The lyric poem aims only at singing its song. But the great narrative poems have their lyric moments and even the lyric itself implies scene, character, and events that precede or follow the song. Here we will not concern ourselves with formal divisions, but simply list them for their possible interest.

Major lyric forms: Song, sonnet, ode, and elegy
Major narrative forms: Epic, romance, ballad, and tale

In the narrative form, Homer—reasonably enough—set the tradition of a national hero who is involved with gods and men in carrying out some great adventure. There is a rich admixture of myth and legend and the working out of a position that supports the national beliefs or traditions. In Greece the *Iliad* and *Odyssey* set the pattern. Virgil's *Aeneid* became the major Roman work, and *Paradise Lost* is the most important English epic. Any one of these reread may well profit the potential storyteller, for in each case the narrative job has been done with a peculiar and consummate skill. Skill has given to each work a life of its own and the power to carry into the work of others. Any writer will also find here a tradition and a set of allusions that may prove useful in the telling of his own tale. Alexander Pope, for example, used the whole epic structure to show up a mini-event for what it was. His *Rape of the Lock* becomes a burlesque by putting hero's garments on trivialities. It is his knowledge and use of the epic tradition that permit his mock epic to work.

The metrical romance of the middle ages is a minstrel's, or gleeman's, tale. These stories were told to sophisticated court audiences. In these tales the power of courtly love and the order imposed by chivalry hold back the forces of evil, man, beast, and the devil. Here decorative verse is used to embroider elaborate stories that capture the beauty of civilized life and the need for heroic deeds if monsters of the dark are to be kept at bay. These are the tales of King Arthur and of Charlemagne. The tradition is brought down to us by Keats, who is the best of the moderns to work in this form. He begins "The Eve of St. Agnes" with a verse that is itself a masterpiece of scene setting.

> St. Agnes' Eve—Ah, bitter chill it was!
> The owl, for all his feathers, was a-cold;
> The hare limped trembling through the frozen
> grass,
> And silent was the flock in woolly fold:
> Numb were the Beadsman's fingers, while he told
> His rosary, and while his frosted breath,
> Like pious incense from a censer old,
> Seem'd taking flight for heaven, without a death,
> Past the sweet Virgin's picture, while his prayer he
> saith.

Story-poems called ballads put in memorable form vital experiences of life. The oral folk-traditions that memorialized these tales of love, death, war, and witchcraft were models of simplicity, and to assist memory, repetition was often built into them. Extraneous detail was deleted. Frequently events were made to speak for themselves by being presented through dialogue without authorial comment. It is a form familiar to us in our own cowboy songs.

Narratives that do not fit the form of epic, romance, or ballad are called tales. They range from fables to short stories.

Chaucer and his *Canterbury Tales* are perhaps the most famous. The poem "Richard Cory" by E. A. Robinson is a modern example of that form.

What is to be learned from narrative verse has been suggested rather than defined—outlined rather than explained. Perhaps this is a fault. You may find it useful to consider a single poem and what may be learned from it. The ballad "Johnie Armstrong" will serve as an illustration. First read this poem and then consider how it relates to story and storytelling.

Johnie Armstrong

There dwelt a man in faire Westmerland,
    Johnie Armstrong men did him call,
He had nither lands nor rents coming in,
    Yet he kept eight score men in his hall.

He had horse and harness for them all,
    Goodly steeds were all milke-white;
O the golden bands an about their necks,
    And their weapons, they were all alike.

Newes then was brought unto the king
    That there was sicke a won as hee,
That livèd lyke a bold out-law,
    And robbèd all the north country.

The king he writt an a letter then,
    A letter which was large and long;
He signèd it with his owne hand,
    And he promised to doe him no wrong.

When this letter came Johnie untill,
    His heart it was as blythe as birds on the tree:
"Never was I sent for before any king,
    My father, my grandfather, nor none but mee.

"And if wee goe the king before,
    I would we went most orderly;
Every man of you shall have his scarlet cloak,
    Lacèd with silver laces three.

"Every won of you shall have his velvett coat,
   Lacèd with silver lace so white;
O the golden bands an about your necks,
   Black hatts, white feathers, all alyke."

By the morrow morninge at ten of the clock,
   Towards Edenburough gon was hee,
And with him all his eight score men;
   Good Lord, it was a goodly sight for to see!

When Johnie came befower the king,
   He fell downe on his knee;
"Oh pardon, my soveraine leige," he said,
   "O pardon my eight score men and mee!"

"Thou shalt have no pardon, thou traytor strong,
   For thy eight score men nor thee;
For tomorrow morning by ten of the clock,
   Both thou and them shall hang on the gallow-
      tree."

But Johnie looke'd over his left shoulder,
   Good Lord, what a grievous look looked hee!
Saying, "Asking grace of a graceles face—
   Why there is none for you nor me."

But Johnie had a bright sword by his side,
   And it was made of the mettle so free,
That had not the king stept his foot aside,
   He had smitten his head from his faire boddë.

Saying, "Fight on, my merry men all,
   And see that none of you be taine;
For rather than men shall say we were hang'd,
   Let them report how we were slaine."

Then, God wott, faire Eddenburrough rose,
   And so besett poore Johnie rounde,
That fowerscore and tenn of Johnie's best men
   Lay gasping all upon the ground.

Then like a mad man Johnie laid about,
    And like a mad man then fought hee,
Until a falce Scot came Johnie behinde,
    And runn him through the faire boddee.

Saying, "Fight on, my merry men all,
    And see that none of you be taine;
For I will stand by and bleed but awhile,
    And then will I come and fight againe."

Newes then was brought to young Johnie Arm-
        strong,
    As he stood by his nurse's knee,
Who vowed if ere he lived for to be a man,
    On the treacherous Scots reveng'd hee'd be.

Reading this poem and reading a story are much alike. Both interest us in a character. Both present us action and an outcome that interprets that character, and both give us a vicarious experience. How does the unknown teller make this more than a "seem" experience? How is the "be" quality of the tale introduced and sustained?

1. Our sympathy and understanding are enlisted in the first two stanzas, which serve as exposition and present the hero.
2. Then after two narrative stanzas, we are presented dramatic scene after dramatic scene (the letter, the company on its way to court, the betrayal, the fight, the vow of revenge).
3. The story has its beginning near the climax. We are shown the key scenes and experience their pace and directness through dialogue.
4. The irony of betrayal is heightened by the joy of receiving the letter.
5. The climax interprets character.
6. Detail is selected for economy and vividness. For example, the king's treachery is not analyzed but presented.
7. The story outcome satisfies our curiosity. There is an end, though not a "happy ending." Through the tale we have seen man meet disaster triumphantly and feel that even the rogues—so perhaps the rest of us—have a potential if

not for greatness at least for fidelity to standards. The story in addition to event and speed has been given an emotional and intellectual dimension.

8. The tale is told without the intrusion of the narrator.
9. In brief, the tale has been told with form (beginning, middle, and end), economy, point, and interest.

Narrative poems are a way of presenting a story. They are not all there is to poetry or all there is to storytelling, but a writer may study the technique with profit.

Assignment 13

1. Read the chapter up to this point.
2. In your own journal do *one* of the following:
   a. Reread a book of the *Odyssey* and then in your own words retell an event from it. Transpose and alter as freely as you wish.
   b. Select one of the major narrative forms for study. Reread a poem that uses the form you have chosen. Explain what may be learned from it about narrative techniques.
   c. The literary ballad "The Highwayman" presents a story of action. T. S. Eliot's "The Love Song of J. Alfred Prufrock" tells of a life of inaction. Discuss the narrative techniques used in both and their appropriateness.

Assignment 14

As a further way of letting the poets help you tell your own story, turn to a translation of *The Canterbury Tales*. Read that portion of "The Pardoner's Tale" that begins on line 199 and ends on line 431.

In your journal do *one* of the following:
a. Tell a portion of the story in prose.
b. Discuss how the three rioters might have been described if they had been presented in "The Great Prologue."
c. Outline a story in which a hypocrite attempts to justify himself by telling the full truth.

Assignment 15

In this short poem there is a long story:

In the Orchard

We sat in the Cambridge orchard drinking tea.
Above, the apples rounded to a fall.
Preserving balance, cup upon a knee,
   we thought no thought at all;

but rumored idly with the idle bees
deep in the heart of flowers, who triggered thus
another generation's histories.
   But what was that to us?

A cheek may flush, a heart may miss a beat.
I am not master of such languages.
I settled back into the rural seat,
   "Another biscuit, please."

Master or not, was she not signaling?
And was I not interpreting her eyes?
For suddenly I felt it like a sting:
   Why, this was Paradise!

and almost dropped my cup. Something was slith-
    ering.
Well, here was one man it could not deceive.
I laughed—as if I hadn't heard a thing.
And she laughed back—as if her name were Eve.

ROBERT FRIEND

1. Read the poem for this assignment.
2. In your journal do *one* of the following:
   a. Turn the events presented in the poem into the open-ing situation of a short story.
   b. Reread the poem, and then find parallels in prose of this basic situation. Give exact sources. Comment briefly on each.
   c. What, if anything, have you learned about narrative from the poets?

2 | Review

The terms given here will aid you in considering poetry. Although there is not a mechanical relationship between your knowledge of the terms and your knowledge of poetry, the terms do help. Look up any unfamiliar terms in a good reference book. Two that are excellent for that purpose are *A Glossary of Literary Terms,* by M. H. Abrams, and *A Handbook to Literature,* by William Flint Thrall, Addison Hibbard, and C. Hugh Holman.

alliteration
antithesis
apostrophe
assonance
ballad stanza
blank verse
cacophony
caesura
consonance
couplet
elegy
end-stopped line
English sonnet
euphony
foot
free verse
heroic couplet
internal rhyme
Italian sonnet
limerick
line
lyric
meter
metonymy

metric foot (various patterns)
metrical feet, type of
metrical lines, kinds of
mock heroic
octave
onomatopoeia
pastoral
Petrarchan sonnet
quatrain
refrain
rhyme
rhyme scheme
run-on line
scansion
sestet
Shakespearean sonnet
sonnet
Spenserian stanza
stanza
stanzas, kinds of
stress (accent)
synecdoche
verse forms

Review Assignment

1. Study the terms and relate them to poems you know.
2. In your journal do *one* of the following:
   a. Make an intensive study of a single poet. Carry this project as far as time permits.
   b. Write a short story based on a poem.
   c. Discuss narrative devices used by Chaucer.

UNIT 3

———◆———

Learn from Drama

---

*"Never keep a secret from the audience!"-
"Never try to fool the audience!"—
"Begin in the thick of the action,
and quit when you are through!"—
"Show everything that is important to
the plot; don't tell about it merely, but
let the spectators see it for themselves!"
—these are all monitions of indisputable
importance; and the 'prentice playwright
will do well to get them by heart and to
take them to heart.*—BRANDER MATTHEWS

3|1

IMPORTANCE OF SCENE

One reason an author works in the dramatic medium is that he wants the deeds he has invented to hit us at the same "gut" level that actualities do.

JAMES MOFFETT
from *Drama*

Writing an entire play is certainly as difficult as writing a novel. The discipline, the condensation, the sense of life that must be captured, contained, and projected is formidable. But it is no more difficult to write a single dramatic scene than it is to write an essay or theme. Indeed, the requirements of time and ability are quite similar. You will learn much about writing and about theater and story if you will approach drama as a visual, vocal, and social experience that is to be presented and absorbed scene by scene. Each scene in a play is, in effect, its own little drama with conflict, action, crisis, and atmosphere. An entire play is, of course, a totality of all these dramatic enactments.

Your writing in this unit will give you more than a spectator's view of the theater. You will by turns be playwright, actor, stage manager, critic, and audience. For in these lessons you will be writing scenes in competition and in collaboration with others—at least that is the ideal approach. The best scenes should, if circumstances permit, be enacted—perhaps informally and right in the classroom with no more staging than your imagination and a few comments can supply. Scenes written by a group or groups should also get their showing. You are accustomed to reading plays and letting your imagination supply the voices, nuances, and actors' interpretations. Here, you will make do with nothing more elaborate than a classroom reading, but because the scenes have been written with a particular audience in mind, they should in spirit and in fact prove dramatic.

Perhaps a good way to start your own "Writer's Theater" is to begin by first reading in class some scenes by established writers; for example, take a scene from *Our Town, Of Mice and Men,* the *Odyssey, Hamlet,* or perhaps a contemporary comedy. In any event, local talent should have a chance to emerge and the class an opportunity to become accustomed to the arrangements and limitations of its own particular class theater. Then, having heard how professional writing sounds on your temporary stage, you will have a fairer basis for judging student writing. In doing your own work for these presentations, remember it is important to keep your audience in mind and to let your material project itself so that the scenes you invent carry the impact of life itself.

If you read Tennessee Williams's short story "Portrait of a Girl in Glass," and then read his play *The Glass Menagerie,* you will gain a sharper sense of the difference between stage and story. The complete short story and a few pages of the play are presented here to demonstrate some of the things a writer can do to intensify the dramatic quality of a short story.

PORTRAIT OF A GIRL IN GLASS

TENNESSEE WILLIAMS

We lived in a third-floor apartment on Maple Street in St. Louis, on a block which also contained the Ever-ready Garage, a Chinese laundry, and a bookie shop disguised as a cigar store.

Mine was an anomalous character, one that appeared to be slated for radical change or disaster, for I was a poet who had a job in a warehouse. As for my sister Laura, she could be classified even less readily than I. She made no positive motion toward the world but stood at the edge of the water, so to speak, with feet that anticipated too much cold to move. She'd never have budged an inch, I'm pretty sure, if my mother who was a relatively aggressive sort of woman had not shoved her roughly forward, when Laura was twenty years old, by enrolling her as a student in a nearby business college. Out of her "magazine money" (she sold subscriptions to women's magazines), Mother had paid my sister's tuition for a term of six months. It did not work out. Laura tried to memorize the typewriter keyboard, she had a chart at home, she used to sit silently in front of it for hours, staring at it while she cleaned and polished her infinite number of little glass ornaments. She did this every evening after dinner. Mother would caution me to be very quiet. "Sister is looking at her typewriter chart!" I felt somehow that it would do her no good, and I was right. She would seem to know the positions of the keys until the weekly speed-drill got under way, and then they would fly from her mind like a bunch of startled birds.

At last she couldn't bring herself to enter the school any more. She kept this failure a secret for a while. She left the house each morning as before and spent six hours walking around the park. This was in February, and all the walking outdoors regardless of weather brought on influenza. She was in bed for a couple of weeks with a curiously happy little smile on her face. Of course Mother phoned the business college to let them know she was ill. Whoever was talking on the other end of the line had some trouble, it seems, in remembering who Laura was, which annoyed my mother and she spoke up pretty sharply. "Laura has been attending that school of yours for two months, you certainly ought to recognize her name!" Then came the stunning disclosure. The person sharply retorted, after a moment or two, that now she *did* remember the Wingfield girl, and that she had not been at the business college *once* in about a month. Mother's voice became strident. Another person was brought to the phone to verify the statement of the first. Mother hung up and went to Laura's bedroom where she lay with a tense and frightened look in place of the faint little smile. Yes, admitted my sister, what they said was true. "I couldn't go any longer, it scared me too much, it made me sick at the stomach!"

After this fiasco, my sister stayed at home and kept in her bedroom mostly. This was a narrow room that had two windows on a dusky areaway between two wings of the building. We called this areaway Death Valley for a reason that seems worth telling. There were a great many alley cats in the neighborhood and one particularly vicious dirty white Chow who stalked them continually. In the open or on the fire escapes they could usually elude him but now and again he cleverly contrived to run some youngster among them into the cul-de-sac of this narrow areaway at the far end of which, directly beneath my sister's bedroom windows, they made the blinding discovery that what had appeared to be an avenue of escape was really a locked arena, a gloomy vault of concrete and brick with walls too high for any cat to spring, in which they must suddenly turn to spit at their death until it was hurled upon them. Hardly a week went by without a repetition of this violent drama. The areaway had grown to be hateful to Laura because she could not look out on it without recalling the screams and the snarls of killing. She kept the shades drawn down, and as Mother would not permit the use of electric current except when needed, her days were spent almost in perpetual twilight. There were three pieces of dingy ivory furniture in the room, a bed, a bureau, a chair. Over the bed was a remarkably bad religious painting, a very effeminate head of Christ with teardrops visible just below the eyes. The charm of the room was produced by my sister's collection of glass. She loved colored glass and had covered the walls with shelves of little glass articles, all of them light and delicate in color. These she washed and polished with endless care. When you entered the room there was always this soft, transparent radiance in it which came from the glass absorbing whatever faint light came through the shades on Death Valley. I have no idea how many articles there were of this delicate glass. There must have been hundreds of them. But Laura could tell you exactly. She loved each one.

She lived in a world of glass and also a world of music. The music came from a 1920 victrola and a bunch of records that dated from about the same period, pieces such as *Whispering* or *The Love Nest* or *Dardanella.* These records were souvenirs of our father, a man whom we barely remembered, whose name was spoken rarely. Before his sudden and unexplained disappearance from our lives, he had made this gift to the household, the phonograph and the records, whose music remained as a sort of apology for him. Once in a while, on payday at the warehouse, I would bring home a new record. But Laura seldom cared for these new records, maybe because they reminded her too much of the noisy tragedies in Death Valley or the speed-drills at the business college. The tunes she loved were the ones she had always heard. Often she sang to herself at night in her bedroom. Her voice was thin, it usually wandered off-key. Yet it had a curious childlike sweetness. At eight o'clock in the evening I sat down to write in my own mousetrap of a room. Through the closed doors, through the walls, I would hear my sister singing to herself, a piece like *Whispering* or *I Love You* or *Sleepy Time Gal,* losing the tune now and then but always preserving the minor atmosphere of the music. I think that was why I always wrote such strange and sorrowful poems in those days. Because I had in my ears the wispy sound of my sister serenading her pieces of colored glass, washing them while she sang or merely looking down at them with her vague blue eyes until the points of gemlike radiance in them gently drew the aching particles of reality from her mind and finally produced a state of hypnotic calm in which she even stopped singing or washing the glass and merely sat without motion until my mother knocked at the door and warned her against the waste of electric current.

I don't believe that my sister was actually foolish. I think the petals of her mind had simply closed through fear, and it's no telling how much they had closed upon in the way of secret wisdom. She never talked very much, not even to me, but once in a while she did pop out with something that took you by surprise.

After work at the warehouse or after I'd finished my writing in the evening, I'd drop in her room for a little visit because she had a restful and soothing effect on nerves that were worn rather thin from trying to ride two horses simultaneously in two opposite directions.

I usually found her seated in the straight-back ivory chair with a piece of glass cupped tenderly in her palm.

"What are you doing? Talking to it?" I asked.

"No," she answered gravely, "I was just looking at it."

On the bureau were two pieces of fiction which she had received as Christmas or birthday presents. One was a novel called the *Rose-Garden Husband* by someone whose name escapes me. The other was *Freckles* by Gene Stratton Porter. I never saw her reading the *Rose-Garden Husband,* but the other book was one that she actually lived with. It had probably never occurred to Laura that a book was something you read straight through and then laid aside as finished. The character Freckles, a one-armed orphan youth who worked in a lumber camp, was someone that she invited into her bed-room now and then for a friendly visit just as she did me. When I came in and found this novel open upon her lap, she would gravely remark that Freckles was having some trouble with the foreman of the lumber camp or that he had just received an injury to his spine when a tree fell on him. She frowned with genuine sorrow when she reported these misadventures of her story-book hero, possibly not recalling how successfully he came through them all, that the injury to the spine fortuitously resulted in the discovery of rich parents and that the bad-tempered foreman had a heart of gold at the end of the book. Freckles became involved in romance with a girl he called The Angel, but my sister usually stopped reading when this girl became too prominent in the story. She closed the book or turned back to the lonelier periods in the orphan's story. I only remember her making one reference to this heroine of the novel. "The Angel is nice," she said, "but seems to be kind of conceited about her looks."

Then one time at Christmas, while she was trimming the artificial tree, she picked up the Star of Bethlehem that went on the topmost branch and held it gravely toward the chandelier.

"Do stars have five points really?" she enquired.

This was the sort of thing that you didn't believe and that made you stare at Laura with sorrow and confusion.

"No," I told her, seeing she really meant it, "they're round like the earth and most of them much bigger."

She was gently surprised by this new information. She went to the window to look up at the sky which was, as usual during St. Louis winters, completely shrouded by smoke.

"It's hard to tell," she said, and returned to the tree.

So time passed on till my sister was twenty-three. Old enough to be married, but the fact of the matter was she had never even had a date with a boy. I don't believe this seemed as awful to her as it did to Mother.

At breakfast one morning Mother said to me, "Why don't you cultivate some nice young friends? How about down at the warehouse? Aren't there some young men down there you could ask to dinner?"

This suggestion surprised me because there was

seldom quite enough food on her table to satisfy three people. My mother was a terribly stringent housekeeper, God knows we were poor enough in actuality, but my mother had an almost obsessive dread of becoming even poorer. A not unreasonable fear since the man of the house was a poet who worked in a warehouse, but one which I thought played too important a part in all her calculations.

Almost immediately Mother explained herself.

"I think it might be nice," she said, "for your sister."

I brought Jim home to dinner a few nights later. Jim was a big red-haired Irishman who had the scrubbed and polished look of well-kept chinaware. His big square hands seemed to have a direct and very innocent hunger for touching his friends. He was always clapping them on your arms or shoulders and they burned through the cloth of your shirt like plates taken out of an oven. He was the best-liked man in the warehouse and oddly enough he was the only one that I was on good terms with. He found me agreeably ridiculous I think. He knew of my secret practice of retiring to a cabinet in the lavatory and working on rhyme schemes when work was slack in the warehouse, and of sneaking up on the roof now and then to smoke my cigarette with a view across the river at the undulant open country of Illinois. No doubt I was classified as screwy in Jim's mind as much as in the others', but while their attitude was suspicious and hostile when they first knew me, Jim's was warmly tolerant from the beginning. He called me Slim, and gradually his cordial acceptance drew the others around, and while he remained the only one who actually had anything to do with me, the others had now begun to smile when they saw me, as people smile at an oddly fashioned dog who crosses their path at some distance.

Nevertheless it took some courage for me to invite Jim to dinner. I thought about it all week and delayed the action till Friday noon, the last possible moment, as the dinner was set for that evening.

"What are you doing tonight?" I finally asked him.

"Not a damn thing," said Jim. "I had a date but her aunt took sick and she's hauled her freight to Centralia!"

"Well," I said, "why don't you come over for dinner?"

"Sure!" said Jim. He grinned with astonishing brightness.

I went outside to phone the news to Mother.

Her voice that was never tired responded with an energy that made the wires crackle.

"I suppose he's Catholic?" she said.

"Yes," I told her, remembering the tiny silver cross on his freckled chest.

"Good!" she said. "I'll bake a salmon loaf!"

And so we rode home together in his jalopy.

I had a curious feeling of guilt and apprehension as I led the lamblike Irishman up three flights of cracked marble steps to the door of Apartment F, which was not thick enough to hold inside it the odor of baking salmon.

Never having a key, I pressed the bell.

"Laura!" came Mother's voice. "That's Tom and Mr. Delaney! Let them in!"

There was a long, long pause.

"Laura?" she called again. "I'm busy in the kitchen, you answer the door!"

Then at last I heard my sister's footsteps. They went right past the door at which we were standing and into the parlor. I heard the creaking noise of the phonograph crank. Music commenced. One of the oldest records, a march of Sousa's, put on to give her the courage to let in a stranger.

The door came timidly open and there she stood in a dress from Mother's wardrobe, a black chiffon ankle-length, and high-heeled slippers on which she balanced uncertainly like a tipsy crane of melancholy plumage. Her eyes stared back at us with a glass brightness and her delicate winglike shoulders were hunched with nervousness.

"Hello!" said Jim, before I could introduce him.

He stretched out his hand. My sister touched it only for a second.

"Excuse me!" she whispered, and turned with a breathless rustle back to her bedroom door, the sanctuary beyond it briefly revealing itself with the tinkling, muted radiance of glass before the door closed rapidly but gently on her wraithlike figure.

Jim seemed to be incapable of surprise.

"Your sister?" he asked.

"Yes, that was her," I admitted. "She's terribly shy with strangers."

"She looks like you," said Jim, "except she's pretty."

Laura did not reappear till called to dinner. Her place was next to Jim at the drop-leaf table and all through the meal her figure was slightly tilted away from his. Her face was feverishly bright and one eyelid, the one on the side toward Jim, had developed a nervous wink. Three times in the course of the dinner she dropped her fork on her plate with a terrible clatter and she was continually raising the water glass to her lips for hasty little gulps. She went on doing this even after the water was gone from the glass. And her handling of the silver became more awkward and hurried all the time.

I thought of nothing to say.

To Mother belonged the conversational honors, such as they were. She asked the caller about his home and family. She was delighted to learn that his father had a business of his own, a retail shoe store somewhere in Wyoming. The news that he went to night school to study accounting was still more edifying. What was his heart set on beside the warehouse? Radio-engineering? My, my, my! It was easy to see that here was a very up-and-coming young man who was certainly going to make his place in the world!

Then she started to talk about her children.

Laura, she said, was not cut out for business. She was domestic, however, and making a home was really a girl's best bet.

Jim agreed with all this and seemed not to sense the ghost of an implication. I suffered through it dumbly, trying not to see Laura trembling more and more beneath the incredible unawareness of Mother.

And bad as it was, excruciating in fact, I thought with dread of the moment when dinner was going to be over, for then the diversion of food would be taken away, we would have to go into the little steam-heated parlor. I fancied the four of us having run out of talk, even Mother's seemingly endless store of questions about Jim's home and his job all used up finally—the four of us, then, just sitting there in the parlor, listening to the hiss of the radiator and nervously clearing our throats in the kind of self-consciousness that gets to be suffocating.

But when the blancmange was finished, a miracle happened.

Mother got up to clear the dishes away. Jim gave me a clap on the shoulders and said, "Hey, Slim, let's go have a look at those old records in there!"

He sauntered carelessly into the front room and flopped down on the floor beside the victrola. He began sorting through the collection of worn-out records and reading their titles aloud in a voice so hearty that it shot like beams of sunlight through the vapors of self-consciousness engulfing my sister and me.

He was sitting directly under the floor lamp and all at once my sister jumped up and said to him, "Oh—you have freckles!"

Jim grinned. "Sure that's what my folks call me —Freckles!"

"Freckles?" Laura repeated. She looked toward me as if for the confirmation of some too wonderful hope. I looked away quickly, not knowing whether to feel relieved or alarmed at the turn that things were taking.

Jim had wound the victrola and put on *Dardanella.*

He grinned at Laura.

"How about you an' me cutting the rug a little?"

"What?" said Laura breathlessly, smiling and smiling.

"Dance!" he said, drawing her into his arms.

As far as I knew she had never danced in her life. But to my everlasting wonder she slipped quite naturally into those huge arms of Jim's, and they danced round and around the small steam-heated parlor, bumping against the sofa and chairs and laughing loudly and happily together. Something opened up in my sister's face. To say it was love is not too hasty a judgment, for after all he had freckles and that was what his folks called him. Yes, he had undoubtedly assumed the identity— for all practical purposes—of the one-armed orphan youth who lived in the Limberlost, that tall and misty region to which she retreated whenever the walls of Apartment F became too close to endure.

Mother came back in with some lemonade. She stopped short as she entered the portieres.

"Good heavens! Laura? Dancing?"

Her look was absurdly grateful as well as startled.

"But isn't she stepping all over you, Mr. Delaney?"

"What if she does?" said Jim, with bearish gallantry. "I'm not made of eggs!"

"Well, well, well!" said Mother, senselessly beaming.

"She's light as a feather!" said Jim. "With a little more practice she'd dance as good as Betty!"

There was a little pause of silence.

"Betty?" said Mother.

"The girl I go out with!" said Jim.

"Oh!" said Mother.

She set the pitcher of lemonade carefully down and with her back to the caller and her eyes on me, she asked him just how often he and the lucky young lady went out together.

"Steady!" said Jim.

Mother's look, remaining on my face, turned into a glare of fury.

"Tom didn't mention that you went out with a girl!"

"Nope," said Jim. "I didn't mean to let the cat out of the bag. The boys at the warehouse'll kid me to death when Slim gives the news away."

He laughed heartily but his laughter dropped heavily and awkwardly away as even his dull senses were gradually penetrated by the unpleasant sensation the news of Betty had made.

"Are you thinking of getting married?" said Mother.

"First of next month!" he told her.

It took her several moments to pull herself together. Then she said in a dismal tone, "How nice! If Tom had only told us we could have asked you *both!*"

Jim had picked up his coat.

"Must you be going?" said Mother.

"I hope it don't seem like I'm rushing off," said Jim, "but Betty's gonna get back on the eight o'clock train an' by the time I get my jalopy down to the Wabash depot——"

"Oh, then, we mustn't keep you."

Soon as he'd left, we all sat down, looking dazed.

Laura was the first to speak.

"Wasn't he nice?" she said. "And all those freckles!"

"Yes," said Mother. Then she turned on me.

"You didn't mention that he was engaged to be married!"

"Well, how did I know that he was engaged to be married?"

"I thought you called him your best friend down at the warehouse?"

"Yes, but I didn't know he was going to be married!"

"How peculiar!" said Mother. "How very peculiar!"

"No," said Laura gently, getting up from the sofa. "There's nothing peculiar about it."

She picked up one of the records and blew on its surface a little as if it were dusty, then set it softly back down.

"People in love," she said, "take everything for granted."

What did she mean by that? I never knew.

She slipped quietly back to her room and closed the door.

Not very long after that I lost my job at the warehouse. I was fired for writing a poem on the lid of a shoe-box. I left St. Louis and took to moving around. The cities swept about me like dead leaves, leaves that were brightly colored but torn away from the branches. My nature changed. I grew to be firm and sufficient.

In five years' time I had nearly forgotten home. I had to forget it, I couldn't carry it with me. But once in a while, usually in a strange town before I have found companions, the shell of deliberate hardness is broken through. A door comes softly and irresistibly open. I hear the tired old music my unknown father left in the place he abandoned as faithlessly as I. I see the faint and sorrowful radiance of the glass, hundreds of little transparent pieces of it in very delicate colors. I hold my breath, for if my sister's face appears among them—the night is hers!

THE GLASS MENAGERIE

TENNESSEE WILLIAMS

SCENE I

The Wingfield apartment is in the rear of the building, one of those vast hivelike conglomerations of cellular living units that flower as warty growths in overcrowded urban centers of lower middle-class population and are symptomatic of the impulse of this largest and fundamentally enslaved section of American society to avoid fluidity and differentiation and to exist and function as one interfused mass of automatism.

The apartment faces an alley and is entered by a fire escape, a structure whose name is a touch of accidental poetic truth, for all of these huge buildings are always burning with the slow and implacable fires of human desperation. The fire escape is included in the set—that is, the landing of it and steps descending from it.

The scene is memory and is therefore nonrealistic. Memory takes a lot of poetic license. It omits some details; others are exaggerated, according to the emotional value of the articles it touches, for memory is seated predominantly in the heart. The interior is therefore rather dim and poetic.

At the rise of the curtain, the audience is faced with the dark, grim rear wall of the Wingfield tenement. This building, which runs parallel to the footlights, is flanked on both sides by dark, narrow alleys which run into murky canyons of tangled clotheslines, garbage cans and the sinister latticework of neighboring fire escapes. It is up and down these side alleys that exterior entrances and exits are made, during the play. At the end of TOM's opening commentary, the dark tenement wall slowly reveals (by means of a transparency) the interior of the ground floor Wingfield apartment.

Downstage is the living room, which also serves as a sleeping room for LAURA, the sofa unfolding to make her bed. Upstage, center, and divided by a wide arch or second proscenium with transparent faded portieres (or second curtain), is the dining room. In an old-fashioned whatnot in the living room are seen scores of transparent glass animals. A blown-up photograph of the father hangs on the wall of the living room, facing the audience, to the left of the archway. It is the face of a very handsome young man in a doughboy's first World War cap.

He is gallantly smiling, ineluctably smiling, as if to say, "I will be smiling forever."

The audience hears and sees the opening scene in the dining room through both the transparent fourth wall of the building and the transparent gauze portieres of the dining-room arch. It is during this revealing scene that the fourth wall slowly ascends, out of sight. This transparent exterior wall is not brought down again until the very end of the play, during TOM'S *final speech.*

The narrator is an undisguised convention of the play. He takes whatever license with dramatic convention as is convenient to his purposes.

TOM *enters dressed as a merchant sailor from alley, stage left, and strolls across the front of the stage to the fire escape. There he stops and lights a cigarette. He addresses the audience.*

TOM: Yes, I have tricks in my pocket; I have things up my sleeve. But I am the opposite of a stage magician. He gives you illusion that has the appearance of truth. I give you truth in the pleasant disguise of illusion.

To begin with, I turn back time. I reverse it to that quaint period, the thirties, when the huge middle class of America was matriculating in a school for the blind. Their eyes had failed them, or they had failed their eyes, and so they were having their fingers pressed forcibly down on the fiery Braille alphabet of a dissolving economy.

In Spain there was revolution. Here there was only shouting and confusion.

In Spain there was Guernica. Here there were disturbances of labor, sometimes pretty violent, in otherwise peaceful cities such as Chicago, Cleveland, St. Louis. . . .

This is the social background of the play.

(MUSIC.)

The play is memory.

Being a memory play, it is dimly lighted, it is sentimental, it is not realistic.

In memory everything seems to happen to music. That explains the fiddle in the wings.

I am the narrator of the play, and also a character in it.

The other characters are my mother, Amanda, my sister, Laura, and a gentleman caller who appears in the final scenes.

He is the most realistic character in the play, being an emissary from a world of reality that we were somehow set apart from.

But since I have a poet's weakness for symbols, I am using this character also as a symbol; he is the long delayed but always expected something that we live for.

There is a fifth character in the play who doesn't appear except in this larger-than-life-size photograph over the mantel.

This is our father who left us a long time ago.

He was a telephone man who fell in love with long distances; he gave up his job with the telephone company and skipped the light fantastic out of town. . . .

The last we heard of him was a picture post card from Mazatlan, on the Pacific coast of Mexico, containing a message of two words—

"Hello—Good-by!" and no address.

I think the rest of the play will explain itself. . . .

(AMANDA's *voice becomes audible through the portieres.*)

(LEGEND ON SCREEN: "OÙ SONT LES NEIGES.")

(*He divides the portieres and enters the upstage area.*)

(AMANDA *and* LAURA *are seated at a drop-leaf table. Eating is indicated by gestures without food or utensils.* AMANDA *faces the audience.* TOM *and* LAURA *are seated in profile.*)

(*The interior has lit up softly and through the scrim we see* AMANDA *and* LAURA *seated at the table in the upstage area.*)

AMANDA (*Calling*): Tom?

TOM: Yes, Mother.

AMANDA: We can't say grace until you come to the table!

TOM: Coming, Mother. (*He bows slightly and withdraws, reappearing a few moments later in his place at the table.*)

AMANDA (*To her son*): Honey, don't *push* with your *fingers.* If you have to push with something, the thing to push with is a crust of bread. And chew—chew! Animals have sections in their stomachs which enable them to digest food without mastication, but human beings are supposed to chew their food before they swallow it down. Eat food leisurely, son, and really enjoy it. A well-cooked meal has lots of delicate flavors that have to be held in the mouth for appreciation. So chew your food and give your salivary glands a chance to function!

(TOM *deliberately lays his imaginary fork down and pushes his chair back from the table.*)

TOM: I haven't enjoyed one bite of this dinner because of your constant directions on how to eat it. It's you that make me rush through meals with your hawklike attention to every bite I take. Sickening—spoils my appetite—all this discussion of—animals' secretion—salivary glands—mastication!

AMANDA (*Lightly*): Temperament like a Metropolitan star! (*He rises and crosses downstage.*) You're not excused from the table.

TOM: I'm getting a cigarette.

AMANDA: You smoke too much.

(LAURA *rises.*)

LAURA: I'll bring in the blancmange.

(*He remains standing with his cigarette by the portieres. . . .*)

Assignment 1

1. Read the chapter up to this point.
2. In your journal do *one* of the following:
   a. Write a dramatic scene for use in class reading.
   b. Take a professional short story and turn a portion of it into a scene for the stage.
   c. Rewrite a portion of one of your own short stories for the classroom stage.

Assignment 2

One kind of playwriting and playacting we all get involved in is monologue. We hear an internal voice that tells us all sorts of things; as the expression goes, we "talk to ourselves." When you were a child, you did not distinguish between talking to yourself and talking to others. What the child thinks, he says; and often his speech repeats the pattern, tone, and direction of the adult world about him. In a short story called "Patricia, Edith, and Arnold," Dylan Thomas makes use of these facts to present a small boy playing trains in his backyard. In the course of the story the child's mind is shown as it absorbs—and fails to absorb—the events. Here is how the tale begins.

> The small boy in his invisible engine, the Cwm-donkin Special, its wheels, polished to dazzle, crunching on the small back garden scattered with breadcrumbs for the birds and white with yesterday's snow, its smoke rising thin and pale as breath in the cold afternoon, hooted under the washline, kicked the dog's plate at the washhouse stop, and puffed and pistoned slower and slower while the servant girl lowered the pole, unpegged the swinging vests, showed the brown stains under her arms, and called over the wall: "Edith, Edith, come here, I want you."
>
> Edith climbed on two tubs on the other side of the wall and called back: "I'm here, Patricia." Her head bobbed up above the broken glass.
>
> He backed the Flying Welshman from the washhouse to the open door of the coal-hole and pulled

hard on the brake that was a hammer in his pocket; assistants in uniform ran out with fuel; he spoke to a saluting fireman, and the engine shuffled off, round the barbed walls of China that kept the cats away, by the frozen rivers in the sink, in and out of the coal-hole tunnel. But he was listening carefully all the time, through the squeals and whistles, to Patricia and the next-door servant, who belonged to Mrs. Lewis, talking when they should have been working, calling his mother Mrs. T., being rude about Mrs. L.

He heard Patricia say: "Mrs. T. won't be back till six."

And Edith next door replied: "Old Mrs. L. has gone to Neath to look for Mr. Robert."

"He's on the randy again," Patricia whispered.

"Randy, sandy, bandy!" cried the boy out of the coal-hole.

"You get your face dirty, I'll kill you," Patricia said absent-mindedly.

She did not try to stop him when he climbed up the coal-heap. He stood quietly on the top, King of the Coal Castle, his head touching the roof, and listened to the worried voices of the girls. Patricia was almost in tears, Edith was sobbing and rocking on the unsteady tubs. "I'm standing on top of the coal," he said, and waited for Patricia's anger.

She said: "I don't want to see him, you go alone."

"We must, we must go together," said Edith. "I've got to know."

"I don't want to know."

"I can't stand it, Patricia, you must go with me."

"You go alone, he's waiting for you."

"Please, Patricia!"

"I'm lying on my face in the coal," said the boy.

"No, it's your day with him. I don't want to know. I just want to think he loves me."

"Oh, talk sense, Patricia, please! Will you come or no? I've got to hear what he says."

DYLAN THOMAS
from "Patricia, Edith, and Arnold"

Drama makes public the interior voice. The convention called monologue is merely that of talking out loud to oneself. Of course the audience is there, but the make-believe of the theater permits the speaker and the audience to suspend fact for the duration, and they share with the speaker his interior thoughts. You will remember James Joyce uses this device in *A Portrait of the Artist as a Young Man*. Stream of consciousness has its place as a device in the theater too. Here is how Arthur Miller makes it work in *Death of a Salesman*.

> BIFF: What's he doing out there?
> LINDA: He's planting the garden!
> BIFF (*Quietly*): Now? Oh, my God!

> (*Biff moves outside, Linda following. The light dies down on them and comes upon the center of the apron as Willy walks into it. He is carrying a flashlight, a hoe, and a handful of seed packets. He raps the top of the hoe sharply to fix it firmly, and then moves to the left, measuring off the distance with his foot. He holds the flashlight to look at the seed packets, reading off the instructions. He is in the blue of night.*)

> WILLY: Carrots . . . quarter-inch apart. Rows . . . one-foot rows. (*He measures it off.*) One foot. (*He puts down a package and measures off.*) Beets. (*He puts down another package and measures again.*) Lettuce. (*He reads the package, puts it down.*) One foot—(*He breaks off as* BEN *appears at the right and moves slowly down to him.*) What a proposition, ts, ts. Terrific, terrific. 'Cause she's suffered, Ben, the woman has suffered. You understand me? A man can't go out the way he came in, Ben, a man has got to add up to something. You can't, you can't—(BEN *moves toward him as though to interrupt.*) You gotta consider, now. Don't answer so quick. Remember, it's a guaranteed twenty-thousand-dollar proposition. Now look, Ben, I want you to go through the ins and outs of this thing with me. I've got nobody to talk to, Ben, and the woman has suffered, you hear me?

BEN (*Standing still, considering*): What's the proposition?

WILLY: It's twenty thousand dollars on the barrelhead. Guaranteed, gilt-edged, you understand?

BEN: You don't want to make a fool of yourself. They might not honor the policy.

WILLY: How can they dare refuse? Didn't I work like a coolie to meet every premium on the nose? And now they don't pay off! Impossible!

BEN: It's called a cowardly thing, William.

WILLY: Why? Does it take more guts to stand here the rest of my life ringing up a zero?

BEN (*Yielding*): That's a point, William. (*He moves, thinking, turns.*) And twenty thousand—that *is* something one can feel with the hand, it is there.

WILLY (*Now assured, with rising power*): Oh, Ben, that's the whole beauty of it! I see it like a diamond, shining in the dark, hard and rough, that I can pick up and touch in my hand. Not like—like an appointment! This would not be another damned-fool appointment, Ben, and it changes all the aspects. Because he thinks I'm nothing, see, and so he spites me. But the funeral—(*Straightening up*) Ben, that funeral will be massive! They'll come from Maine, Massachusetts, Vermont, New Hampshire! All the old-timers with the strange license plates—that boy will be thunderstruck, Ben, because he never realized—I am known! Rhode Island, New York, New Jersey—I am known, Ben, and he'll see it with his eyes once and for all. He'll see what I am, Ben! He's in for a shock, that boy!

BEN (*Coming down to the edge of the garden*): He'll call you a coward.

WILLY (*Suddenly fearful*): No, that would be terrible.

BEN: Yes. And a damned fool.

WILLY: No, no he mustn't, I won't have that! (*He is broken and desperate.*)

BEN: He'll hate you, William.

(*The gay music of the Boys is heard.*)

WILLY: Oh, Ben, how do we get back to all the great times? Used to be so full of light, and comradeship, the sleigh-riding in winter, and the ruddiness on his cheeks. And always some kind of good news coming up, always something nice coming up ahead. And never even let me carry the valises in the house, and simonizing that little red car! Why, why can't I give him something and not have him hate me?

ARTHUR MILLER
from *Death of a Salesman*

1. Read the two excerpts for this assignment.
2. In your journal do *one* of the following:
   a. (1) Transcribe an interior monologue just as it in fact occurs, writing out your own thoughts as they come. (You need not do this particular piece of writing in your journal.)
   (2) Edit what you have written so that it has point and direction but still retains the ease and flow of the actual event. Do the section of the assignment in your journal.
   b. Locate a scene in a play that makes use of monologue. Copy out a few of the speeches. Then seek to duplicate or parallel your model, writing on a different subject but keeping the voices and characters intact.
   c. Write an interior monologue that shapes itself into a dramatic moment or scene.

Assignment 3

Writing for the stage is writing to be seen and to be heard; action accompanies speech. Such writing is interpreted by the actor's voice and gestures—two dimensions that make an incalculable difference to the words. Still, the play is the vehicle that permits the actor to move; it gives him his reason for being seen and heard. The reason does not need to be a serious one. Indeed, comedy permits an actor scope, and an audience fun.

Here is a scene from Clarence Day's novel, *Life with Father*. Imagine the variety of interpretations it would permit if it were to be dramatized.

But Mother was one of those persons for whom charge accounts were invented. When she bought something and charged it, the first of the next month seemed far away, and she hoped that perhaps Father wouldn't mind—he might be nice about it for once. Her desire for the thing was strong at that moment, the penalty was remote, and she fell.

She was a different woman entirely when she had to pay cash. It was hard to get cash out of Father, she never got much at one time, and as she looked in her pocketbook she could see her precious little hoard dwindling. She fingered a purchase and thought twice about it before she could bear to part with the money. But shopping on a charge account was fun. She tried not to let herself be tempted, but of course she was, all the time, and after she had conscientiously resisted nine lovely temptations, it didn't seem really wicked to yield to the tenth.

Father did his level best to take all the fun out of it for her. Once every month regularly he held court and sat as a judge, and required her to explain her crimes and misdemeanors. When she cried, or showed that she was hurt, it appeared that Father, too, felt hurt and worried. He said again and again at the top of his voice that he wished to be reasonable but that he couldn't afford to spend money that way, and that they would have to do better.

Once in a while when Father got low in his mind and said that he was discouraged, Mother felt so sorry that she tried hard to keep count of the cash for him. She put down all sorts of little expenses, on backs of envelopes or on half-sheets of letter paper of different sizes, and she gave these to Father with many interlineations and much scratching out of other memoranda, and with mystifying omissions. He would pore over them, calling out to her to tell him what this was, or that, in a vain attempt to bring order out of this feminine chaos.

Mother could sometimes, though not very often, be managed by praise, but criticism made her rebellious, and after a dose of it she wouldn't put down any figures at all for a while. She had to do the mending and marketing and take care of the children, and she told Father she had no time to learn to be a bookkeeper too. What was the use of keeping track of anything that was over and done with? She said that wasn't her way of doing things.

"Well," Father said patiently, "let's get at the bottom of this, now, and work out some solution. What *is* your way of doing things? Tell me."

Mother said firmly that her way was to do the very best she could to keep down expenses, and that all her friends thought she did wonderfully, and the Wards spent twice as much.

Father said, "Damn the Wards! They don't have to work for it. I don't wish to be told what they spend, or how they throw money around."

Mother said, "Oh, Clare, how can you! They don't. They just like to have things go nicely, and live in a comfortable way, and I thought you were so fond of Cousin Mary. You know very well she is lovely, and she gave the baby a cup."

Father declared that he might be fond of Cousin Mary without wanting to hear so damned much about her. He said she cropped up every minute.

"You talk of your own family enough," Mother answered.

Father felt this was very unjust. When he talked of his own family he criticized them, and as severely as he knew how. He held tightly onto himself in an effort to keep to the subject. He said that the point he was trying to make was that Cousin Mary's ways were not his ways, and that consequently there was no use whatever discussing them with him.

Mother said, "Goodness knows *I* don't want to discuss things, it's always you who are doing it, and if I can't even *speak* of Cousin Mary——"

"You can, you can speak of her all you want to,"

Father hotly protested. "But I won't have Cousin Mary or anyone else dictating to me how to run things."

"I didn't say a word about her dictating, Clare. She isn't that kind."

"I don't know what you said, now," Father replied. "You never stick to the point. But you implied in some way that Cousin Mary——"

"Oh, Clare, please! I didn't! And I can't bear to have you talk so harshly of her when she admires you so."

Something like this happened to every financial conversation they had. Father did his best to confine the discussion to the question at issue, but somehow, no matter how calmly he started, he soon got exasperated and went galloping fiercely off in any direction Mother's mind happened to take; and in the middle of it one of the babies would cry and Mother would have to go off to see what was wrong, or she would have to run down to leave word for Mrs. Tobin, the washerwoman, to do Father's shirts differently, and when Father complained Mother reminded him reproachfully that she had to keep house.

Father was baffled by these tactics. But every time he went back down to the basement and ruled neat lines in his ledgers, he made up his mind all over again that he wouldn't give up.

CLARENCE DAY
from *Life with Father*

1. Read the excerpt for this assignment.
2. In your journal do *one* of the following:
   a. Copy out a scene you regard as a comic success. Then write on a different but parallel topic; in your imitation use the style and approach supplied by the model.
   b. Write a comic scene of your own invention.
   c. From memory re-create a scene presented by a comic you enjoy, or from a TV show that amused you. Try to provide what you think the original script might have carried.

3|2

USE OF DIALOGUE

Your concern in this unit is not only to learn about drama, but to learn from it. Drama, itself, offers potent lessons in ways to manage scene, develop thought, get outside yourself, direct audience interest, and to present plot, character, and dialogue. All these matters should be part of your concern as you read and watch plays. Such concerns are a way of realizing the value of what Robert Frost meant when he said, "Don't work. Worry!" In this particular chapter your work and worry will be with dialogue, for dialogue embraces many aspects of theater and, except for action, is the key dramatic device. Dialogue creates much of the action and interaction that gives a story or a play vitality, and at the same time creates the believability necessary even to the world of make-believe. Here is an excellent analysis of dialogue:

Diction is simply the dialogue of the play, the combination of words into speeches. Formerly, it is controlled by the thought of the characters; that is, what the characters say and how they say it are determined by what they feel and think. Diction, in turn, is the primary material out of which they construct and render their thoughts. It is the central means of drama and, since drama is in a major sense an art of language, it is a significant part of the play as a whole. It is, however, subordinate to and dependent upon plot, character, and thought. The first requisite of dramatic diction is clearness. The second is that it be not flat and commonplace, but arresting, colorful, exciting, memorable—in short, rich and beautiful.

A spoken word is a single sound or a combination of sounds. When a series of words is skillfully patterned into a speech and properly spoken by an actor, it will have a rhythm and a melody which aids in conveying its feeling and thought. This is the "music" of dramatic diction. The diction may be in realistic and colloquial prose, or at the other extreme it may be so highly formalized in rhythm and melody that it is best rendered in song. The experienced actor knows that the simplest prose speech may be altered through the music of speech melody to convey a variety of meanings. Take such a simple speech as "Close the door." Speak it as a stern command; then speak it as a simple request to a friend; then speak it as a question; finally, speak it as an exclamation of startled surprise. In all these utterances the diction remains the same, while the changing music—or melody—gives a variety of meanings and effects. Music is a means through which diction serves thought. In a great dramatic speech the music becomes highly complex and subtle. Whole scenes, as well as single speeches, have their variations of rhythm and melody. Indeed, a play as a whole may be considered as a tonal composition, and some directors are keenly aware of the fine effects to be gained through rhythm and melody in the staging of certain plays.

HUBERT HEFFNER
from *The Nature of Drama*

Assignment 4

1. Read the preceding excerpt by Heffner.
2. In your journal do *one* of the following:
   a. Find a dialogue you enjoy and copy a portion of it into your journal. Then write your comments on how it succeeds.
   b. Make an adaptation of a dialogue from *Oedipus Rex*. Have the speakers deal with a contemporary situation.
   c. Write a comic dialogue that also reveals character.

Assignment 5

The action and interaction that is drama goes beyond script and involves the mind and emotions of audience or reader. Something of the complexity of this interaction is suggested by the following statement. As you read the statement, consider at how many points action and character must reveal themselves through dialogue.

> The story which a drama tells is not merely a random series of incidents and episodes such as may make up a travel narrative or a tale of adventures. In such stories the agent who undergoes or experiences the succession of events may in no sense cause them. In drama what happens to its agents is partly caused by what those agents are, by their characters; hence character in drama, as in novel and epic, is a basic determinant of action. What happens in a play, what characters say and will and do, is made to seem in large measure the outcome of what they are. On the other hand, character in drama is shaped by action in that the kind of action which the playwright chooses will determine the formulation of the characters he creates to perform that action and make it probable. For purposes of emphasis, this reciprocal relationship of character and action may be stated thus: Character in drama is formally determined by the whole action, whereas action has characters as its material cause. A dramatic action is one which would probably or necessarily result from the kind of characters who are the agents in it. Because of this intricate relationship of character and action, and because plays are written to be performed by actors on a stage before audiences, the structure of drama is complex indeed.
>
> Since plays are written to be performed, that is to "happen" in a place and time in which the reader or spectator imaginatively participates as though he were actually present as the events take place, the action of drama has always the illusion of being present action. Even though the action of the play

ostensibly occurs in the past and in a distant place, the spectator in viewing it imagines himself to be "there." The action of an epic or a novel, on the other hand, always gives the sensation of being past action, even though the novel may be about contemporary events and characters. Its action is narrated by an omniscient author, by one of the agents, or by an observer who is not an agent in the plot. Hence, even though he purports to be telling about contemporary events as they occur, obviously for him to be able to narrate them they have already occurred. Thus the novel always presents a past action leading toward the present, whereas the drama always presents present action leading toward the future. It is, perhaps, this immediacy of drama, even more than the fact that the individual spectator is part of a mass audience participating in mass responses, that accounts for the powerful effect which may be realized not only by seeing a play in the theater, but by the trained reader reading a play.

HUBERT HEFFNER
from *The Nature of Drama*

1. Read the excerpt for this assignment.
2. In your journal do *one* of the following:
   a. (1) Make a tape recording of an actual dialogue, and then transcribe just enough of it in your journal to suggest its actual flavor.
   (2) If time permits, shape the recording into a few moments of dramatic dialogue for the classroom stage.
   b. Discuss the difference between talk on-stage and talk off-stage. Illustrate.
   c. Discuss drama as an intensified story of the momentous present, or characterize and discuss it from another point of view.

Assignment 6

Practice in listening to and in constructing dialogue makes you a better reader and a better writer. Dialogue is a central feature of the novel and short story as well as of the play. Becoming familiar with a variety of styles and voice possibilities is a marvelous way of improving your own range of compositional choice. To collect excerpts from real and fictional dialogues has interest and value. For example, if you are given just a snatch of conversation, what can you make of it? Can you construct stories, thoughts, discourses? These lines, for instance, take you where?

> E: You have some hidden motive in this, H.!
> H: Yes, I have. I want for once in my life to have
>   power to mold a human destiny.

In these lines you may find destruction, futility, maladjustment, rebellion, scandal, boredom. A full year's work for any psychoanalyst is caught up in these lines from Ibsen's *Hedda Gabler*. Listen to dialogue and see what you can invent and construct from it.

1. Read the material for this assignment.
2. In your journal do *one* of the following:
   a. (1) Take a piece of dialogue and write the story you feel it implies, or
      (2) Extend a piece of dialogue until it makes a story.
   b. Discuss and explain the differences and similarities between drama and story.
   c. Write on a topic of your own choice.

3|3

STAGING AN IDEA

All I want is to speak simply; for this grace I pray.
For we have loaded even the song with so many
    kinds of music
That gradually it sinks.
And our art we so decorated that beneath the gilt
Its face is eaten away.
And it is now time for us to say the few words we
    have to say
Because tomorrow our soul sets sail.
                GEORGE SEFERIS
            from "An Old Man on the River Bank"

Writing is a dramatic act. You put yourself and your ideas
on stage every time you write. The analogy extends even to
lighting, as you can see by tracing that motif in Hawthorne's
House of the Seven Gables. Words are the actors in the drama
of the page, and you are playwright, stage manager, and director. Admittedly a laundry list does not record much more than
dirty clothes, but an essay or story is singularly your production.

The question then is how best to stage an idea. Clearly
there is no single right answer, either in composition or
drama. Yet one constant remains. You do have to know or
discover what it is you want to say—flutter, charm, or flourish
lasts only so long and then the audience gets up and goes out.
Unless you are writing comedy or just being entertaining—
both considerable feats—you need a core idea around which
to move your acts or paragraphs, for thoughts are needed to
sustain an essay. Perhaps a brief example will illustrate some
of the ways in which an idea may be directed so as to occupy
center stage. As you read these paragraphs by E. B. White,
what do you find as idea? What unifies the writing and makes
it a successful production?

It was a fine clear day for the Fair this year, and I went up early to see how the Ferris wheel was doing and to take a ride. It pays to check up on Ferris wheels these days: by noting the volume of business, one can get some idea which side is ahead in the world—whether the airborne freemen outnumber the earthbound slaves. It was encouraging to discover that there were still quite a few people at the Fair who preferred a feeling of high, breezy insecurity to one of solid support. My friend Healy surprised me by declining to go aloft; he is an unusually cautious man, however—even his hat was insured.

I like to watch the faces of people who are trying to get up their nerve to take to the air. You see them at the ticket booths in amusement parks, in the waiting room at the airport. Within them two irreconcilables are at war—the desire for safety, the yearning for a dizzy release. My *Britannica* tells nothing about Mr. G. W. G. Ferris, but he belongs with the immortals. From the top of the wheel, seated beside a small boy, windswept and fancy free, I looked down on the Fair and for a moment was alive. Below us the old harness drivers pushed their trotters round the dirt track, old men with their legs still sticking out stiffly round the rumps of horses. And from the cluster of loud speakers atop the judges' stand came the "Indian Love Call," bathing heaven and earth in jumbo tenderness.

This silvery wheel, revolving slowly in the cause of freedom, was only just holding its own, I soon discovered; for farther along in the midway, in a sideshow tent, a tattoo artist was doing a land-office business, not with anchors, flags, and pretty mermaids, but with Social Security numbers, neatly pricked on your forearm with the electric needle. He had plenty of customers, mild-mannered pale men, asking glumly for the sort of indelible ignominy that was once reserved for prisoners and beef cattle. Drab times these, when the bravado and the exhibitionism are gone from tattooing and it be-

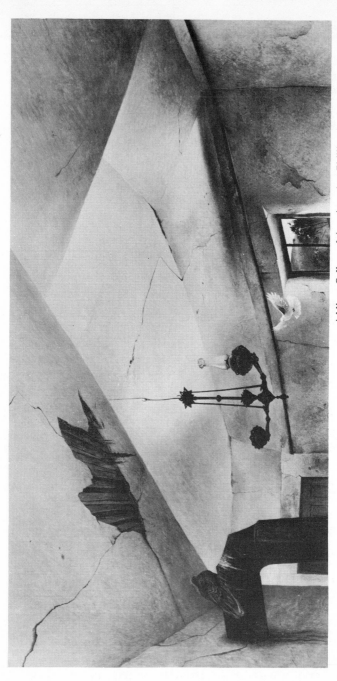

Addison Gallery of American Art, Phillips Academy, Andover, Mass.

Andrew Wyeth: *Mother Archie's Church*

comes simply a branding operation. I hope the art which produced the bird's eye view of Sydney will not be forever lost in the routine business of putting serial numbers on people who are worried about growing old.

The sight would have depressed me had I not soon won a cane by knocking over three cats with three balls. There is no moment when a man so surely has the world by the tail as when he strolls down the midway swinging a prize cane.

E. B. WHITE
from One Man's Meat

Assignment 7

1. Read the chapter up to this point.
2. In your journal do *one* of the following:
   a. Write an essay of your own in which a single idea is made the chief actor and given center stage.
   b. Write an essay in which you explain how a professional writer has dramatized an idea. Be specific.
   c. By referring to a play studied in class, show the parallels you find between drama and essay.

Assignment 8

The picture that accompanies this assignment is "Mother Archie's Church" by Andrew Wyeth. This picture suggests ideas on stage. Look at this picture carefully and consider what is being said and what is happening.

1. Study the picture.
2. In your journal do *one* of the following:
   a. Discuss the ideas you find suggested by the picture.
   b. Write dialogue you feel belongs with this picture.
   c. Comment on the relation you find between problems suggested by the picture, and problems presented in daily life.

Addison Gallery of American Art, Phillips Academy, Andover, Mass.

Thomas Eakins: *Prof. Henry Rowland*

Assignment 9

The picture that accompanies this assignment is a portrait of Professor Henry Rowland by Thomas Eakins. As you can see, the painter found his own way of staging a particular idea. Consider the picture and then write about it. At the same time, consider the possibility of making continued use of this device of moving from picture to idea; also consider some of your own ideas, and think about ways of putting them on stage.

In your journal do *one* of the following:

a. Collect and paste into your journal three or more pictures of paintings you think would be interesting to write about. Then indicate briefly the questions and ideas each suggests to you.

b. Start a story based on your observation of a picture. Name the picture and, if possible, paste a copy of it into your journal.

c. Write an essay on a topic of your own choice.

3|4

FOCUS OF INTEREST

Drama that does not succeed in its own time never succeeds. Plays are for people, people in the present. If that present extends itself into a future, then the play carries greatness that permits classics to endure. But remember that the play, unlike most art forms, must first live in its own time and place if it is to live in the future. In your own writing let the future take care of itself. Speak to your present audience. Say your say, but say it so that they applaud. But how, you may well ask, can such a thing be done? To that question you will not find any ultimate answer here—or perhaps elsewhere. But you will find answers all the same, and in the end, when you write, you will be obliged to take those best answers and your own talent and use them both as best you can.

The first answer offered here is no answer at all, but a dramatic and amusing statement that may have in it more truth than one likes. What follows, reprinted from Brander Matthews's *Papers on Playmaking,* is a portion of a letter by Alexandre Dumas *fils,* a nineteenth-century novelist and dramatist.

My dear fellow craftsman and friend:

. . . You ask me to tell you how a play is made, and I tell you, or rather I try to tell you, what must be put into it.

Well, my dear friend, if you want me to be quite frank, I'll own up that I don't know how to write a play. One day a long time ago, when I was scarcely out of school, I asked my father the same question. He answered: "It's very simple; the first act clear, the last act short, and all the acts inter-esting."

The recipe is in reality very simple. The only thing that is needed in addition is to know how to carry it out. There the difficulty begins. The man to whom this recipe is given is somewhat like the cat that has found a nut. He turns it in every direc-tion with his paw because he hears something mov-ing in the shell—but he can't open it. In other words, there are those who *from their birth* know how to write a play (I do not say that the gift is hereditary); and there are those who do not know at once—and these will never know. You are a dram-atist, or you are not; neither will power nor work has anything to do with it. The gift is indispensable. I think that everyone whom you may ask how to write a play will reply, if he really can write one, that he doesn't know how it is done. It is a little as if you were to ask Romeo what he did to fall in love with Juliet and to make her love him; he would reply that he did not know, that it simply hap-pened.

Truly yours,
A. DUMAS *fils*

Assignment 10

1. Read the chapter up to this point.
2. In your journal do *one* of the following:
   a. Agree or disagree with the statement by Dumas *fils*. In either case, explain why skill and technique can be taught in arts other than drama.
   b. Review a play you have read and see if you can explain its audience appeal.
   c. Take a few dull lines from a classic and see if you can give them new life.

Assignment 11

Here are two more letters reprinted from Matthews's *Papers on Playmaking*. Each purports to explain how one writes a successful play. See if you find merit in either of these statements.

Everyone writes in accordance with his inspiration and his temperament. Some sing a gay note, others find more pleasure in making people weep.

As for me, this is my procedure:

When I have no idea, I gnaw my nails and invoke the aid of Providence.

When I have an idea, I still invoke the aid of Providence—but with less fervor, because I think I can get along without it.

It is quite human, but quite ungrateful.

I have then an idea, or I think I have one.

I take a quire of white paper, linen paper—on any other kind I can imagine nothing—and I write on the first page:

PLAN

By the plan I mean the developed succession, scene by scene, of the whole piece, from the beginning to the end.

So long as one has not reached the end of his play he has neither the beginning nor the middle. This part of the work is obviously the most laborious. It is the creation, the parturition.

As soon as my plan is complete, I go over it and ask concerning each scene its purpose, whether it prepares for or develops a character or a situation, and then whether it advances the action. A play is a thousand-legged creature which must keep on going. If it slows up, the public yawns; if it stops, the public hisses.

To write a sprightly play you must have a good digestion. Sprightliness resides in the stomach.

EUGÈNE LABICHE

You ask me how a play is made.

By beginning at the end.

A novel is quite a different matter.

I could mention several illustrious novelists who have often started out without knowing where they are going.

Walter Scott, the great Walter Scott, sat down of a morning at his study table, took six sheets of paper, and wrote "Chapter One," without knowing anything else about his story than the first chapter. He set forth his characters, he indicated the situation; then situation and characters got out of the affair as best they could. They were left to create themselves by the logic of events.

Eugène Sue often told me that it was impossible for him to draw up a plan. It benumbed him. His imagination needed the shock of the unforeseen; to surprise the public he had to be surprised himself. More than once at the end of an installment of one of his serial stories he left his characters in an inextricable situation of which he himself did not know the outcome.

George Sand frequently started a novel on the strength of a phrase, a thought, a page, a landscape. It was not she who guided her pen, but her pen which guided her. She started out with the intention of writing one volume and she wrote ten. She might intend to write ten and she wrote only one. She dreamed of a happy ending, and then she concluded with a suicide.

But never [has] Scribe, or Dumas *père,* or Dumas *fils,* or Augier, or Labiche, or Sardou, written "Scene One" without knowing what they were going to put into the last scene. A point of departure was for them nothing but an interrogation point. "Where are you going to lead me?" they would ask it; and they would accept it only if it led them to a final point, or to a central point which determined all the stages of the route, including the first.

The novel is a journey in a carriage. You make stops, you spend a night at the inn, you get out to look at the country, you turn aside to take breakfast in some charming spot. What difference does it make to you as a traveler? You are in no hurry. Your object is not to arrive anywhere, but to find amusement while on the road. Your true goal is the trip itself.

A play is a railway journey by an express train—forty miles an hour, and from time to time ten minutes' stop for the intermissions; and if the locomotive ceases rushing and hissing you hiss.

All this does not mean that there are no dramatic masterpieces which do not run so fast or that there was not an author of great talent, Molière, who often brought about his ending by the grace of God. Only, let me add that to secure absolution for the last act of *Tartuffe* you must have written the first four.

ERNEST LEGOUVÉ

1. Read the two letters for this assignment.
2. In your journal do *one* of the following:
   a. Write your own letter explaining how a dramatist has made his play successful.
   b. Respond to the statements made by the writers of the letters above.
   c. Revise or extend a previous entry.

Assignment 12

Perhaps the best answer to our fundamentally unanswerable question of how to write a successful play is to turn to plays that people have liked. As you read and consider them, see if you can find for yourself some of the ingredients that keep people listening. Here is one man's answer: a description of a germinal idea.

I think the real-life experience from which the idea of *Beyond the Horizon* sprang was this: On the British tramp steamer on which I made a voyage as ordinary seaman, Buenos Aires to New York, there was a Norwegian A.B., and we became quite good friends. The great sorrow and mistake of his life, he used to grumble, was that as a boy he had left the small paternal farm to run away to sea. He had been at sea twenty years, and had never gone home once in that time. . . . Yet he cursed the sea and the life it had led him—affectionately. He loved to hold forth on what a fool he had been to leave the farm. There was the life for you. . . . At exactly the right moment . . . he turned up in my memory. I thought: "What if he had stayed on the farm, with his instincts? What would have happened?" But I realized at once he never would have stayed. . . . It amused him to pretend he craved the farm. He was too harmonious a creature of the God of Things as They Are. . . . And from that point I started to think of a more intellectual, civilized type from the standpoint of the above-mentioned God—a man who would have my Norwegian's inborn craving for the sea's unrest, only in him it would be conscious, too conscious, intellectually diluted into a vague, intangible wanderlust. His powers of resistance, both moral and physical, would also probably be correspondingly watered. He would throw away his instinctive dream and accept the thralldom of the farm for—why, for almost any nice little poetical craving—the romance of sex, say.

EUGENE O'NEILL

1. Read the excerpt by O'Neill.
2. In your journal do *one* of the following:
    a. Review a few plays with which you are familiar and

see if you can discover any common denominators for success.

b. In listening and responding to your work in a class theater, have you made any discoveries about what makes a scene work?

c. Write on a topic of your own choice.

3|5

STYLE

Young writers often suppose that style is a garnish for the meat of prose, a sauce by which a dull dish is made palatable. Style has no such separate entity; it is nondetachable, unfilterable. The beginner should approach style warily, realizing that it is himself he is approaching, no other; and he should begin by turning resolutely away from all devices that are popularly believed to indicate style —all mannerisms, tricks, adornments. The approach to style is by way of plainness, simplicity, orderliness, sincerity.

WILLIAM STRUNK, JR., and E. B. WHITE
from *The Elements of Style*

The word "style" refers to excellence in matching method to medium—means to ends—words to ideas. When you say of a writer that he has a finished style, you are indicating accomplishment on an implied scale. The term is also used in a second sense to classify analytically by type or school, as when you say a writer is pedantic, Miltonic, and so on. In the final analysis, style presents itself as an expression of its author.

These same distinctions apply to "style" when it is used in describing drama. In theater, "style" describes the performance of all participants—playwright, actors, director, and stage designer. Indeed, successful production requires a harmonizing of individual styles in the interest of the total dramatic production, and one of the lessons to be learned from drama is this need for harmony of parts without loss of individuality or distinction. The successful play, like the successful essay, is a total production—a harmony of parts.

Style is an abstraction that theater presents as a concrete

reality. Drama shows you the difference in ways of saying and doing. For example, you can see the difference in style between a traditional Shakespearean production and the same play presented in modern dress, and you can hear and see the differences in style when plot and script are updated, as in moving from the opera *Carmen* to the musical *Carmen Jones*. The fundamental difference in each case is not of plot and character, but of conception that reflects itself in style. The relation of an idea to its expression is reflected in every aspect of theater. How idea affects style can be seen by considering tradition within the theater itself. For example, are you for the "box" set and the theater of tradition, or do you support the theater of revolt, or are both choices absurd? Is the best of both theaters to be encouraged?

Perhaps to condemn today's theater out of hand as uncentered trash may be as unfair as to demand a Shakespeare from a theater without a tradition. You need to remember that today's theater says, "Mind is not enough—the past has proven that; theater should involve the total person." And yet, to that statement a reasonable playgoer may join in the reservation raised by Benjamin DeMott in his essay called "Tickle-Touch Theater":

> Absorption, attentiveness, concentration on otherness—these are hard for a playgoer to sustain in a situation in which the immediate urgent question inside him is: Does that actor heading my way mean to hit (kiss, fondle, solicit) me? Security vanishes, and, with it, guarantees of continuous outward focus. It's not all loss, naturally. Challenge and interruption are values, when sparingly, pointedly used; they can awaken the mind to action. But are there not limits to this action? Could a man write a chapter of a novel amid the uncertainty thus aroused, amid such promptings to nervous self-regard? Yet the good playgoer is, for the length of *his* performance, like a novelist: he is an interpreter, a provider, filler-in, reader-creator of motives, an active, strenuous, comprehensive intelligence.
>
> BENJAMIN DE MOTT
> from *Supergrow*

As you know, the popular and the enduring are not always synonymous, and yet the enduring in the theater has always been popular, as Shakespeare has shown. Does the failure of the new to find a profound voice in itself nullify the attempts and the trying? Doesn't theater need to experiment, keep in touch, and discover and rediscover itself? Can theater, like Antaeus, who, we are told, was constantly renewed by touching the earth, also find its way to the roots of our lives and give itself a new strength?

You are invited to see and to support all manner of entertainments and experiments. You have a wide if not altogether free choice, for time and money are necessarily involved. The theater you support deserves your best judgment. Perhaps the following brief statement will start you thinking about theater as a place in which to study styles in ideas as well as styles in expression, and at the same time to see something of their interrelation.

> Revolt is the energy which drives the modern theater, just as faith drove the theater of the past. Revolt, however, is not simply an energy but also a body of ideas, a system of values; and these have both their implicit and explicit aspects. In order to emphasize similarities rather than differences among the various playwrights, I have primarily examined the negative side of their revolt: inclined to disagree about what they are for, these playwrights are generally agreed about what they are against. My emphasis sounds like special pleading —but it is an emphasis very frequently made by the playwrights themselves. The theater of revolt occasionally houses positive ideas and revolutionary programs—especially, as we have seen, in its messianic phase. But more often, its values are implicit. In its negative critique of existing conventions and institutions, it rarely offers any substitute ideas or ideals.
>
> Such destructive criticism accounts, in part, for the unpopularity of this drama, for the modern world wants affirmations. The man who knocks the props out from under the shaky structure of our

beliefs is expected to provide us with a new foundation: it is for this reason, perhaps, that the artist in our time has become the focus of so much expectation, and so much chagrin. Revolt is all very well, but revolt on behalf of what, in support of whom? If all our hopes are illusions, what hopes can he give us in return? Such questions the rebel dramatist is stubbornly disinclined to answer, or proceeds to answer with impossible programs and fantastic demands. To those who labor on behalf of the world, this man is an exasperating figure and a false prophet—radical when the world needs moderation, fanatic when the world needs men of goodwill, acrimonious when the world needs harmony.

But in demanding of him the positive values that they themselves possess, the men of action mistake his function.

ROBERT BRUSTEIN
from *The Theatre of Revolt:*
An Approach to the Modern Drama

Assignment 13

The best way of learning how to write a play is to see one of your own produced. That will teach you how to write lines that the actors find easy to say and, if you have an ear, how far you can carry the rhythm of a sentence without losing the spontaneity of conversation. It will show you what sort of speech and what sort of scene are effective. But I think the secret of playwriting can be given in two maxims: stick to the point and whenever you can, cut.

W. SOMERSET MAUGHAM
from *The Summing Up*

1. Read the chapter up to this point.
2. In your journal do *one* of the following:
   a. Discuss the new theater.

b. Start (if you have time, finish) a one-scene happening that you think presents significance. Have your audience in mind. Remember their need for entertainment and for something more than entertainment.

c. Do some reading about theater and report briefly on it.

Assignment 14

Probably not many would join Mr. Bennett Cerf in denying that the situation of the theater is today very problematic. Most discussions of the problem go wrong not in denying its existence but in regarding it as new and peculiar to our generation, and thus in attributing it to some localized cause, such as the rise of movies or the high Manhattan rents. The theater is always a problem. Over a century ago Carlyle wrote: "Nay, do not we English hear daily for the last twenty years, that the Drama is dead, or in a state of suspended animation: and are not medical men sitting on the case, and propounding their remedial appliances, weekly, monthly, quarterly, to no manner of purpose?" Such statements are to be found not only in times of dramatic drought but also in the harvest seasons. Looking back on the eighteen-nineties today, we regard them as years of dramatic achievement; Bernard Shaw's *Dramatic Opinions,* written at the time, tell another story. We think of the Restoration as the age of Congreve, yet the great comedian was very inconspicuous in his own day, and his now acknowledged masterpiece was a total failure on the stage. Shakespeare, the most read and the most performed of all dramatists, may have been best known in his lifetime for his cheapest and rawest plays (such as *Titus Andronicus* and *Henry VI*), and a contemporary boasts that one of his best plays (*Troilus*) was "never clapper-clawed by the palms of the vulgar."

The theater is always in trouble because its success depends upon too rare a set of coincidences. A poem needs only an author and a reader. A sonata needs a composer, a performer, and a listener. Closer to the drama is the symphony, which requires teamwork, coordination at the hands of a conductor, a large audience, and a heap of money. The drama, however, boasting of being a meeting place of all the arts, requires a too rare conjunction of economic, social, and artistic elements. Especially in its synthetic manifestations, which include everything in musical-choreographic-spectacular-mimetic-rhetorical theater from the Greeks to *Tannhäuser* and beyond, drama is the most impossible of the arts.

Yet the very citation of titles reminds us of its possibility. The fact is that, while high theater has a harder time than any other high art, the popular theater, dedicated to entertainment, and today functioning chiefly on the screen and over the air, is perpetually the most flourishing of the arts. It is the art which most excites children, savages, and all who are least conscious of artistic leanings. It seems to be an inextinguishable and indispensable art, an addiction more universal than smoking. It followed the doughboys to foxholes on tropical islands. It followed the doubly mechanized divisions of the Third Reich. It lures the schoolboy twice a week to the movies; it entices the student to turn on the radio while pretending to study.

ERIC BENTLEY
from *The Playwright as Thinker*

1. Read the excerpt for this assignment.
2. In your journal do *one* of the following:
   a. Rewrite or complete a previous entry.
   b. Respond to Bentley's statement, or make one of your own.
   c. Write your predictions for the theater of 1980.

Assignment 15

However they may be experienced, comedy and tragedy are constants in life and in drama. You should learn all you can about these terms and the expressions of them.

1. Look up a literary definition of comedy and of tragedy.
2. In your journal do *one* of the following:
   a. Write a tragic scene (not melodrama).
   b. Write a comic scene.
   c. Write a scene based on a dramatic model of your own choice.

3 | Review

Drama resembles lyric poetry in its concern for sensations, feelings, emotions, moods, thoughts—in short, the inner life of characters who are the agents in dramatic action. It differs from the lyric in that it is concerned with these inner states not as ends in themselves but as motivations toward actions. It more closely resembles narrative literature—the epic, novel, short story, and tale—by the fact that it is organized in terms of a story.

HUBERT HEFFNER
from *The Nature of Drama*

The following terms are an essential part of the vocabulary of the stage. They are the words commonly used in discussing the construction and working out of a play. Like any listed words, they represent only an inert grouping until the mind reaches for them and makes them a part of personal experience. To make such identification real, first establish a precise understanding of the definition of each word, and then use the words in talking and writing. Many of these terms will already be a part of your active vocabulary, but now is the time to master those that are not.

act (*noun*)
antagonist
anticlimax
apostrophe
bathos
bowdlerize
canonical plays
catastrophe
catharsis
chronicles
climax
comedy
comic relief
Commonwealth period
conflict
dénouement
dialogue
drama
dramatic monologue
Elizabethan age
folio
heroic drama
Jacobean age
miracle *and* morality plays
objective correlative

pathos	scene
plot	slapstick
protagonist	soliloquy
quarto	style
Renaissance	tragedy
Restoration period	unities
rising action	Victorian period

Another way of improving your understanding of the theater is, of course, to read about it and to participate actively in it. There are usually a good many opportunities to take part in play presentations provided you are willing to start as stagehand rather than star. And then the number of good books about theater is really impressive. For your convenience, a half-dozen representative titles in paperback are listed here:

Bentley, Eric. *The Playwright as Thinker: A Study of Drama in Modern Times.* New York: Harcourt Brace Jovanovich, 1967.

Brustein, Robert. *The Theatre of Revolt: An Approach to the Modern Drama.* Boston: Little, Brown, 1964.

Burton, E. J. *The Student's Guide to World Theatre.* Elmsford, N.Y.: London House & Maxwell, 1964.

Fergusson, Francis. *The Idea of a Theater: The Art of Drama in Changing Perspective.* Garden City, N.Y.: Doubleday, 1954.

Gaster, Theodor H. *Thespis: Ritual, Myth and Drama in the Ancient Near East.* New York: Harper & Row, 1966.

Heffner, Hubert. *The Nature of Drama.* Boston: Houghton Mifflin, 1959.

Review Assignment

In your journal do *one* of the following:
a. Write a one-act play about drama, or create the script and assemble pictures for a filmstrip about drama. Be sure that what you present is itself dramatic.
b. Revise scenes that you have previously written so as to give them a cumulative shape and impact.
c. Read a book on drama and review it.

UNIT 4

Reading
for Writing

*I tell my hearers: Reading a book is
like dropping chemicals into a test tube.
It is dropping ideas into a brain.
There should be a reaction,
some kind of explosion. No explosion,
no brain.*—ROBERT E. ROGERS

41

READ WITH IMAGINATION

> But it fortunately happens that what we call our education supplies to all of us the first basis for writing, the ability to read and to spell.
>
> STEPHEN LEACOCK

As a writer, you must have something to say and say it effectively. Both parts of this requirement will take you back to "the first basis for writing, the ability to read and to spell." The spelling part will be left to you and your dictionary. Here the focus is on ways reading may serve your writing.

At the start of your reading experience or perhaps even before that, when you were only old enough to listen to stories, you had one great advantage: vivid imagination. Because you have grown away from childhood, you may have forgotten how real were those fictional experiences. Can you recall looking at the pictures in a book and being incensed that the hero did not look as you had imagined him, and then experiencing a comforting awareness that the book picture simply reflected someone else's imagination and that you were free to go on using yours? Memories like that suggest how important imagination is to reading. Imagination is the part that makes a story come alive. Imagination is the part that makes you care.

From the first, and for all readers, reading is an imaginative experience. Perhaps writers develop their imaginative powers through the exercise of writing, or perhaps their imaginative responses are initially more intense. However it is, all writers are readers, but why aren't all readers writers? In the nonwriter something has probably been snuffed out or has gotten neglected, and the act of writing itself goes uncared for.

If you would strengthen your own response to writing, start by letting your imagination become involved. How important and lasting an experience this can be for the writer is explained by Elizabeth Bowen.

What do I mean by . . . books making myself? In the first place, they were power-testing athletics for my imagination—cross-country runs into strange country, sprints, long and high jumps. It was exhilarating to discover what one could feel: the discovery itself was an advance. Then, by successively "being" a character in every book I read, I doubled the meaning of everything that happened in my otherwise constricted life. Books introduced me to, and magnified, desire and danger. They represented life, with a conclusiveness I had no reason to challenge, as an affair of mysteries and attractions, in which each object or place or face was in itself a volume of promises and deceptions, and in which nothing was impossible. Books made me see everything that I saw either as a symbol or as having its place in a mythology—in fact, reading gave bias to my observations of everything in the between-times when I was not reading. And obviously, the characters in the books gave prototypes under which, for evermore, to assemble all living people. This did not by any means simplify people for me; it had the reverse effect, and I was glad that it should—the characters who came out of my childish reading to obsess me were the incalculable ones, who always moved in a blur of potentialities. It appeared that nobody who mattered was capable of being explained. Thus was inculcated a feeling for the dark horse.

The child lives in the book; but just as much the book lives in the child. I mean that, admittedly, the process of reading is reciprocal; the book is no more than a formula, to be furnished out with images out of the reader's mind. At any age, the reader must come across: the child reader is the most eager and quick to do so; he not only lends to the story, he flings into the story the whole of his sensuous experience which from being limited is the more intense. Book dishes draw saliva to the mouth; book fears raise gooseflesh and make the palms clammy; book suspense make the cheeks burn and the heart thump. Still more, at the very touch of a phrase there is a surge of brilliant visual images: the child rushes up the scenery for the story. When the story, as so often happens, demands what has not yet come into stock, indefatigable make-shifts are arrived at—as when a play that calls for elaborate staging is performed by an enterprising little company with scanty equipment and few drop scenes. Extension (to draw an iceberg out of a fishmonger's ice block) or multiplication (to make a thin, known wood into a trackless forest) goes on. For castles, gorges, or anything else spectacular out of art or nature, recollections of picture post cards, posters or travel albums are drawn on; and, of course, the child today has amassed a whole further scenic stock from the cinema. This provision of a convincing *where* for the story is a reflex.

For the child, any real-life scene that has once been sucked into the ambience of the story is affected, or infected, forever. The road, crossroads, corner of a wood, cliff, flight of steps, town square, quayside or door in a wall keeps a transmuted existence: it has not only given body to fiction, it has partaken of fiction's body. . . .

In reverse, there are the real-life places—towns, seaports, suburbs of London—unknown to the child, though heard of, which become "real" through being also in books. For instance, after *David Copperfield* I could not hear either Dover or Yarmouth mentioned, in the most ordinary context, without excitement: I had a line on them. . . . Historic places one was taken to see meant no more and no less to me than this; history was fiction —it took me a long time to be able to see that it gained anything further from being "true."

Though not all reading children grow up to be writers, I take it that most creative writers must in their day have been reading children. All through creative writing there must run a sense of dishonesty and of debt. In fact, is there such a thing, any more, as creative writing? The imagination, which may appear to bear such individual fruit, is rooted in a compost of forgotten books. The apparent choices of art are nothing but addictions, predispositions: where did these come from, how were they formed? The esthetic is nothing but a return to images that will allow nothing to take their place; the esthetic is nothing but an attempt to disguise and glorify the enforced return. All susceptibility belongs to the age of magic, the Eden where fact and fiction were the same; the imaginative writer was the imaginative child, who relied for life upon being lied to—and how, now, is he to separate the lies from his consciousness of life? If he be a novelist, all his psychology is merely a new parade of the old mythology. We have relied on our childhoods, on the sensations of childhood, because we mistake vividness for purity; actually, the story was there first—one is forced to see that it was the story that appareled everything in celestial light. It could lead to madness to look back and back for the true primary impression or sensation; those we did ever experience we have forgotten—we only remember that to which something was added. Almost no experience, however much simplified by the distance of time, is to be vouched for as being wholly my own—*did* I live through that, or was I told that it happened, or did I read it? When I write, I am re-creating what was created for me. The gladness of vision, in writing, is my own gladness, but not at my own vision. I may see, for instance, a road running uphill, a skyline, a figure coming slowly over the hill—the approach of the figure is momentous, accompanied by fear or rapture or fear of rapture or a rapture of fear. But who and how is this? Am I sure this is not a figure out of a book?

ELIZABETH BOWEN
from *Collected Impressions*

Assignment 1

1. Read the chapter up to this point.
2. In your journal do *one* of the following:
   a. Write an entry in which you review your experience with a particular book, one you lived with as a child. Insofar as you can, trace its influence on your imagination.
   b. The portion of Elizabeth Bowen's essay that appears here may prompt you to your own reflections about the relation of reading to writing. Consider what you have to say. Then say it.
   c. Take the "figure coming slowly over the hill" and see what your invention can tell of him.

Assignment 2

   Q. Do you just take it from what you read?
   A. Sure, you can get a lot of it. That's a very good way to learn the craft of writing—from reading. Just like a very good way to be a carpenter is from watching a seasoned carpenter do it. So you have been gaining experience all your life, and you will gain more as you get older. But you should have a pretty good size filing case or junk box of your own by now. You've been reading twelve, fifteen years—that's the main source, because there are so few plots and what you read—the plot has not changed too much, only the people involved in it have changed, and to see this same plot repeated time after time with different people motivated by it or trying to cope with it, you can learn about people that way, to match against your own experience with living people. So that you can remember things that you read when you were twelve, fourteen years old that you've forgotten. Suddenly at twenty-one you say, Why yes, that's so, because I saw that yesterday. That was so.

   WILLIAM FAULKNER
   from *Faulkner in the University*
   edited by F. L. Gwynn and J. L. Blotner

You will be saved a trip to the dictionary by reading this definition.

> **imagination:** 1. *a*) the act or power of forming mental images of what is not actually present. *b*) the act or power of creating mental images of what has never been actually experienced, or of creating new images or ideas by combining previous experiences; creative power. *Imagination* is often regarded as the more seriously and deeply creative faculty, which perceives the basic resemblance between things, as distinguished from *fancy,* the lighter and more decorative faculty, which perceives superficial resemblances. . . .
> **4.** the ability to understand and appreciate imaginative creations of others, especially works of art and literature.
>
> from *Webster's New World Dictionary*

In your own reading—especially in poetry and fiction—the use of imagination is a must. No set of directions can be given. No equivalency table can be established for those who do and those who do not read with imagination, but the results are clear and real. The unimaginative reader reads little, and that little principally in the realm of fact. The unimaginative reader does not enlarge his perceptions. He simply increases statistical control. By reading only the words on the page, he misses the connotations of those words, and by reading only words, he keeps himself from the involvement that reading with imagination requires. Reading with imagination creates a fusion of the past with the present, of the page with the self, of the old with the new. It creates its own images and brings with it the excitement of experience and perception.

Leigh Hunt points to the difference between imaginative and unimaginative readers in these words:

> There are two worlds; the world that we can measure with line and rule, and the world that we feel with hearts and imaginations. To be sensible

of the truth of only one of these is to know truth but by halves. . . .

To love matter of fact is to have a lively sense of the visible and the immediate; to love fiction is to have as lively a sense of the possible and the remote. Now these two senses, if they exist at all, are of necessity as real, the one as the other. The only proof of either is in our perception. To a blind man, the most visible colors no more exist than the lines of a fairy tale to a man destitute of fancy. To a man of fancy, who sheds tears over a tale, the chair in which he sits has not truer existence in its way than the story that moves him. His being touched is his proof in both instances.

Mechanical knowledge is a great and a glorious tool in the hands of man and will change the globe. But it will still leave untouched the invisible sphere above and about us; still leave us all the great and all the gentle objects of poetry—the heavens and the human heart, the regions of genie and fairies, the fanciful or passionate images that come to us from the seas, and from the flowers, and all that we behold.

LEIGH HUNT
from *Men, Women, and Books*

Constructive imagination is an act of self that takes you out of your limited physical self, and puts you into a larger, even limitless, world. Literature is only a part of that total world; but because it presents the voice of imagination, it is worth listening to. Literature performs a dual function. It projects the writer's imagination; and at the same time it invites you to use your own. Here is such an invitation.

The following statement is from the Preface of *Steppenwolf* by Hermann Hesse:

This book contains the records left by a man whom, according to the expression he often used himself, we called the Steppenwolf. Whether this manuscript needs any introductory remarks may be open to question. I, however, feel the need of adding a few pages to those of the Steppenwolf in which I try to record my recollections of him. What I know of him is little enough. Indeed, of his past life and origins I know nothing at all. Yet the impression left by his personality has remained, in spite of all, a deep and sympathetic one.

Some years ago the Steppenwolf, who was then approaching fifty, called on my aunt to inquire for a furnished room. He took the attic room on the top floor and the bedroom next it, returned a day or two later with two trunks and a big case of books and stayed nine or ten months with us. He lived by himself very quietly, and but for the fact that our bedrooms were next door to each other—which occasioned a good many chance encounters on the stairs and in the passage—we should have remained practically unacquainted. For he was not a sociable man. Indeed, he was unsociable to a degree I had never before experienced in anybody. He was, in fact, as he called himself, a real wolf of the Steppes, a strange, wild, shy—very shy—being from another world than mine. How deep the loneliness into which his life had drifted on account of his disposition and destiny and how consciously he accepted this loneliness as his destiny, I certainly did not know until I read the records he left behind him. Yet, before that, from our occasional talks and encounters, I became gradually acquainted with him, and I found that the portrait in his records was in substantial agreement with the paler and less complete one that our personal acquaintance had given me.

By chance I was there at the very moment when the Steppenwolf entered our house for the first time and became my aunt's lodger. He came at noon. The table had not been cleared and I still had half an hour before going back to the office. I have never forgotten the odd and very conflicting impressions he made on me at this first encounter. He came through the glazed door, having just rung the bell, and my aunt asked him in the dim light of the hall what he wanted. The Steppenwolf, however, first threw up his sharp, closely cropped head and sniffed around nervously before he either made any answer or announced his name.

"Oh, it smells good here," he said, and at that he smiled and my aunt smiled too. For my part, I found this manner of introducing himself ridiculous and was not favorably impressed.

"However," said he, "I've come about the room you have to let."

I did not get a good look at him until we were all three on our way up to the top floor. Though not very big, he had the bearing of a big man. He wore a fashionable and comfortable winter overcoat and he was well, though carelessly, dressed, clean-shaven, and his cropped head showed here and there a streak of gray. He carried himself in a way I did not at all like at first. There was something weary and undecided about it that did not go with his keen and striking profile nor with the tone of his voice. Later, I found out that his health was poor and that walking tired him. With a peculiar smile—at that time equally unpleasant to me—he contemplated the stairs, the walls, and windows, and the tall old cupboards on the staircase. All this seemed to please and at the same time to amuse him. Altogether he gave the impression of having come out of an alien world, from another continent perhaps. He found it all very charming and a little odd. I cannot deny that he was polite, even friendly. He agreed at once and without objection to the terms of lodging and breakfast and so forth, and yet about the whole man there was a foreign and, as I chose to think, disagreeable or hostile atmosphere. He took the room and the bedroom too, listened attentively and amiably to all he was told about the heating, the water, the service and the rules of the household, agreed to everything, offered at once to pay a sum in advance—and yet he seemed at the same time to be outside it all, to find it comic to be doing as he did and not to take it seriously.

It was as though it were a very odd and new experience for him, occupied as he was with quite other concerns, to be renting a room and talking to people in German. Such more or less was my impression, and it would certainly not have been a good one if it had not been revised and corrected by many small instances. Above all, his face pleased me from the first, in spite of the foreign air it had. It was a rather original face and perhaps a sad one, but alert, thoughtful, strongly marked and highly intellectual. And then, to reconcile me further, there was his polite and friendly manner, which though it seemed to cost him some pains, was all the same quite without pretension; on the contrary, there was something almost touching, imploring in it. The explanation of it I found later, but it disposed me at once in his favor.

By means of these comments we are introduced to the narrator and to a man by the name of Harry Haller. It happens that Haller's records fall into the narrator's hands. He makes these comments about them:

He left nothing behind but his manuscript. It was written during the time he was here, and he left it with a few lines to say that I might do what I liked with it.

It was not in my power to verify the truth of the experiences related in Haller's manuscript. I have no doubt that they are for the most part fictitious, not, however, in the sense of arbitrary invention. They are rather the deeply lived spiritual events which he has attempted to express by giving them the form of tangible experience. The partly fantastic occurrences in Haller's fiction come presumably from the later period of his stay here, and I have no doubt that even they have some basis in real occurrence.

HERMANN HESSE
from *Steppenwolf*

1. Read the material for this assignment.
2. In your journal do *one* of the following:
   a. Take up the description of the roomer, and present one or more additional impressions he might have supplied the narrator.
   b. Present your own version of a single entry from Harry Haller's records.
   c. Present as tangible experience some fanciful or vital image that comes to you from your reading or from your observation of nature.

Assignment 3

The toughest thing, for a writer, is to maintain the vigor and fertility of his imagination.

ERNEST HEMINGWAY

To read with imagination is to prompt creativity. The spark may be struck by a character, a scene, or an idea. Here is a brief statement that illustrates the connection between reading with imagination and subsequent writing.

When—perhaps I was fourteen at the time—I took Miss Marjorie Bowen's *The Viper of Milan* from the library shelf, the future for better or worse really struck. From that moment I began to write. . . . Why? On the surface *The Viper of Milan* is only the story of a war between Gian Galeazzo Visconti, Duke of Milan, and Mastino della Scala, Duke of Verona, told with zest and cunning and an amazing pictorial sense. Why did it creep and color and explain the terrible living world of the stone stairs and the never quiet dormitory? . . . As for Visconti, with his beauty, his patience and his genius for evil, I had watched him pass by many a time in his black Sunday suit smelling of mothballs. His name was Carter. He exercised terror from a distance like a snowcloud over the young fields. Goodness has only once found a perfect incarnation in a human body and never will again, but evil can always find a home there. Human nature is not black and white but black and gray. I read all that in *The Viper of Milan* and I looked around and saw that it was so.

GRAHAM GREENE
in *Paris Review*

The writer can only be fertile if he renews himself and he can only renew himself if his soul is constantly enriched by fresh experience. There is no more fruitful source of this than the enchanting exploration of the great literatures of the past.

W. SOMERSET MAUGHAM
from *The Summing Up*

1. Read the excerpts in this assignment.
2. In your journal do *one* of the following:
   a. Report your own experience of an insight prompted by reading.
   b. Comment in a full entry on the statement, "Human nature is not black and white but black and gray." Illustrate your point from your reading.
   c. Present a sketch based on this line, "He exercised terror from a distance like a snowcloud over the young fields."

4|2

LET READING
PROMPT WRITING

The truth is that, if reading is to affect writing immediately, it must be reading that has writing in mind.

ROBERT M. GAY

Reading should prompt writing, but that does not mean you're obliged to write about every book you encounter. Such an approach would be as pointless as giving a close reading to all the print you see. But to read from day to day without keeping a record of your perceptions is also foolish. When you are on the alert for ideas and distinctions, the quality of your reading improves, and it improves further if you hold yourself accountable for keeping a record of those perceptions. Not to keep such a record is to deny yourself exercise of the very powers you seek to develop. When you read, if you know you are soon to write, you stay on the alert for material to which you can respond. Reading in this way helps you see what is junk, or unimportant, and where the center of the experience is for you.

Another advantage to reading that anticipates writing is the attention it brings to style. Because you know you are soon to write, you give extra thought to the way the other fellow has done his job. You are prompted to read with imagination because of this interest in how a thing is said. No longer do you accept the words on the page as the only possibility. You speculate about other ways the story might have been told. You do not look on the print as a finality but as the expression of one possibility. Such reading permits you to see how others have used their imaginations to produce a given effect, and it leaves you free to speculate, practice, and produce your own. Reading in itself gives you something to say, a point to move from, and attention to style suggests a variety of ways in which it may be said.

Journal entries and notes are ideal for recording what happens in the laboratory of your mind. Record there the discoveries to which your reading led you. What is the point of exposure without response? How clear are your thoughts about a book, or any experience, if you can't talk and write about it? True, a child may perceive and intuit more than he can express or explain, but this is the precise point. You are moving from inarticulateness—nonsaying—to an educated expression of self. That is the presumed direction, but if you don't move, time and opportunity are lost. Read and respond—that is the way of the writer.

Assignment 4

1. Read the chapter up to this point.
2. In your journal do *one* of the following:
   a. Do a specific piece of reading with writing in mind. Record your responses.
   b. Turn to the journal of an established writer and copy out some of the observations he has made about the books he has read.
   c. Respond here to a piece of reading you have done this week. Name the source from which your writing moves.

Assignment 5

Like every young man, I was strongly under the influence of writers I admired. One of the chief writers at that time was Mr. James Joyce with his book *Ulysses*. The book that I was writing was much influenced, I believe, by his own book, and yet the powerful energy and fire of my own youth played over and, I think, possessed it all. Like Mr. Joyce, I wrote about things that I had known, the immediate life and experience that had been familiar to me in my childhood. Unlike Mr. Joyce, I had no literary experience. I had never had anything published before.

THOMAS WOLFE
from *The Story of a Novel*

Professor Gay in the following statement suggests a practical way of improving writing. What the method lacks in glamor is in part compensated for by the certainty that the job can be done, and that the results will be rewarding. Not an overnight method to writing success, it nonetheless has the virtue of beginning with reading and ending with writing.

If I were called upon, then, to suggest to a busy man or woman one way of improving his writing, I should advise as follows: copy every day, with preliminary *oral* reading, a passage of good contemporary prose, using the dictionary faithfully, and keeping always in mind the fact that you are not merely copying words but are transcribing thoughts. Further than this, so far as your time permits, memorize short passages of the very finest prose and poetry, and vary your practice with translating, paraphrasing and condensing. Have faith in the great natural principle of unconscious imitation, believing that what you learned in your practice will eventually affect profoundly your original writing.

ROBERT M. GAY
from *Writing Through Reading*

1. Read the two excerpts in this assignment.
2. In your journal do *one* of the following:
   a. After careful preliminary reading, copy a passage of prose or poetry that you particularly admire. Then comment on your reactions to the passage.
   b. Copy into your journal the opening page and a half of James Joyce's *A Portrait of the Artist as a Young Man.* Then give a detailed statement of your response to it.

Assignment 6

The paragraph below completes the quotation placed at the opening of this unit. You will find it suggests agreeable ways to think and to talk about books. The ideas presented in the paragraph may assist you when you turn to the more formal work of the book review, which will be taken up in the next chapter. Now, here is the full statement.

> I tell my hearers: Reading a book is like dropping chemicals into a test tube. It is dropping ideas into a brain. There should be a reaction, some kind of explosion. No explosion, no brain. The book *may* be at fault, but ten to one it is the brain which is inert. Every book contains at least one point where an idea touches your personality and your life, is of immediate interest to you. It may be an idea, it may be an experience. There is the springboard for your dive into your own spirit. No book but contains a text which you can illustrate from your own interests and memories. A good book will contain dozens. You must jot them down as you come to them. Then, while the book is still fresh in your memory, play solitaire with your jottings. Out of them will emerge a main theme, a critical conception. The others will hang on that main theme like cooking pots on a crane. And presently you will be sure in your own mind what you think about that book and why you think it.
>
> ROBERT E. ROGERS
> from *The Fine Art of Reading*

The influence a book may have on a writer, or any reader, is difficult to determine. But the work of most writers does reflect their own reading as well as their experience of life. As John Erskine pointed out long ago, "very few great books ever had what we should call an original plot. I say 'very few,' to be prudent—I know of none. . . ."

> Once you have understood the tendency of both reader and writer to rework old and familiar images of life, you can reason back from the experience we

have today, and imagine how people received the classics when they first appeared. If Mr. Shaw writes about Caesar and Cleopatra, we say he has modernized the old story, and if we don't like Mr. Shaw, we imply that he has taken a great liberty with sacred things. But all great writers, it would seem, have modernized famous material—not always in the direction of humor, but sometimes so. Chaucer's *Troilus and Criseyde* and Shakespeare's *Troilus and Cressida* no doubt shocked the classical antiquarian of their day. What extraordinary liberties Virgil took with Homer's plot and his characters! How Tennyson changes Malory around! How presuming of Mr. Robinson to cut up Tennyson and Malory both, into his beautiful poem *Lancelot!*

If we usually feel in a great work of literature that the tradition has been modernized, our feelings are guiding us correctly, I believe. In the finest books there will always be some elements of alloy, something contemporary and local, which readers in another time and place cannot recognize, and if the book continues to be read, the wish grows in us to get rid of the dead parts. We wish to see only our own face. The reader achieves this end by skipping. The publisher does it by getting someone to edit the text. The creative genius does it by rewriting the book.

JOHN ERSKINE
from *The Delight of Great Books*

Hawthorne gives us an example of this kind of imaginative reading and rewriting in "The Celestial Railroad." Randall Stewart in his biography of Hawthorne puts the matter this way:

The story is an adaptation from Bunyan's *Pilgrim's Progress,* with modern improvements. Instead of going to the Celestial City on foot like Bunyan's pilgrim, Hawthorne's characters ride comfortably on the railroad train. Burdens are no longer carried on the back but checked in the baggage car. A bridge spans the Slough of Despond, a tunnel cuts through the Hill Difficulty, modern gas lamps illuminate the Valley of the Shadow of Death. But the train stops short of the Celestial City owing to a limitation of franchise. Bunyan's way, Hawthorne thought, was still the best. The railroad in Hawthorne's story becomes a symbol of those contrivances—whether philosophical systems or mechanical inventions—which promise an easy and ready way to perfection.

RANDALL STEWART

from *Nathaniel Hawthorne*

1. Read the three excerpts in this assignment.
2. In your journal do *one* of the following:
   a. Look at Shakespeare's *Romeo and Juliet* and then look at Jean Anouilh's *Romeo et Jeannette*. Note similarities and comment on them.
   b. "Every book contains at least one point where an idea touches your personality and your life. . . ." From your own reading, illustrate this "one point" theory, and show how it applies to you.
   c. Let a masterwork consciously influence a piece of your own writing. Name the text and passage from which you are working.

4|3

ANALYTICAL WRITING

Story and analyses are more closely linked than most beginning writers realize. Unless you are working for unadulterated flattery when you show a person something you have written, you are asking for criticism. You want an expression of judgment. But this is right, for how can a writer improve if he is unable to compare one thing with another? This matter of comparison is at the heart of analysis. The ideal or the real way will be the standard against which you and the critic move, but without a standard for comparison, improvement is impossible. As you compare one theme with another, one story with previous stories, you begin to exercise those analytical faculties that permit improvement. You see what is and what is not as it should be. Too often analysis is equated with tearing down, slashing, dissecting, pulling apart. A story, a poem, or a painting is quite as much a physical entity when you finish verbalizing as when you started. In making an analysis, you project your own awareness clearly enough to permit another person to understand your emotional and intellectual response to the material. You have answered the basic question all writers want answered: "How do you like what I have written?" But instead of lumping your response in one word—good, bad, or indifferent—you sort out the parts; you identify the strengths and weaknesses; you take the pains to provide analysis.

Analysis is indispensable to improvement. It is a constant correction factor in sports and in the arts. Unexamined writing is like an unexamined life—when it's all over you don't know what has happened. The failure of the novice to improve is too often attributable to a failure to use analysis—self-analysis and objective analysis. There is a difference, but you need to have faith in your own basic judgments, for in the end you by yourself will be obliged to do whatever creative work you accomplish. But because artistic expression is an expression of self there is a real point in turning *to* rather than *from* thoughtful, detailed analysis. Like a mirror, it shows you what you can not otherwise see. Mirrors vary in quality, but you know when you are in a fun house or looking into a cracked glass.

You may find it helpful at this point to consider three pieces of student writing. Each is an analysis of the Conrad passage you earlier used as a model. Each of the student's comments is followed by a teacher's comment. But before you read the analysis of others, you may like to pause a moment and consider just what you, yourself, might say were you called upon for an analysis of the passage. Make a few notes if you wish. Then consider the others' statements. As you read, remember the point of the exercise is to become more analytical. That skill may develop slowly, but it will help you judge the writing of others and it will help you improve your own.

For your convenience, the Conrad paragraph is presented first and then the analytical statements.

And this is how I see the East. I have seen its secret places and have looked into its very soul; but now I see it always from a small boat, a high outline of mountains, blue and afar in the morning; like faint mist at noon; a jagged wall of purple at sunset. I have the feel of the oar in my hand, the vision of a scorching blue sea in my eyes. And I see a bay, a wide bay, smooth as glass and polished like ice, shimmering in the dark. A red light burns far off upon the gloom of the land, and the night is soft and warm. We drag at the oars with aching arms, and suddenly a puff of wind, a puff faint and tepid and laden with strange odors of blossoms, of aromatic wood, comes out of the still night—the first sigh of the East on my face. That I can never forget. It was impalpable and enslaving, like a charm, like a whispered promise of mysterious delight.

JOSEPH CONRAD
from "Youth"

Student's Unsatisfactory Analysis of Conrad's "East"

In this paragraph, Joseph Conrad uses good rhetorical techniques which help persuade the reader of the author's point of view. While he never once says in so many words, "I like the East," he not only convinces the reader that that is the case, but he also causes the reader to share in his feelings. Through the use of extremely colorful and descriptive language, Joseph Conrad literally paints a picture out of which radiate the senses of sight, smell, and touch. This picture is so tantalizing it leaves the reader himself eager for the "mysterious delight" it promises.

Comment on Student's Analysis

This paper is marked "unsatisfactory" because it lacks insight, precision, and support. The comments give a blanket blurb of approval but examine nothing in detail. The piece depends on clichéd thought; substitute another author and title and the comments work about as well as they do here. Statements such as "through the use of extremely colorful and descriptive language, Joseph Conrad literally paints a picture out of which radiate the senses of sight, smell, and touch" are as trite as the book report which begins: "This is one of the best books I ever read" and ends "I think everyone should read it, and I recommend it to you." Such mindless comments suggest the writer is incapable of either close observation or supported statement.

Student's Useful Analysis of Conrad's "East"

Conrad's paragraph aims at presenting the whole East in one glimpse. We know, and he affirms, that there is a great deal more to the East than this one view. Therefore, we may expect some persuasion of the meaningfulness of this view from Conrad. Looking carefully, we find that his description is calculated to expand this glimpse by contrasts. He contrasts the interior with the exterior, the very soul with the view from a small boat. He describes the mountains as they appear at all times of day, thereby expanding the time element. He moves systematically, from top to bottom, contrasting the jagged mountains with the glassy bay. Here, he captures the varied topography of the East. He also captures not one but many sensual appeals: he smells blossoms; and he feels, above these, a mysterious attraction. Finally, by changing constantly from present visions to past experiences, he expands the focus of time forward and backward. Thus, Conrad effectively expands this one glimpse by expanding the time element, the topography, the sensual appeals, and the focus—all by contrast. As a result, this one view of the East catches the variety, mystery, and eternity of the area.

RICHARD H. BRODHEAD

Comment on Student's Analysis

This writer makes some good points. He is sensitive to Conrad's use of contrast and the interrelation of time and focus within the description. Unfortunately, the student mars his own writing by a lack of terseness.

Transitions within the paper are well managed. Expressions such as "looking carefully," "finally," "thus," and "as a result" make for coherence and easy reading.

The total comment says something significant about the structure of the paragraph, but the writing lacks force.

Student's Outstanding Analysis of Conrad's "East"

Joseph Conrad once remarked, "My task which I am trying to achieve is, by the power of the written word, to make you hear, to make you feel—it is, before all, to make you see. That—and no more, and it is everything." In this passage from "Youth" Conrad is directing his appeal primarily to the sense perceptions; he feels the puff of wind in his face, he senses the strange odors of aromatic wood, and he hears a whispered promise of mysterious delight. Yet, as the first sentence suggests, he wants, above all, to make us see. His primary imagery, then, is of color and of shape.

The effectiveness of this imagery in conveying the sense impression is typical of the author's descriptive technique. Recognizing the power of a concrete image, he does not lapse into abstractions, but, instead, tells us of momentary impressions of actual objects—a jagged wall of purple, a red light in the gloom, a wide bay in the dark. Indeed, even in his selection of these images, he is careful to choose words whose connotations enhance the treatment of his romantic subject; thus, the East wind is heralded by an odor—but not by just any smell— by the mysterious and romantic aroma of strange blossoms. Finally, he strengthens our impression of the incomprehensible and overwhelming nature of the East by a series of imagistic contrasts with the familiar world—the sight of a small boat and the huge outline of mountains, the feel of one small oar and the vision of the all-encompassing sea, the heavy toil of dragging at the oars and the easy relief of a gentle puff of the East wind.

Another aspect of Conrad's descriptive technique is the putting together of materials from several different points of view; this passage, for example, is narrated both in the past and the present and in the singular and the plural. Although this method may create a feeling of discontinuity, it does serve to convey the inexplicable character of life and the shifting quality of the human mind. Closely akin to the workings of the mind, this style, then, like a stream of consciousness, is unified by whatever is logical and orderly in the human thought process. Furthermore, a sense of unity may be achieved by a logical progression within the apparent disorder; here, for instance, we first see the East in the early morning, then at noon, at sunset, and finally at night.

Moreover, any form which is so close to the human mind as this one, is bound to reflect the attitude of its creator; in this passage the tone is one of incomprehensible mystery. Thus, although the author may wander from his original subject, he is inevitably drawn back by the urge to attempt to understand the mystery more fully. Conrad is not describing his subject—he is becoming personally involved in it—he is penetrating it.

JOHN F. SEEGAL

Comment on Student's Analysis

This paper sees into the model further than the others. The student begins with a quotation that reveals his awareness of the principle that underlies Conrad's work in general and this paragraph in particular. He moves from Conrad's desire to evoke reader perception, to his use of imagery, and then to his primary imagery, color, and shape. This sense of order, transition, and movement proves characteristic of the paper as a whole. But the student does not rely on broad generalities. His second paragraph is a detailed study of the effectiveness, color, and shape of the primary imagery. In the next paragraph the writer faces the problem of discontinuity and explains how Conrad transcends seeming disorder by employing the stream of consciousness as a unifying force.

Assignment 7

1. Read the chapter up to this point.
2. In your journal do *one* of the following:
    a. Write an analysis of the following student theme.

In your request for an essay about a rewarding experience, I have taken the word in a light sense and have not written about any moral lesson which I have learned or something similar, but have applied it to a visit that was rewarding because it was very enjoyable.

About a year ago my family was on vacation in

Michigan. When the time came to head back for home, we decided to make a small detour to a little known but, nevertheless, often visited attraction. This was the Abbott's Magic Company in the town of Colon. A gas-station attendant gave us directions, which led us eventually to what is proudly advertised as being "The Magic Capital of the World." It was nestled at the back of a food store. We discovered it to be a plain brick building with a modest sign saying "Abbott's" and the entire front covered with white painted skeletons!

Upon entering, we found ourselves in a small room containing one counter, some autographed photographs of magicians, and a beaming, mustached man puffing contentedly on a cigar. We asked if *this* room was the "magic capital of the world." He, without a word, ushered us into an adjoining room.

Imagine this now: going into a small building, entering a tiny room, and then being swept into an inner sanctum as large as a gymnasium—no, three times as large—with rows of glass counters filled to overflowing with colored silks twelve-inches to six-feet wide, silver and gold palming coins in foot-high stacks, painted guillotines and armchoppers that miraculously never harm the occupant, giant cards, Chinese rings that link together though they are solid metal, chrome chains and handcuffs, milk pitchers that make their contents vanish, shiny red billiard balls that multiply mysteriously, and more tricks by the thousand! At the other end of the room was a stage. As we approached, we saw that on it were shop assistants performing illusions for the customers. We stared, in a slightly dazed manner, at the way they made wands vanish and appear again, the silks tie themselves into knots, and at the unconcerned air they took when juggling bubbles or taking the flame off a candle and calmly proceeding to light each of their fingers, one by one.

A vigorous business was being conducted over

the counters also. I would not be surprised if a hundred dollars changed hands every hour, for I learned that magic is not an inexpensive hobby by any means. Our friend with the cigar and mustache inquired what branch of magic I was interested in. I asked how many branches were there—he took a deep breath and said, "Oh! We have rope tricks, egg tricks, dove tricks, card tricks, silk tricks, cane tricks, ball tricks, candle tricks. . . ." I interrupted hastily and asked to see some coin tricks. He pulled a silver dollar out of my mother's ear, in a maddening sort of way, and did things with that coin that I never would have believed possible. For five minutes his flying fingers made coins, cards, and at last my long-saved allowance disappear!

At length the lunch bell sounded and we had to continue our journey home. Perhaps you feel I have exaggerated somewhat. I have—although I'm not sure how much. There is the reason that I found our visit rewarding. The nature of the Abbott's Company is such that one can twist the facts about everything one sees there and still not be lying. This is because at Abbott's there is only magic, and in magic, anything can happen.

ALEX VAN OSS

b. Select a picture you admire and write an analysis of it.
c. From your reading in literature, or from your work in another subject, select a passage and make an analysis of it. Be sure to place a copy of the original passage in your journal.

Assignment 8

The first step in analysis is close reading, or what the French call *explication de texte*. The process involves the breaking into parts—that is, the identification of key words, phrases, ideas, devices, and so on, and then an evaluation of the parts in relation to each other and to the work as a whole. Analysis should provide a statement of the significant insights the reader has arrived at as the result of his thoughtful examination of the material read. But remember, analysis is always for a particular purpose and from a particular point of view. For example, a tapestry might be studied from an artistic, a historic, or a chemical point of view, and each analysis will sharply differ from the others.

In making an analysis, explain what effects have been achieved and how they have been arrived at. Analysis requires a clear statement of the means by which a piece of writing succeeds or fails. Here is a check list of the qualities desired in an analysis. It is a guideline, not a life line. Skill in analysis depends on judgment and experience, not on formulas or adherence to rules.

1. Be clear.
   a) Identify your major and minor points.
   b) Preplan your statement.
      (1) Unify the total analysis around a central perception or idea.
      (2) Unify each paragraph around a topic sentence.
   c) State first things first.
   d) Give supporting evidence.
   e) Show relationships and subordination.
   f) Avoid the irrelevant.
   g) Make sure your judgments are reasonable, good tempered, relevant, fair, supported, and clear.
2. Observe these five steps when dealing with argument or exposition:
   a) State the writer's generalization.
   b) State whether the generalization is true or false and explain why.
   c) State whether the generalization is worth making or not worth making. Be specific.
   d) State what support the author has given for his generalization.
   e) State whether the writer has done what he set out to do and estimate the degree of skill he has shown in doing it. Give specific evidence in support of your estimation of his accomplishment.
3. Read and revise to improve mechanics and readability. The following points are worth considering when you un-

dertake a piece of critical writing. Again and again, failure at one or more of these points produces poor work.

a) Limited length: Even if each sentence is precise and excellent in itself, limited length often precludes the possibility of reasonable coverage. Too much simply gets omitted.

b) Lack of supporting evidence: The writer must distinguish between fact and opinion and at all points seek to evaluate and support both.

c) Errors of fact: Here, haste or misinterpretation is usually the culprit.

d) Shoddy word choice.

e) Failure to identify and treat problems presented in the original.

f) Failure to identify and treat strengths presented in the original.

g) Failure to understand or explain the significance of major points and hence the disposition to draw limited or faulty conclusions.

1. Read the material for this assignment.
2. In your journal do *one* of the following:
   a. Read a critical review in a scholarly journal and prepare notes for an oral report.
   b. Write a piece of analysis based on a short selection by a favorite author.
   c. Write an analysis of your own writing as represented by your best journal work.

Assignment 9

> Criticism should not be querulous and wasting,
> all knife and root-puller, but guiding, instructive,
> inspiring, a south wind not an east wind.
>
> RALPH WALDO EMERSON

Book reviews should be lively or highly informative, or both. Here is an example of a lively review taken from *Time* Magazine. Such reports on books are not intended to be scholarly, but rather to inform a potential reader about what he is or is not missing. You will note that the popular review does not assume its reader is familiar with the volume under discussion. The scholarly essay or analysis, on the other hand, assumes the reader has a knowledge of the work. Here is *Time*'s review of *The Dorp*, a novel by Frieda Arkin:

> Frieda Arkin has found a real, snug little place for herself in northern New York State, name of Kuyper's Dorp, halfway between the Adirondacks and the Catskills. Or—if you prefer to chart it on another map—halfway between the delicate perceptions of *Our Town* and the guff of *Peyton Place*.
>
> Up to now a craftswomanly short-story writer, Miss Arkin in this book has not so much composed a novel as arranged a tableau, then methodically violated it with sudden disasters. Give Miss Arkin a road and she'll give you an accident. Give her a decent storm and she'll burn at least one house down. Give her a lovable set of old bones and bingo, bango, she'll supply a fatal disease and buy the funeral.
>
> There is no design to *The Dorp*, no misguided attempt to unify it around a central character or theme. It all flaps as loosely (and engagingly) as the gossip columns of a small-town newspaper. The author obediently follows the ancient code of the village novelist. Her spinsters come in only two styles: dotty or drunk. Her clergyman predictably wrestles with doubt. The young girls are either uptight virgins or "fast." Most of the time the novel seems to take place—and to be written—around the turn of the century.
>
> "What was the village doing at such an hour?" Miss Arkin likes to ask herself periodically. Well, Country Editor J. C. Barrows could be playing chess as usual. Old Helen Trombley, the town hypochondriac, could be counting her twinges to old Vebber Stevens at the pig farm. Elizabeth Rust, who truly loves her husband, might be making love

to Jimmy Clancy at the motel. Down by the quarry, Kenneth Borgstrom, a schoolboy, might be making love to Eunice Dewsnap, a nurse. And Tony Di-Luzio, teen-age Lothario, might be making love to just about anybody just about anywhere.

It isn't *Winesburg, Ohio*. Rather it is soap opera, a sort of superserial in which the lovable characters are sometimes handled with such consummate affection by the author, with such descriptive refinement of feeling that it approaches art. Of course, there are those organ-tone poems about the seasons. Characters inexplicably appear and just as inexplicably disappear. Chapter after chapter goes absolutely nowhere. But the reader gets hooked nevertheless.

Now here is an example of a scholarly consideration of a novel. The writer is Clinton S. Burhans, Jr.; the paper, reproduced here in part, appeared in *American Literature*.

In *Death in the Afternoon,* Hemingway uses an effective metaphor to describe the kind of prose he is trying to write: he explains that "if a writer of prose knows enough about what he is writing about he may omit things that he knows and the reader, if the writer is writing truly enough, will have a feeling of those things as strongly as though the writer had stated them. The dignity of movement of an iceberg is due to only one eighth of it being above water." [1]

Among all the works of Hemingway which illustrate this metaphor, none, I think, does so more consistently or more thoroughly than the saga of Santiago. Indeed, the critical reception of the novel has emphasized this aspect of it: in particular, Philip Young, Leo Gurko, and Carlos Baker have stressed the qualities of *The Old Man and the Sea*

[1] Ernest Hemingway, *Death in the Afternoon* (New York, 1932), p. 183.

as allegory and parable.[2] Each of these critics is especially concerned with two qualities in Santiago—his epic individualism and the love he feels for the creatures who share with him a world of inescapable violence—though in the main each views these qualities from a different point of the literary compass. Young regards the novel as essentially classical in nature; [3] Gurko sees it as reflecting Hemingway's romanticism; [4] and to Baker, the novel is Christian in context, and the old fisherman is suggestive of Christ.[5]

Such interpretations of *The Old Man and the Sea* are not, of course, contradictory; in fact, they are parallel at many points. All are true, and together they point to both the breadth and depth of the novel's enduring significance and also to its central greatness: like all great works of art it is a mirror wherein every man perceives a personal likeness. Such viewpoints, then, differ only in emphasis and reflect generally similar conclusions—that Santiago represents a noble and tragic individualism revealing what man can do in an indifferent universe which defeats him, and the love he can feel for such a universe and his humility before it.

True as this is, there yet remains, I think, a deeper level of significance, a deeper level upon which the ultimate beauty and the dignity of movement of this brilliant structure fundamentally rest. On this level of significance, Santiago is Harry Morgan alive again and grown old; for what comes to Morgan in a sudden and unexpected revelation as he lies dying is the matrix of the old fisherman's

[2] On the other hand—though not, to me, convincingly—Otto Friedrich, "Ernest Hemingway: Joy Through Strength," *The American Scholar*, XXVI, 470, 513–30 (Autumn, 1957), sees Santiago's experience as little more than the result of the necessities of his profession.
[3] Philip Young, *Hemingway* (New York, 1952), p. 100.
[4] Leo Gurko, "The Old Man and the Sea," *College English*, XVIII, 1, 14 (Oct., 1955).
[5] Carlos Baker, *Hemingway* (Princeton, 1956), p. 299.

climactic experience. Since 1937, Hemingway has been increasingly concerned with the relationship between individualism and interdependence; [6] and *The Old Man and the Sea* is the culminating expression of this concern in its reflection of Hemingway's mature view of the tragic irony of man's fate: that no abstraction can bring man an awareness and understanding of the solidarity and interdependence without which life is impossible; he must learn it, as it has always been truly learned, through the agony of active and isolated individualism in a universe which dooms such individualism.

II

Throughout *The Old Man and the Sea,* Santiago is given heroic proportions. He is "a strange old man," [7] still powerful and still wise in all the ways of his trade. After he hooks the great marlin, he fights him with epic skill and endurance, showing "what a man can do and what a man endures" (p. 64). And when the sharks come, he is determined " 'to fight them until I die' " (p. 116), because he knows that " 'a man is not made for defeat. . . . A man can be destroyed but not defeated' " (p. 103).

In searching for and in catching his big fish, Santiago gains a deepened insight into himself and

[6] This direction in Hemingway's thought and art has, of course, been pointed out by several critics, particularly by Edgar Johnson in the *Sewanee Review,* XLVIII, 3 (July–Sept., 1940) and by Maxwell Geismar in *Writers in Crisis* (Cambridge, Mass., 1942). With prophetic insight, Johnson says that "the important thing about Hemingway is that he has earned his philosophy, that he has struggled to reach it, overcome the obstacles to attaining it. . . . He has earned the right to reject rejection. For the good, the gentle and the brave, he now tells us, if they do not try to stand alone and make a separate peace, defeat is not inevitable. His life-blood dripping into the bottom of the boat, Harry Morgan realized it at the end of his career. Philip Rawlings realized it in the blood and terror and tragedy and splendor even of a dying Madrid. Hemingway has realized it there too, and the realization may well be for him the very beginning of a new and more vital career."

[7] Ernest Hemingway, *The Old Man and the Sea* (London, 1952), p. 10.

into his relationship to the rest of created life—an insight as pervasive and implicit in the old fisherman's experience as it is sudden and explicit in Harry Morgan's. As he sails far out on the sea, Santiago thinks of it "as feminine and as something that gave or withheld great favors, and if she did wild or wicked things it was because she could not help them" (p. 27). For the bird who rests on his line and for other creatures who share with him such a capricious and violent life, the old man feels friendship and love (pp. 26, 46). And when he sees a flight of wild ducks go over, the old man knows "no man was ever alone on the sea" (p. 59).

Santiago comes to feel his deepest love for the creature that he himself hunts and kills, the great fish which he must catch not alone for physical need but even more for his pride and his profession. The great marlin is unlike the other fish which the old man catches; he is a spiritual more than a physical necessity. He is unlike the other fish, too, in that he is a worthy antagonist for the old man, and during his long ordeal, Santiago comes to pity the marlin and then to respect and to love him. In the end he senses that there can be no victory for either in the equal struggle between them, that the conditions which have brought them together have made them one. And so, though he kills the great fish, the old man has come to love him as his equal and his brother; sharing a life which is a capricious mixture of incredible beauty and deadly violence and in which all creatures are both hunter and hunted, they are bound together in its most primal relationship.

Beyond the heroic individualism of Santiago's struggle with the great fish and his fight against the sharks, however, and beyond the love and the brotherhood which he comes to feel for the noble creature he must kill, there is a further dimension in the old man's experience which gives to these their ultimate significance. For in killing the great marlin and in losing him to the sharks, the old man learns the sin into which men inevitably fall by going far out beyond their depth, beyond their true place in life. In the first night of his struggle with the great fish, the old man begins to feel a loneliness and a sense almost of guilt for the way in which he has caught him (p. 48); and after he has killed the marlin, he feels no pride of accomplishment, no sense of victory. Rather, he seems to feel almost as though he has betrayed the great fish; "I am only better than him through trickery," he thinks, "and he meant me no harm" (p. 99).

Thus, when the sharks come, it is almost as a thing expected, almost as a punishment which the old man brings upon himself in going far out "beyond all people. Beyond all people in the world" (p. 48) and there hooking and killing the great fish. For the coming of the sharks is not a matter of chance nor a stroke of bad luck; "the shark was not an accident" (p. 99). They are the direct result of the old man's action in killing the fish. He has driven his harpoon deep into the marlin's heart, and the blood of the great fish, welling from his heart, leaves a trail of scent which the first shark follows. He tears huge pieces from the marlin's body, causing more blood to seep into the sea and thus attract other sharks; and in killing the first shark, the old man loses his principal weapon, his harpoon. Thus, in winning his struggle with the marlin and in killing him, the old man sets in motion the sequence of events which take from him the great fish whom he has come to love and with whom he identifies himself completely. And the old man senses an inevitability in the coming of the sharks (p. 101), a feeling of guilt which deepens into remorse and regret. "I am sorry that I killed the fish . . ." (p. 103), he thinks, and he tells himself that "You did not kill the fish only to keep alive and to sell for food. . . . You killed him for pride and because you are a fisherman" (p. 105).

CLINTON S. BURHANS, JR.
from "*The Old Man and the Sea:*
Hemingway's Tragic Vision of Man"

In writing your own reviews, you may find help in these comments by professionals. The first excerpt that follows was taken from an essay by Joseph Wood Krutch.

> But the book review as a literary form implies completeness; it has not really performed its function unless, to begin with, it puts the reader in possession of the facts upon which the criticism is based, and unless—no matter upon how small a scale—its consideration is complete. However penetrating a piece of writing may be, it is not a good review if it leaves the reader wondering what the book itself is like as a whole or if it is concerned with only some aspects of the book's quality.
>
> . . . Whatever other qualities they [well-written reviews] may have, they accomplish the three minimum tasks of the book review: they describe the book, they communicate something of its quality, and they pass a judgment upon it.
>
> . . . It is not easy to do within the space of 1000 words or less, the three things enumerated. It is less easy still to combine the description, the impression, and the judgment into a whole which seems to be, not three things at least, but one.
>
> Yet a first-rate review, despite its miniature scale, raises precisely the same problems as long narratives or exposition raise, and each must be solved as artfully if the review is to have such beauty of form as it is capable of.
>
> JOSEPH WOOD KRUTCH
> from *The Nation*

Now, here are "ten commandments":

1. Don't use loose words—thrilling, intriguing, cute, grand, swell—in talking or writing of books. There are some readers who don't know any better; you do.
2. Practice humility in stating your opinion of a book. Allow for the possibility that your judgment may not be infallible.

3. Don't give away the contents, or the plot, of the book you are discussing. The author has taken a year to prepare its entertainment and surprise. You have absolutely no right to give the show away in three desiccated paragraphs.
4. Read the book; don't skim it.
5. When you read, allow 60 percent of your thoughts to be swept into the main current of the story; keep the other 40 percent detached and observant on the river bank. Pause whenever a note seems worth taking.
6. In conclusion, ask yourself what the author is trying to do.
7. Ask yourself how well he has done it.
8. Ask yourself—in your opinion—was it worth doing?
9. If possible, hold what you have written for twenty-four hours and show it to someone whose judgment you respect. Second thoughts will often modify the first flush of enthusiasm.
10. Avoid superlatives: a Shakespeare, a Keats, a Kipling, or a Galsworthy does not reproduce himself every ten years.

EDWARD WEEKS
from *The Atlantic Monthly*

1. Read the excerpts and discussion for this assignment.
2. In your journal do *one* of the following:
   a. Make a study of the current reviews in the Sunday book review section of *The New York Times*. Note your observations.
   b. Write a lively review of a book you have recently read.
   c. Write a scholarly analysis about a portion of a literary work studied in class.

4|4

SUGGESTIONS FOR READER
AND WRITER

Rules can be tedious and constricting, but the ones offered here are not. They are presented simply as aids, not as edicts. If you find you can write faster and better by disregarding those rules on writing, go to it.

As far as the rules on reading are concerned, they are really not rules at all but questions—questions to ask yourself. Again, as to how well they work, you'll have to be the judge. It's easier to fool yourself about the reading part, though. Once you have finished a book you tend to feel on an equal footing with anyone else who has finished the same pages. But, in fact, the experience for each of you may be far from equivalent. As a way of checking on the value of the reading you have done, you might consider its long-range effect. Do you find yourself responding to what you have read? Do you think about it, allude to it, relive any part of it? Does it come to mind or emotions as a real experience? Specifically, has reading invigorated your imagination, and prompted you to write? If few or none of these things are happening, then you better give the key questions presented in the following excerpt a close look. Perhaps you can find ways of letting them help you respond more fully to the things you read.

> Observe the paradox here. On the one hand, I say that skill in reading fiction is more difficult to analyze; on the other, it seems to be a fact that such skill is more widely possessed than the art of reading science and philosophy, politics, economics, and history. It may be, of course, that people deceive themselves about their ability to read novels intelligently. If that is not the case, I think I can explain the paradox another way. Imaginative literature delights primarily rather than instructs. It

is much easier to be delighted than instructed, but much harder to know *why* one is delighted. Beauty is more elusive, analytically, than truth.

From my teaching experience, I know how tongue-tied people become when asked to say what they liked about a novel. That they enjoyed it is perfectly clear to them, but they cannot give much account of their enjoyment or tell what the book contained which caused them pleasure. This indicates, you may say, that people can be good readers of fiction without being good critics. I suspect this is, at best, a half-truth. A critical reading of anything depends upon the fullness of one's apprehension. Those who cannot say what they like about a novel probably have not read it below its most obvious surfaces.

If the principles of literary criticism were firmly established, and generally agreed on, it would be easy to enumerate briefly the main critical remarks that a reader could make about an imaginative book. Unfortunately—or fortunately—that is not the case, and you will sympathize with my discretion in hesitating to rush in. I shall, however, risk suggesting five questions which will help anyone form a critical judgment on fiction. (1) To what degree does the work have unity? (2) How great is the complexity of parts and elements which that unity embraces and organizes? (3) It is a likely story, that is, does it have the inherent plausibility of poetic truth? (4) Does it elevate you from the ordinary semiconsciousness of daily life to the clarity of intense wakefulness, by stirring your emotions and filling your imagination? (5) Does it create a new world into which you are drawn and wherein you seem to live with the illusion that you are seeing life steadily and whole?

I shall not defend these questions beyond saying that the more they can be answered affirmatively, the more likely it is that the book in question is a great work of art. I think they will help you to discriminate between good and bad fiction, as well as to become more articulate in explaining your likes and dislikes. Although you must never forget the possible discrepancy between what is good in itself and what pleases you, you will be able to avoid the extreme inanity of the remark: "I don't know anything about art, but I know what I like."

MORTIMER J. ADLER

from *How to Read a Book*

Assignment 10

1. Read the chapter up to this point.
2. In your journal do *one* of the following:
   a. In a full entry write about rules for reading. Be sure to make as many additions and commentaries on what is offered here as your own experience permits.
   b. Read a short piece of imaginative prose or poetry. Ask the key questions and report your answers.
   c. Do some independent study on reading techniques. Report your experience and discoveries.

Assignment 11

Here are suggestions about theme writing. You may well have read them all before. Perhaps this rereading will remind you of what you are still not doing, or perhaps it will prompt you to more rigorous revisions. Personal editing and clean copy will upgrade almost any theme.

Not included in the listed suggestions, but a major factor in successful theme writing, is time. You need time to think about your topic, and time between first draft and final copy. The following brief note could have been penned by many a student:

> Dear Sir,
> I have just made a real discovery about short stories. They write better if one gives them plenty of time—time between story idea and story writing, and especially time for the writing job itself.

I am not happy about this paper. It's late and it's rushed. Still I hope you find it worth reading. I'm on my way home to get some rest.

Sincerely,

Joe

As you start a theme or essay it is well to remind yourself that you do not need confidence, or talent, or genius. What you do need is a clear, reasonable path of progress. You need to explore a theme that will act as a unifying force for the paper, and then you need a quantity of interesting examples, facts, and other supporting material.

Theme Writing—A Step-by-Step Plan for Progress

1. Think in terms of single pages—estimate number needed.
2. Think a paragraph to a page—but adjust to realities.
3. Think two examples per topic sentence—aim at the human or humorous, always the concrete.
4. Write a thesis sentence.
5. Write four or five sentences that are the main subtopics of the thesis sentence. These sentences should be of parallel importance and show some logical order of division. These four or five sentences are now the main divisions of your paper.
6. Write (the number depends on desired length of section) sentences that expand, prove, probe, illustrate, analyze or describe, observe, or reflect on some aspect of your topic sentence.
7. After you have your topic sentence, in a sentence—or phrase—indicate your two illustrations, but be sure you really have or can find what you indicate.
8. Plan transitions. Ask, will the reader read on? Ask yourself what you have done to make the movement within the paragraph and from one paragraph to the next convenient for the reader.
9. Find a model that approximates what you want to do in your paper.
   a) Make an outline of it.
   b) Note its features.
   c) Determine which if any you can emulate.

10. Write. Keep it clear, simple, honest. Write with as much vigor and variety as you can manage. Write quickly. Revise rigorously.

After the thesis statement has been written and the major divisions of your paper planned, focus on one page at a time.

Start with your topic sentence. See how it can be expanded. Usually a word or idea in one sentence will serve as the foundation or keystone of the next. This technique helps both coherence and unity. Topic sentences are simply your principal points. Your principal points should add up to your thesis statement.

A topic sentence is a direct statement of your main idea. It puts the main point squarely before the reader. It is what you will show him in the paragraph itself.

Make your major policy decisions before you start: determine your topic—how narrow, how long, and so on. Determine your plan of development—that is, narration, description, observation, argument, or combination, but don't be too fussy about this.

Focus attention upon a main idea and then give reasons for, or illustrations, or examples, or details, or explanations in support.

Facts are the secret to length Keep talking about them. Statements that are conclusions should be limited to one per three hundred words. *Support* and *develop* statements of fact by explaining, describing, proving, or illustrating the issues raised by your topic sentence. If you can't find the examples you want, try for the next best thing, a related illustration. For example, if you don't know what happened in art that year, tell what happened in science.

Show what you promised in vivid, concrete, if possible, dramatic form. In the body of the paragraph you keep your promise to your reader by providing a series of sentences that give specific evidence and that, added together, qualify or substantiate your general statement. These may be developed by example, analogy, comparison, or cause and effect. The material itself will suggest the best method of development. It is well to employ some variety of method from paragraph to paragraph.

Make frequent use of a narrative structure within paragraphs, though preserving the frame of argument for the paper as a whole.

The search for good material and illustrations may be endless. Set a deadline to your efforts. When you have reached your deadline, stop. Then make the most imaginative and original use of the material you have. Look for more material only after you have put what you have to creative use.

Whether you are addicted to outlining or not, you may find the following statement a useful guide in shaping your writing.

Plan your work before you do it, but don't *overplan* it. Don't set yourself up a mold that is so rigid you can't wriggle out of it on your way through the mill. I myself always jot down a structural outline before I begin. In fact, I get something of the sort on paper the moment I decide to do a story. It is a good guide. It usually covers a page, no more. The outline for this present chapter, which I scratched down before beginning, has fourteen items in it. They give the names of the subjects I will tackle, a few sentences I think I'd like to use, an idea, a phrase. The outline is not pretty. It is full of boxes around items, with lines and arrows shifting them to other positions. Its value is that it visualizes my problem. It is not rigid. If I find as I write that it is leading me astray, I immediately make another outline correcting the trouble. Quickies of this kind can be done in five minutes. This present paragraph, in my first outline, was scheduled to come in sooner. When I'd written it, I found it was out of place. I am just now transplanting it to what I hope will turn out to be its proper place. What happened was that I got a new view of the logic of the chapter as I wrote it. Early planning had been wrong, a little.

If you know about what you want to say, your outline won't be seriously in error. Whether it is right or wrong is unimportant. The vital thing is to avoid spending hours on an elaborate structural plan, worrying out supposed mistakes till you think every part is in its place. It won't be any righter after a day than after five minutes. If you find yourself sweating over the arrangement of your piece, chances are you don't know what you're talking about and should go back and get more information from the sources. When you are really full of your subject, the order of presentation will come to you naturally.

DAVID O. WOODBURY
from *Writers on Writing*
edited by Herschel Brickell

1. Read the suggestions on theme-writing for this assignment.
2. In your journal do *one* of the following:
   a. Using the suggestions given here, outline a projected theme. Choose your own topic.
   b. Read a *Time* Magazine "Essay" or some other article that interests you. Make an outline of the material you have read. Does the experience suggest the addition or deletion of rules? Be specific.
   c. Write an entry that has the conversational spirit and lightness of a letter or personal essay.

Assignment 12

I too often wait for the sentence to have finished taking shape in me before writing it. It is best to take it by the end that first offers itself, head or foot, without yet knowing the rest; then to pull; the rest will follow along.

from *The Journals of André Gide,* Vol. III
translated by Justin O'Brien

The following excerpts are from an essay titled "Calamophobia, or Hints Toward a Writer's Discipline," by Jacques Barzun. Again, what you are given are not quite rules, but if you are one of those writers who occasionally get stuck, or daily can't start, these thoughts may help.

Obviously, if one were starving or in danger of assault, words would come fast enough, the inner censorship lifted and all sense of affectation gone. This, then, is the desirable situation to create for oneself every morning at nine, or every evening at five. The hopelessly stuck would find it expensive but worth it to hire a gunman to pound on the door and threaten death as a spur to composition. Ideas would come thick and fast and yet be sorted out with wonderful clarity in that final message to one's literary executors.

The sober application of this principle suggests that the writer needs an equivalent of this urgency, this pressure. It cannot help being artificial, like any pulmotoring but, although it need have nothing to do with danger, it must generate some form of excitement. Most of those who have written extensively under varying conditions would say that the true healthful pressure and excitement comes from a belief that the things one wants to say form a coherent whole and are in some way needed; that is, the urge is a mixture of the esthetic and the utilitarian impulses. This seems to be borne out by the observation frequently made that if one can only get something down on paper—anything—one feels no further hindrance to working. The final product may not contain a single sentence of the original, but in the successive drafts one has only a sense of pleasure at molding a resistant lump of clay —cutting away here and adding there in the double light of utility and harmony. It is at the outset, before the matter exists, that the great void paradoxically objectifies one's fear, one's conviction that "they don't want to hear about it."

To know how to begin, then, is the great art—no very profound maxim—but since in any extended piece of work one must begin many times, this is the art which it is essential to master. There is only one way: to study one's needs and quirks, and circumvent one's tricks for escape. The guidebooks will tell you that you should be full of your subject

—a very good notion but too abstract. Fullness requires moral and mechanical aids and stout controls. For nothing is more common than to feel a stream of excellent ideas racing past and never a hook to lure them out into the open. This is especially true if one has previously tried to capture them and failed. We may say that our ideas feel like a whole world which is too big and whirling too fast to be pulled out in one piece. True, and this is why first aid at this point consists in not trying to have it born whole. Convince yourself that you are working in clay not marble, on paper not eternal bronze: let that first sentence be as stupid as it wishes. No one will rush out and print it as it stands. Just put it down; then another. Your whole first paragraph or first page may have to be guillotined in any case after your piece is finished: it is a kind of "forebirth." But as modern mathematics has discovered, there can be no second paragraph (which contains your true beginning) until you have a first.

The alternative to beginning stupidly, with a kind of "Er-ah," is to pick out during the earliest mental preparation for the work some idea which will make a good beginning, whether for intrinsic or topical reasons, and let it pull the rest along. Thus I began this essay on the cheering note that those mighty engines, Scott and Dickens, also stalled, and I had this in mind long before I knew what would come next. The danger of this procedure is that a picturesque idea can lead one too far back of the true starting line, and the cleverness or the charm of the idea make one unwilling to sacrifice it.

Some writers, it is true, are able once started to shape their sentences whole in their heads before putting them down—Gibbon was one of those. But most, I believe, do not. Hence it is fatal for them to feel the entire system of ideas, feelings, and tenuous associations which is now in motion come to a dead stop because some adjective which means "boring" and begins with n eludes them. Forget it. Leave a blank. The probability is that there is no such word; if there is, it will come up of itself during revision or be rendered unnecessary by it. This sets the rule, by the way, for revision itself: keep going at a reasonable pace to the end, skipping the impossible; then start afresh until you have solved the true problems and removed the insoluble. Remember Barrie's schoolboy who chewed a pencil to splinters and failed the examination because he sought a word halfway between mickle and muckle.

The same law of momentum applies to the search for transitions, to perfecting the rhythm and shape of sentences, even occasionally to the ordering of paragraphs. Don't haggle and fuss but reassure yourself with the knowledge that when you come back to settle these uncertainties and fill these blanks you will still have your mind with you. Especially for young writers who have experienced difficulty and discouragement, the proper aim is that of the learner on the bicycle—keep going, which means a certain speed. Cutting slow capers will come later.

JACQUES BARZUN

1. Read the excerpt by Barzun.
2. In your journal, do *one* of the following:
   a. Write as rapidly as possible for a continuous half-hour. Do not stop to revise.
   b. Defend or attack Barzun's statements in light of your own writing habits.
   c. Write on a topic of your own choice.

4|5

THE PRÉCIS

What you will be asked to do in this chapter is not in any sense busy work, and yet it may strike you as just that. Because there is apt to be a lack of understanding on this point, take a few moments to consider the purpose of the précis, the focus of this lesson.

A précis, more than any other writing exercise, allows you to see structure and substance. Outlining would seem to offer as much, but in fact does not because the real writing part is too light. In précis work, as you know, writing follows reading and the pressure on each of these skills is about equal.

Précis-writing is a study skill and a marvelous way to marshal material. Its utility in doing college work can hardly be overstated. The ability to read and then restate the core of the matter has obvious application in the study of history and related subjects. When you have developed enough proficiency to carry out précis-making in your mind page after page, you will indeed have done much to make yourself not only a better student but also a better reader and writer.

Précis-making requires that you think about writing as you read, and that you think about reading as you write. The combination can be magic. The central problem is the amount of sheer hard work involved. But if you understand the value of this work and dedicate yourself to it long enough to become proficient, you will profit hugely. Précis-writing is excellent as an aid to retention and as a way of sharpening your own appreciation of style and content.

Assignment 13

1. Read the discussion of the précis.
2. In your journal do *one* of the following:
   a. Write a précis of an editorial in today's paper. (Paste the editorial into your journal.)

b. Write a précis of reading you are doing for another course.

c. Write a précis of the following material.

Let me begin with the ever-vexed and important subject of criticism; for by criticism, intelligently applied, the reader makes the story his own or rejects it. When I had collected my short stories, I wrote, to follow each one, a commentary on it, giving its origin, its purpose, and occasionally my own opinion of it, favorable or otherwise. This was, as any writer will readily see, a most interesting exercise, and I hoped it would enhance the interest in the stories. But apart from the interest in the stories themselves, I hoped also that these short commentaries might suggest to the intelligent reader an approach to true criticism, providing him with as much ammunition as possible with which to shoot at the story he had just completed.

I have held for many years that criticism should confine itself to a judgment, not of what the writer might have written, but of what he did write; and that within that compass, its function was to discover whether what was written had been successful or not. That is to say, if a story was patently written to entertain, to amuse, the object of criticism was not to bewail the fact that the author was spending his time on this, but to determine if he did in fact entertain or amuse his readers. If the author's intention was evidently a more serious one—such as to exhibit a moral truth, to propagandize, to satirize—the same rule holds good; though I conceive that the critic has a full right—and the professional critic a duty—to determine whether the author has allowed his overall purpose to becloud and confuse, to weaken, or even to destroy, the essential element of all good stories, the accomplished telling of the story itself.

CHRISTOPHER LA FARGE
from "Fiction: Some Personal Beliefs"

Assignment 14

The two paragraphs that follow are from a letter by Robert P. Knapp, Jr. He, himself, is a lawyer and writer. His training for these professions and in other fields prompted these observations. The paragraphs were not intended for publication, but his permission has generously been granted. You will see that what is said about organization and cutting is very much at the center of your work with précis.

As an enthusiastic amateur but formally trained carpenter, cabinet-maker, and electrician, I can see that writing is precisely like the construction of anything. The builder starts with an idea; he makes rough plans, then detailed plans, and goes to work. He does not as so many people do (particularly in my profession) hammer some jerrybuilt contraption together and then go around sawing a bit off here, redrilling a hole there, planing down one part and building up another. It seems to me that at each step of writing, the writer should do the very best that he can. Naturally he will find that his plan can be improved upon and that some parts don't fit as he had hoped they would. In my eyes there is nothing to commend the widely held notion that going through numberless drafts produces a fine result. This process reflects either mental laziness that makes it more attractive to toss off a rough draft than to come to grips with the intellectual and verbal problems presented, or for an over-conscientious person it becomes a matter of lily-gilding with most of the effort put in on the wrong side of the point of diminishing returns.

Finally, in regard to cutting, the most necessary and beneficial practice is also the most painful. There is some deep paternal instinct that draws a writer often to defend with the greatest passion what are really the worst parts of his writing. It is absolutely essential not to equate the time one has put in or the pleasure one feels upon reading his own words with their essentiality to what one is trying to say. It has been my experience that once I had become accustomed to cuts, I became much more discriminating in avoiding passages that would be cut.

ROBERT P. KNAPP, JR.

1. Read the excerpt for this assignment.
2. In your journal do *one* of the following:
   a. Make a précis of the following material.

. . . My subject is the educated imagination, and education is something that affects the whole person, not bits and pieces of him. It doesn't just train the mind: it's a social and moral development too. But now that we've discovered that the imaginative world and the world around us are different worlds, and that the imaginative world is more important, we have to take one more step. The society around us looks like the real world, but we've just seen that there's a great deal of illusion in it, the kind of illusion that propaganda and slanted news and prejudice and a great deal of advertising appeal to. For one thing, as we've been saying, it changes very rapidly, and people who don't know of any other world can never understand what makes it change. If our society in 1962 is different from what it was in 1942, it can't be real society, but only a temporary appearance of real society. And just as it looks real, so this ideal world that our imaginations develop inside us looks like a dream that came out of nowhere, and has no reality except what we put into it. But it isn't. It's the real world, the real form of human society hidden behind the one we see. It's the world of what humanity has done, and therefore can do, the world revealed to us in the arts and sciences. . . .

A hundred years ago the Victorian poet and critic Matthew Arnold pointed out that we live in two environments, an actual social one and an ideal one, and that the ideal one can only come from something suggested in our education. Ar-

nold called this ideal environment culture, and
defined culture as the best that has been thought
and said. The word culture has different overtones
to most of us, but Arnold's conception is a very
important one, and I need it at this point. We live,
then, in both a social and cultural environment,
and only the cultural environment, the world we
study in the arts and sciences, can provide the kind
of standards and values we need if we're to do anything better than adjust.

> NORTHROP FRYE
> from *The Educated Imagination*

b. Make a précis of one of your own journal entries.
c. Make a précis of this paragraph by Stevenson.

A strange picture we make on our way to our
Chimaeras, ceaselessly marching, grudging ourselves the time for rest; indefatigable, adventurous
pioneers. It is true that we shall never reach the
goal; it is even more than probable that there is no
such place; and if we lived for centuries and were
endowed with the powers of a god, we should find
ourselves not much nearer what we wanted at the
end. O toiling hands of mortals! O unwearied feet,
traveling ye know not whither. Soon, soon, it seems
to you, you must come forth on some conspicuous
hilltop, and but a little way farther, against the
setting sun, descry the spires of El Dorado. Little
do ye know your own blessedness; for to travel
hopefully is a better thing than to arrive, and the
true success is to labor.

> ROBERT LOUIS STEVENSON
> from *Virginibus Puerisque*

Assignment 15

The following comment by Robert M. Gay suggests yet
another method for the study of sentence patterns and sentence rhythm. Like the précis, this approach calls attention

to paragraph form. You may wish to adapt it to your present study of the précis.

About the simplest and most completely controlled methods of learning to write are transcription and writing from dictation. Let us take these as an example. Suppose you made a resolution (and kept it) to copy carefully every day twenty lines of good prose, after having read them aloud slowly and expressively two or three times [and] while . . . transcribing keeping your attention concentrated upon the values and placing of the words, noting the relations among the words, and asking yourself the reason for the choice and placing of all important words. Suppose, moreover, you resolved to learn by heart some lines of first-rate prose or verse every week. And finally suppose you planned to take down from dictation a complete paragraph once or twice a week—a paragraph read to you by someone who knew how to break up the sentences into their natural and rhetorical phrasing. Can there be any doubt that by the end of a year you would have learned more about the craft of writing than you have ever learned in an equal time by following rules?

ROBERT M. GAY
from *Reading and Writing*

1. Read the excerpt by Robert M. Gay.
2. In your journal do *one* of the following:
   a. Make a précis of the following statement.

The particular myth that's been organizing this talk, and in a way the whole series, is the story of the Tower of Babel in the Bible. The civilization we live in at present is a gigantic technological structure, a skyscraper almost high enough to reach the moon. It looks like a single worldwide effort, but it's really a deadlock of rivalries; it looks very impressive, except that it has no genuine human dignity. For all its wonderful machinery, we know it's really a crazy ramshackle building, and at any time may crash around our ears. What the myth tells us is that the Tower of Babel is a work of human imagination, that its main elements are words, and that what will make it collapse is a confusion of tongues. All had originally one language, the myth says. That language is not English or Russian or Chinese or any common ancestor, if there was one. It is the language of human nature, the language that makes both Shakespeare and Pushkin authentic poets, that gives a social vision to both Lincoln and Gandhi. It never speaks unless we take the time to listen in leisure, and it speaks only in a voice too quiet for panic to hear. And then all it has to tell us, when we look over the edge of our leaning tower, is that we are not getting any nearer heaven, and that it is time to return to the earth.

NORTHROP FRYE
from The Educated Imagination

b. If you elected Choice **b** in Assignment 14 of this unit, now rewrite the entry paying particular attention to material that should be cut.
c. Make a précis of a statement that interests you.

4 | Review

These usages of written English which are seldom or never abandoned remain simply because no better fashion of expressing ideas has yet been discovered.

BURGES JOHNSON

The list of literary terms given here are worth your attention. Knowledge of them will help you discuss and write about the things you read. The terms themselves are part of a writer's technical vocabulary. Doubtless, you already know many of them. But if there are any with which you are not familiar, now is the time to learn them. You will find a glossary of literary terms more useful than a dictionary for this study and review.

abstract; concrete
allegory
allusion
ambiguity
archaism
archetype
article; essay
atmosphere
Augustan age
autobiography; biography
bombast
burlesque; parody
caricature
character
chorus
cliché
connotation; denotation

convention; tradition
criticism
deus ex machina
diction
didactic; propaganda
empathy; sympathy
epic
epigram
euphemism
euphuism
explication de texte
fable
fabliau; short story
figurative language
genre
Gothic novel
hubris
humanism
hyperbole

in medias res	romance
irony	sarcasm; invective
lampoon	satire
metaphor	sensibility
myth	sentimentalism
novel	setting
objective; subjective	simile
parable	stock characters
paradox	stream of consciousness
plot	symbol
point of view	theme
purple passage	travesty
realism; naturalism	understatement
rhetorical figure	wit; humor

Review Assignment

1. Study the list of literary terms given here and make certain you have a precise knowledge of them.
2. In your journal do *one* of the following:
   a. Read, with imagination, a poem or a play. Make an extended entry in which you report what you can of that experience.
   b. Do an extended piece of critical writing about a single author. In the course of your writing, refer to the literary tradition within which he worked and explain the extent of its influence on him. Give special attention to the one or two writers who most sharply affected his work.
   c. Write an extended entry on a topic of your own choice. In the course of the entry make a number of literary allusions that add to your treatment of the subject, but limit your allusions to works that you, yourself, have read.

UNIT 5

Fiction

> . . . *it* [*a story*] *can only have one merit:*
> *that of making the audience want to know*
> *what happens next.*
> *And conversely it can only have one fault:*
> *that of making the audience not want*
> *to know what happens next.*—E. M. FORSTER

5|1

YOUR STORY'S FIRST PARAGRAPH

The true creator may be recognized by his ability always to find in the most common and humble things about him items which he may use.

IGOR STRAVINSKY
from *Poetics of Music*

You should have great fun with fiction; after all, it is a playground for the imagination. In a story, life can be shaped and clarified and made to explain itself. Writing fiction is a way of discovering the world, and of sharing your discoveries.

Don't tense up or make a big deal out of any of these assignments. You'll not be asked to do more than you can manage. If you are—if you find that you are stumped or scared—then write out your own assignment and do it. The point here is for you to develop your appreciation of fiction, but that is apt to happen only if you know the problems of story writing from the inside—from trying to write stories yourself. No one expects you to prove yourself a professional writer, but the closer you come to professional standards the better will be your understanding of fiction. The intention is for you to see story from a writer's point of view. You've read a great many short stories, but once you start to write any part of one yourself, you'll begin to look at the work of others in a new way. Give this approach a try, and see if it doesn't work for you. Help yourself to a greater appreciation of fiction by writing it.

For the purpose of these lessons and as a way of getting started, aim at writing a story that has a beginning, a middle, and an end. Write a story that has a clear theme (not to be confused with moral), and one that is within the range of your own first-hand emotional experience. In this way you will avoid from the start some of the problems that attend the free story. Elizabeth Bowen points out the pitfalls of that game in these words:

In this country, within the past fifteen years, the noncommercial or free short story—that is to say, the story unsuitable, not meant to be suitable, for the popular, well-paying magazines, and free, therefore, not to conform with so-called popular taste—has found a wider opening: it has come to have an eclectic vogue. Production in this department has consequently increased. But, unhappily, the free story is being fostered with less discrimination than good faith. It is too generally taken that a story by *being* noncommercial may immediately pretend to art. Emancipation from commercial conventions was excellent—but now a fresh set of conventions threatens to spring up and to prove as tyrannous, dangerous to living work. Too many free stories show, both in technique and subject, a desolating and nerveless similarity. The public gets slated by the free short story's promoters for not giving such stories a more grateful reception, or supporting the magazines in which they appear. But why should anyone tolerate lax, unconvincing or arty work—work whose idiom too often shows a touch of high-hat complacency? The commercial short story writer had his own, hard-learned, competence: the new, noncommercial story, if it is to be important, should be able to make its way, any distance, on its intrinsic merits—it still has to be, in one sense or another, subsidized. Subsidy dishonors what ought to be, in the great sense, a popular art. At present, a very large number of free stories lack verisimilitude, are pompous, dissatisfying—they are not up to the mark. . . .

ELIZABETH BOWEN
from *Collected Impressions*

You may wish to experiment with the free form later. But for now satisfy yourself by first showing mastery over the traditional form. Perhaps the following explanation by Jesse Stuart will help you discover your own story.

Often when you read a story and look at the printed page, you feel that something wonderful has been created. It is an art to be able to make the characters in a story seem like real people to the reader.

It takes a skilled author to make a fictional story seem to be true. As you read such a story, your mind eagerly follows the pictures his words have painted. He describes a rising cloud of dust, a cloud in the sky, a tree beside a road, a highway, or a mountain path so that his reader is able to visualize it.

The people the author is writing about may be similar to your neighbors or to your own family. He is writing about people like those you have seen and those you know. This makes the story so real you might even believe that the author has slipped into your neighborhood to obtain his story. Yet, you have the feeling that you could never write anything as good as this story, which is so funny, so sad, so romantic, or so frightening.

You might say writing a short story is not for you. Well, perhaps it isn't, but you'll never know until after you have tried to write one. Forget about all the stories you have read when you try to write a story of your own. Just sit down, start writing, and be your natural self. Of course when you sit down to write it on a typewriter or with a pen or pencil, you should have some idea about what you are going to write. Write the story as if you were telling it to a friend who is sitting across the table from you.

How can you find a story, and how do you know whether your material is the stuff a story should be made of? There are hundreds of impressions that flash through your mind and some of these you think will make short stories. First let us think of themes we might call eternal. How many of your impressions fit into the category of eternal themes? Love is one of the great themes, but it is not necessarily boy meeting girl. Love is a great word; love your neighbor, love wild animals and wildlife, love your home, your country . . . and most of all, love people.

Then there are stories that can be written about families and family life—your family, or a family that lives close to you. Families are a constant source of stories. There is the man who tries to build his neighborhood to a higher level while one of his neighbors is a man who is trying to tear it down. This creates a conflict and a story with an eternal theme. We have these themes now; our ancestors had them five thousand years ago, and future generations will have them two thousand years hence.

You might overlook these themes because you think they are small ones and no one will want to read about them. But, because they are eternal, people will read them, depending on how well you write the story, hundreds of years from now. For example, read the play *Antigone* by Sophocles, written about twenty-four hundred years ago. Why has *Antigone* survived all these centuries? Sophocles tells of a sister's love for her brother, of the complications that arise, and the tragedy that results. There is both love and hate in this short play, and in the end those who caused the trouble pay for their sins. This is an eternal plot and it will never grow old from overuse. So, find out what is good and durable, something that has lasted for the ages, and it will still be a good theme to use.

When I was a small boy, my parents had a falling out and my mother planned to leave my father. She had packed my sister's, my brother's, and my clothes and had planned to go to her father's, taking us with her. But a rainstorm came up from nowhere, one of the hardest rains I have ever seen fall. While it was raining so hard, we couldn't leave; my mother's and father's tempers cooled, they ironed out their differences, and lived together for forty-nine years. Many years later, in 1937, during a tempest as I was crossing the English Channel for the first time, I wrote this story and called it "The Storm." After World War II, when so many families were torn apart as a result of the war, this story was published all over Europe. It was liked because it had universal appeal.

There are stories in your family and in the family next door to you for you to write about. To people in all countries of the world, family is an important unit. There is love, but not enough, throughout the world. There is hate, too, among people in our country and people in countries over the earth. In every country there are those who want to destroy. These are themes of universal appeal for you to use for stories in your high school, or in college, or when you have finished school. Write on the universal themes, and if you weave them through your stories they will have meaning for all people.

Today I am most grateful to my gray-haired English teacher, Mrs. R. E. Hatton, who taught in Greenup High School, because she made me aware of creative expression on paper. She encouraged me and helped me to become a writer and teacher. She told the members of our little English class back in 1923: "Write what you know most about." Out of my English class in Greenup High School came my first short story, "Nest Egg," about my pet rooster. It was written as a theme and published twenty years later in the *Atlantic Monthly;* since then it has been reprinted in college and high school textbooks. Years later, the associate editor of one of America's best magazines said to me: "The finest material sent to us is written by people from the country. Usually this material comes from a journalist who is writing about agricultural products or something about the land. Unfortunately we can only use a small portion of this writing since our magazine must have a balance for readers from all walks of life." Then I said to him, "Why do you think the best writing is coming from writers who live and work on the land?" He replied quickly, "Because they know what they are writing about." This very same thing had been told to me twenty years before by my English teacher, Mrs. Hatton.

It stands to reason, doesn't it, that you can write more and better about something you know well than something you know little about? I am speaking only of creative writing. This principle doesn't apply to research work for which writers must study and read all they can about a person who lived long ago to do a biography of him, or to create an atmosphere of an ancient country, like Greece or Egypt, for a play or a novel. It often takes an author years to get the material for such books.

When you write a short story, it is not difficult to know what the first paragraph should include. When you write or speak a simple sentence, such as "John Smith went to town," you know that John Smith is your subject, that he is the one you are talking about, that he is your main interest. So it is with the short story.

You should manage to mention the principal character in the first paragraph, even in the first sentence if you can. There is no need to say: "The road is a winding one from here to Blakesburg. It is five miles long. John Smith went to Blakesburg this morning over this road." This would change the whole setting and make the road the subject instead of John Smith.

If you reverse the order and say that John Smith went to Blakesburg, he went in his car, or he rode horseback, or he walked five miles over a winding road, then you are on your way to the interesting beginning of a short story. Your reader will want to know why he went, and he will want to know what is going to take place when John Smith gets to Blakesburg. You will have the beginning of a story in a few simple sentences.

The procedure is simple if you will think of your story line instead of thinking about how to write it, for your words will fall into place. If some of the words and sentences are not right, you can revise the story later. What you want to do first is tell your story.

Along with establishing the main character in the first paragraph, mention a few of the minor characters, too, if possible. Once when I was young, I received a bit of advice along this line from Elizabeth Maddox Roberts, who was at that time one of the best known novelists and short-story writers in America. She knew that I was from the Hill country of Eastern Kentucky, and she gave me an illustration about using a main character and minor characters. "Let the backbone of the mountain be your main character," she said. "Let the small ridges that extend from the backbone of the mountain be your minor characters."

While handling your characters you can drop in, with one word, with a sentence, or with a paragraph, the background of your story. If you mention the name of a town or city, whether real or fictitious, the reader knows immediately that the story has something to do with village, town, or city life. If you should write a story with a Western setting, you should mention desert or plain, and for a Southern setting, you could mention a cotton field. And it doesn't hurt to mention the name of the state where the story takes place. I have mentioned "hills" or "mountains" and "Kentucky" in the majority of my stories.

It should be very easy for you, the young would-be short-story writer, to write in simple, communicative language. Do not feel you must use words so difficult that your readers will have to look them up in a dictionary. When you read the stories that have been carefully selected for this volume [*Short*

Stories for Discussion], note the simplicity of the language that the authors have used.

Although each author considers his ideas first, his language is important, too, for it is the author's means of conveying the story to he reader. There are few words in the stories in this book for which you will have to use a dictionary to understand their meaning. The ancient Greeks, who have given more cultural heritage to the world than any other country, said simple art is great art. Ernest Hemingway's *The Old Man and the Sea* is an outstanding example of powerful, but simple, writing.

Try to listen to the ordinary conversation of people. You certainly won't want to reproduce all the trivia of the usual conversation, but you can get the feel of the right language for your story. After you get it down on paper, remove all the excess words when you revise your story.

Where did Hemingway get his true-to-life language in *The Old Man and the Sea*? Remember, he was a great fisherman and he absorbed this language from other fishermen who were his friends. Hemingway is noted for his ability to use simple words and weave them into powerful sentences. And it didn't matter if he wrote a story with a setting in Spain, Africa, Cuba, or the United States; he became acquainted with the people he wrote about and listened carefully to their language. When he wrote about war, as he did in two powerful novels, *A Farewell to Arms* and *For Whom the Bell Tolls,* he used the ordinary language of soldiers in combat.

Once I had a college professor who taught creative writing. He said to the class: "Make your language simple. Stop trying to use big words. If you write using big words and stilted language, no one will read what you have written. Try using nouns as verbs and verbs as nouns. And for fast action in a story, use short, simple sentences." I didn't think he knew what he was talking about, but I followed his instruction and at least twenty short stories I wrote for his class in college have sold to large circulation magazines in America. His pupils from that small class, up to the present time, have published over one hundred books.

There is also the *feeling* for words that one who writes should have. This sensitivity must be a part of your physical make-up; nobody can give it to you, nor can it be taught to you by your teachers. Since you as the writer must project yourself into your characters, you must feel the joy a character feels when he is happy about something, and you must be able to weep with a character you are writing about who has lost his best friend. You have to project yourself into every character you put down on paper and tell your story with feeling, in simple, communicative language. You might, by writing many short stories, tell one of the more powerful stories that will become a classic in American literature.

After the story is down on paper comes the job I am most reluctant to perform—the revising or rewriting, the drudgery of the process of story writing. But it must be done. In the process of revising, remove the repetitious lines; change verbs and modifiers. Switch nouns to verbs and verbs to nouns. Play with the language, remembering always to keep it simple. A simple adjective may have to be changed half a dozen times. In paragraphs of action, shorten the sentences. In rewriting paragraphs you may want to switch their order. Nearly all of my stories are revised twice, and very often three times. I have revised a few stories seven and eight times. As a rule, don't do all of your revising at a single sitting. If it isn't quite right, and by being quite right I mean if it doesn't suit you, if it doesn't excite and communicate, lay it aside for another revision at another time.

All around you, wherever you live, are stories that are going to waste every day. This world is full of unwritten stories. It is up to you to utilize this

raw material, to select the important from the unimportant, and to weave it into the fabric of polished short stories to be added to America's literary
heritage.

JESSE STUART
from *Short Stories for Discussion*
edited by Albert K. Ridout
and Jesse Stuart

Assignment 1

. . . everywhere the everyday is only a surface that
conceals an eternal miracle.

JOHN CANADAY
from *Keys to Art*

1. Read the chapter up to this point.
2. In your journal do *one* of the following:
   a. Copy out the first paragraph of a short story you know
      and like. Then imitate or emulate your model.
   b. Look through a short-story collection with which you
      are familiar. List some of the universal themes the
      writers have used. Give story titles, authors, and in your
      own words state the themes. Then select one of the
      themes you find congenial and sketch out an incident
      from your own experience that illustrates the theme.
   c. Read the opening paragraph of half a dozen short
      stories. Note two or three openings that you like. Then
      explain how and why the story openings work and
      what, if anything, they have in common. Be specific. If
      time permits, copy out the best of the three opening
      paragraphs into your journal.

Assignment 2

The most obvious truth about art, yet the one least
considered by most people, is that if an artist has
nothing to say, it makes little difference how great
his mastery over the means of saying it, and that no

matter how much he may have to say, and no matter how great a man he may be within himself, he is of no consequence as an artist except to the degree that he has mastered the most appropriate way of communicating with the rest of us.

JOHN CANADAY
from *Keys to Art*

Just how difficult it is to find the most appropriate way of communicating is thoughtfully explained by Dorothy Canfield Fisher, a distinguished novelist and one long interested in encouraging young writers. She says:

Scientists tell us it is harder to start a stone moving than to keep it going after it gets started. And every writer can bear witness that the most unyielding stone is mobile as thistledown compared to the inertia of the average human mind confronted with a blank sheet of paper.

It is hard to write. It is infinitely harder to begin to write. Don't I know it? I have been earning my living by my pen for twenty-five years. I shouldn't like to guess how many hundred thousand words I've put on paper, and I have never in my life sat down at my desk and started off without hesitation, repugnance, and wild flounderings. Other authors confess that it is much the same with them. There are exceptions—stories, even novels, where the opening words pop right into one's mind, part of the first conception, but these inspirations are far between.

I set down all this not to discourage those of you who are wondering if perhaps it might not be possible to become an author, still less to add to the gloom of wrestling with the English compositions you all have to write. On the contrary, I hope to encourage you by letting you know that those hopeless moments of inhibition before the blank page, those chewed, balky penholders are only the common lot. There is nothing the matter if you can't start writing without effort. Nobody can.

But perhaps this sounds a little bit like the fortune teller who predicted, "You will have forty years of bad luck and then—then you will be used to it." It is not so bad as that. It is quite true that no one ever learns to write both well and easily. But there are tricks to every trade and some of the most useful of them all are ways of tricking your own rebellious nerves. Perhaps it would help you to know of one that works with most writers. Whenever they have a piece of writing to do, *they begin to write*—to write something, anything. They conquer the inertia of their minds by a spasm of effort, just as a man might give a great heave to a boulder that blocks his way. Grimly, doggedly, they keep on writing. Often what they are setting down is flat, stale balderdash, and they know it. No matter! If they are experienced writers they keep right on, do not stop—not to sharpen a pencil, or get a drink of water, or go to look out of the window, although they yearn to do all these things. They have learned by experience that if they sit and stare at the paper they are lost. The rosy, hazy half-thoughts which flit about the back of the mind always vanish when one tries to think them out. The only way to catch them is to put down on the paper as many of them as possible.

So the struggling author plods ahead, filling page after page with horrible, unwieldy sentences, haphazard, unleavened ideas, and after a time it begins to move more smoothly. Is it because of habit, or because the subconscious mind wakes up, or is it something similar to physical momentum? Nobody knows, but it almost always works. The great boulder begins to roll evenly and more and more in the desired direction. Apter phrases suggest themselves. The whole subject begins to take on shape. Even now it is not good. But there is something there, some stuff which can later be licked into shape.

DOROTHY CANFIELD FISHER
from "Theme Writing"

With the writing of your own story it does not much matter how you get up momentum—just so long as you do get started. One way to start is to begin at the beginning, though there is no reason not to start in the middle or at the end if that suits you better. But at some point you will have to write your story's first paragraph. Edgar Allan Poe in his review of Hawthorne's *Twice-Told Tales* makes an important point about the short story and its first paragraph. You will do well to read and consider his comments. See if you can apply them to your own stories.

> A skillful literary artist has constructed a tale. If wise, he has not fashioned his thoughts to accommodate his incidents; but having conceived, with deliberate care, a certain unique or single *effect* to be wrought out, he then invents such incidents—he then combines such events as may best aid him in establishing this preconceived effect. If his very initial sentence tends not to the outbringing of this effect, then he has failed in his first step. In the whole composition there should be no word written, of which the tendency, direct or indirect, is not to the one preestablished design. And by such means, with such care and skill, a picture is at length painted which leaves in the mind of him who contemplates it with a kindred art, a sense of the fullest satisfaction. The idea of the tale has been presented unblemished, because undisturbed; and this is an end unattainable by the novel. Undue brevity is just as exceptional here as in the poem; but undue length is yet more to be avoided.
>
> from *The Works of Edgar Allan Poe,* Vol. VII

1. Read the three excerpts for this assignment.
2. In your journal do *one* of the following:
   a. Copy out a first paragraph from a Poe story, and explain in about a page how he does or does not follow his own advice.
   b. Copy out a first paragraph of a nonhorror story that makes use of the single *effect*. Show how the author has

caused sentences and events in that first paragraph to contribute to establishing his preconceived effect.

c. State at the top of a page the unique or single effect that you have "conceived with deliberate care." Then try your own hand at writing a first paragraph that follows Poe's advice.

Assignment 3

For an idealism, however noble its aims in the abstract, is a mistaken idealism if it destroys human ties, if it rends apart the social fabric. The examples in Hawthorne's stories are legion of those who, in their quest of some imagined good, violate human relationships, depart from the broad highway of mixed and varied humanity, and discover, sometimes too late, the error of their ways.

RANDALL STEWART
from *Nathaniel Hawthorne*

In part, Hawthorne's stories still interest us because he found a universal theme, one that is far from exhausted. Perhaps Randall Stewart's statement of that theme in the preceding paragraph will suggest to you ideas for a story of your own. In any case, you'll want to give further thought to your story's theme and to its first paragraph. Here are some exercises that should help.

1. Read the excerpt by Stewart.
2. In your journal do *one* of the following:
   a. Copy out a story opening written by a professional. Now recount the same events, but make a sharp change in one of these items: tone, point of view, character. Note how much one change influences all that follows.
   b. Reread a short story you know and like. Copy out its first paragraph. Then write one or two different openings for the same story.
   c. Write out the beginning of your own short story. Your actual first paragraph may be brief or extended, but in any case present here one or two pages of your own work.

5|2

WHAT COMES NEXT?

If a writer has not determined his key event, or if the key event is not truly a key, the structure of the story will be loose and vague, the effect will be one of diffuseness, and the reader will be puzzled rather than enlightened. We can examine any satisfactory story and locate the key event, or the key moment. . . .

Such a moment brings into focus all previous events and interprets all previous events. It is the moment of illumination for the whole story. It is the germ of the story, and contains in itself, by implication at least, the total meaning of the story.

CLEANTH BROOKS and ROBERT PENN WARREN
from *Understanding Fiction*

After your first paragraph, what comes next—or should come—is a scene that advances plot toward the story's key moment and at the same time makes your reader ask, "What happens next?" If you can make your reader ask that question and be concerned about the answer, you're well on your way to successful short-story writing. Stories are read primarily for entertainment; readers want to have their curiosity and interest aroused, and they want to have it satisfied by arriving at a moment of illumination. They also want to have a good time with your prose in the interval between story beginning and story end. But you can't sell your reader description or characterization alone. First, you must involve him in your story. He has to care. Your reader must ask with interest and eagerness, "What comes next?" or he'll stop reading. Teachers, lawyers, and other professionals may have to read, but readers of short fiction don't have to.

In writing fiction don't assume reader interest—earn it. And remember that even as you tell your reader what happens in one scene, you must further engage his curiosity so that he will want to know what happens in the next.

Here is an example taken from the short story "The Lotus-Eater." You will note Maugham establishes a clear beginning that is interesting enough to deserve your attention. Consider how his first reflective, accurate, and rather amusingly expressed observation—an observation that is made to seem casual enough—might in fact prepare for the end of the story, and contribute to its sense of rightness and inevitability. Also ask yourself how this beginning might contribute to theme.

Most people, the vast majority in fact, lead the lives that circumstances have thrust upon them, and though some repine, looking upon themselves as round pegs in square holes, and think that if things had been different they might have made a much better showing, the greater part accept their lot, if not with serenity, at all events with resignation. They are like tramcars traveling forever on the selfsame rails. They go backward and forward, backward and forward, inevitably, till they can go no longer and then are sold as scrap iron. It is not often that you find a man who has boldly taken the course of his life into his own hands. When you do, it is worthwhile having a good look at him.

That was why I was curious to meet Thomas Wilson. It was an interesting and a bold thing he had done. Of course the end was not yet, and until the experiment was concluded it was impossible to call it successful. But from what I heard it seemed he must be an odd sort of fellow, and I thought I should like to know him. I had been told he was reserved, but I had a notion that with patience and tact I could persuade him to confide in me. I wanted to hear the facts from his own lips. People exaggerate, they love to romanticize, and I was quite prepared to discover that his story was not nearly so singular as I had been led to believe.

And this impression was confirmed when at last I made his acquaintance. It was on the Piazza in

Capri, where I was spending the month of August at a friend's villa, and a little before sunset, when most of the inhabitants, native and foreign, gather together to chat with their friends in the cool of the evening. There is a terrace that overlooks the Bay of Naples, and when the sun sinks slowly into the sea the island of Ischia is silhouetted against a blaze of splendor. It is one of the most lovely sights in the world. I was standing there with my friend and host watching it, when suddenly he said:

"Look, there's Wilson."

"Where?"

"The man sitting on the parapet, with his back to us. He's got a blue shirt on."

I saw an undistinguished back and a small head of gray hair, short and rather thin.

"I wish he'd turn round," I said.

"He will presently."

"Ask him to come and have a drink with us at Morgano's."

"All right."

W. SOMERSET MAUGHAM
from "The Lotus-Eater"

You'll have to get a copy of the story to find how Maugham arrives at the story's key moment. But the point of interest here is how does he or any author get readers started and then keep them interested in a piece of fiction? The answer, in part, is sharpness in selection of detail and skill in suggesting appearance, character, and idea. Then too there is the ability to manage emphasis and subordination so that the items selected for use have meaning for the story and contribute to its final statement of "truth" or illumination.

And another part of the answer is to be found in one word, "scene." Scene is minidrama, and every story is made up of a series of these little presentations that happen right in front of you—all else is summary and staging. Scene builds on scene to the very end of the story. Scenes themselves should be dramatically arranged so that tension and curiosity are heightened up to the point of the story's climax. Then the closing scene should resolve matters as quickly and clearly as possible.

Scene presents character, and character is the directing and dynamic force behind plot. You see how all this happens in the story opening you have just read. Despite the need for getting started, introducing time, place, circumstance, central character, narrator, point of view, and problem, the author manages to use scene to make you wonder what Wilson is like, and to make you ask "What comes next?" In "The Lotus-Eater," as in most good fiction, scene is used to ask and answer questions in a dramatic way, and to put conflict on stage. In the Maugham story, reader interest in Wilson is sustained through the end of the final scene, which presents the ultimate discovery to be made about Wilson and his odyssey.

As you write scenes for your own story, remember character should be their directing and dynamic force. True, event, chance, circumstance, and the acts of desperate men may play an important part in the turn of events, but the reader's interest should be focused on character and how it responds to the pressures to which it is exposed. Story—at least the good ones —shows character development or change. As in life, events impinge and affect plans; a rainy day may cancel a picnic, but reader and writer find their real concern not with the rain but with how the characters respond to it. In "The Lotus-Eater," for example, what happens to Thomas Wilson would never happen to "most people." That is a fact told at the start of the story and is one of the devices used to gain reader interest. Another is the fact that the narrator, a sophisticated world traveler, found Wilson and his story curious, memorable, and worth retelling. But note from the start that story focus is on character. What happens to Wilson in the physical sense is event; how Wilson responds to event produces plot and character development. But let the author of the story, Maugham, tell you himself how plots works and how it relates to character; then perhaps you will be ready to start your own story character on an odyssey. When you do, use scene to present character and to keep the reader asking, "What comes next?"

It is a natural desire in the reader to want to know what happens to the people in whom his interest has been aroused, and the plot is the means by which you gratify this desire. A good story is obviously a difficult thing to invent, but its difficulty is a poor reason for despising it. It should have coherence and sufficient probability for the needs of the theme; it should be of a nature to display the development of character, which is the chief concern of fiction at the present day, and it should have completeness, so that when it is finally unfolded no more questions can be asked about the persons who took part in it. It should have like Aristotle's tragedy a beginning, a middle, and an end. The chief use of a plot is one that many people do not seem to have noticed. It is a line to direct the reader's interest. That is possibly the most important thing in fiction, for it is by direction of interest that the author carries the reader along from page to page and it is by direction of interest that he induces in him the mood he desires. The author always loads his dice, but he must never let the reader see that he has done so, and by the manipulation of his plot he can engage the reader's attention so that he does not perceive what violence has been done him.

W. SOMERSET MAUGHAM
from *The Summing Up*

Assignment 4

1. Read the chapter up to this point.
2. In your journal do *one* of the following:
   a. Write a full page in which you explain how a story you like involves reader interest.
   b. Use a short story you have read—give title and author. Outline the story and show at just what points the reader is made to ask, "What happens next?" Consider the use of detail and suggestion in presenting character.
   c. Write an original paragraph or two showing how transitions within a story can be employed to engage reader interest.

Assignment 5

Art and genius, so Voltaire asserted, consists in finding all that is in one's subject, and in not seeking outside it.

BRANDER MATTHEWS
from *Novel and Other Essays*

In your journal do *one* of the following:
a. Reread a short story with which you are familiar. Then explain in a full-page entry how its key moment ". . . brings into focus all previous events and interprets all previous events."
b. Pick a key scene from a short story. Use it as a model for emulation.
c. Write several narrative paragraphs. Do your best to create and sustain reader interest.

Assignment 6

You abuse me for objectivity, calling it indifference to good and evil, lack of ideals and ideas, and so on. You would have me, when I describe horse-thieves, say: "Stealing horses is an evil." But that has been known for ages without my saying so. Let the jury judge them; it's my job simply to show what sort of people they are. I write: "You are dealing with horse-thieves, so let me tell you that they are not beggars but well-fed people, that they are people of a special cult, and that horse-stealing is not simply theft but a passion." Of course it would be pleasant to combine art with a sermon, but for me personally it is extremely difficult and almost impossible, owing to the conditions of technique. You see, to depict horse-thieves in seven hundred lines I must all the time speak and think in their tone and feel in their spirit, otherwise, if I introduce subjectivity, the image becomes blurred and the story will not be as compact as all short stories ought to be. When I write, I reckon entirely upon the reader to add for himself the subjective elements that are lacking in the story.

ANTON CHEKHOV
from *Letters on the Short Story,
the Drama and Other Literary Topics*
edited by L. B. Friedland

Chekhov makes it clear that what comes next in a short story is a reflection of the writer's concern and interest quite as much as the reader's. Chekhov clearly has a purpose and a way for himself of achieving it. You will find it helpful to reread his statement and determine how it applies to your own writing—even if you never intend to write about horse-thieves.

1. Read the excerpt by Chekhov.
2. In your journal do *one* of the following:
   a. In your own words explain what Chekhov has said. Explain how his statement relates to your own writing.
   b. Write a scene or two in which you present a class or type of people. Be objective; show what sort of people they are by speaking and thinking in their tone and spirit.
   c. Find an author who, unlike Chekhov, is interested in combining art with a sermon. Consider how he sustains reader interest from scene to scene. Write a full page of explanations. Use specific examples.
   d. Write a statement of your own in which you tell what you hope to accomplish in a short story and the means by which you seek to achieve your goal. Use the Chekhov statement as a pattern if you wish.

5|3

PARTS AND PATTERNS

This chapter will carry you further into ways of constructing a story. It will thus help you understand how story
parts make a pattern. If you look at the parts first, you will
see that they, like the pieces of a puzzle, fit together to make
a total picture or statement. If you find it helpful to look at
the full picture or statement first and then see how the parts
fit in, you'll want to begin by turning to page 267 and reading
"The Death of the Dauphin," a short story that has the
strength and clarity of a parable. If you do begin in that way,
be sure to return to this page and then read through the entire
chapter with an eye to parts and their relation to the total
pattern of a story.

Here are terms frequently used in discussing the short story.
See if you can note a key term missing from the list:

allegory	focus
atmosphere	foreshadowing
cliché	inevitability
climax	irony
coincidence	melodrama
complication	motivation
conflict	objective; subjective
cutback; flashback	parable
dénouement	paradox
exposition	pathos

To be sure, every word on the list is used in discussing and
analyzing the short story. If you are uncertain about any of
these terms, look them up and write out the definition in
your journal. You'll find Abrams's *A Glossary of Literary
Terms* a useful reference.

But as you have noticed, the key term in story construction
does not appear on the list. It has been held out for special

attention and emphasis. The word is "scene." A scene is always what is in front of you in fact or imagination. It's the way we see events, and it's the unit of focus a writer uses to report them. In the short story, as in a play, scene is the basic unit of plot development.

Scene also occurs regularly in poetry. For example, Robert Frost's " 'Out, Out—' "

"Out, Out—"

Scene I: The buzz saw snarled and rattled in the yard
And made dust and dropped stove-length sticks of wood,
Sweet-scented stuff when the breeze drew across it.
And from there those that lifted eyes could count
Five mountain ranges one behind the other
Under the sunset far into Vermont.
And the saw snarled and rattled, snarled and rattled,
As it ran light, or had to bear a load.
And nothing happened: day was all but done.
Call it a day, I wish they might have said
To please the boy by giving him the half hour
That a boy counts so much when saved from work.

Scene II: His sister stood beside them in her apron
To tell them "Supper." At the word, the saw,
As if to prove saws knew what supper meant,
Leaped out at the boy's hand, or seemed to leap—
He must have given the hand. However it was,
Neither refused the meeting. But the hand!
The boy's first outcry was a rueful laugh,
As he swung toward them holding up the hand,
Half in appeal, but half as if to keep

The life from spilling. Then the boy saw
    all—
Since he was old enough to know, big boy
Doing a man's work, though a child at heart—
He saw all spoiled. "Don't let him cut my
    hand off—
The doctor, when he comes. Don't let him,
    sister!"
So. But the hand was gone already.

Scene III: The doctor put him in the dark of ether.
He lay and puffed his lips out with his
    breath.
And then—the watcher at his pulse took
    fright.
No one believed. They listened at his heart.
Little—less—nothing!—and that ended it.
No more to build on there. And they, since
    they
Were not the one dead, turned to their af-
    fairs.

ROBERT FROST

You will note that the poem falls into three scenes. One may argue about the shift of a line here or there; one may suggest that the last sentence marks a new scene—"And they, since they / Were not the one dead, turned to their affairs." But the essential point is clear; a scene is the focus of attention. It's the place where action happens and to which the narrator and reader attend.

You will see how completely story development depends on scene as you read "The Death of the Dauphin." At the same time you will profit by considering each of the points listed below and its relation to scene and story.

Points to Consider

1. Author's point of view
2. Use of detail
3. Use of conversation
4. Use of irony
5. Use of pathos

Your analysis of "The Death of the Dauphin" and perhaps your own story will be clearer if you use the check points below as a guide in considering story structure, for they should help you see what the author has done in laying out his scenes.

Check Points

1. *Title:* A stopper; also carries meaning and in some way summarizes the story.
2. *Actors:* (Usually three)
   - A.   Hero or central character (Dauphin)
   - B.   Opposes A (Death)
   - C.   Foil to avenge A (Chaplain)
3. *Staging, time, place, social background*
4. *Purpose of actor A:* To solve story problem (here: how to meet death) and to deal with alternate solutions that are proposed.
5. *Villain forces*
6. *Factors for success*
7. *Factors against success*

THE DEATH OF THE DAUPHIN

ALPHONSE DAUDET

The little Dauphin is sick; the little Dauphin is going to die. In all the churches of the realm the Blessed Sacrament is exposed night and day, and tall candles are burning for the recovery of the royal child. The streets in the old residence are sad and silent, the bells no longer ring, and carriages go at a foot-pace. About the palace the curious citizens watch, through the iron grilles, the porters with gilt paunches talking in the courtyards with an air of importance.

The whole château is in commotion. Chamberlains, major-domos, run hastily up and down the marble staircases. The galleries are full of pages and of courtiers in silk garments, who go from group to group asking news in undertones. On the broad steps weeping maids of honor greet one another with low courtesies, wiping their eyes with pretty embroidered handkerchiefs.

In the orangery there is a great assemblage of long-robed doctors. Through the windows they can be seen flourishing their long black sleeves and bending majestically their hammerlike wigs. The little Dauphin's governor and equerry walk back and forth before the door, awaiting the decision of the faculty. Scullions pass them by without saluting them. The equerry swears like a heathen, the governor recites lines from Horace. And meanwhile, in the direction of the stables one hears a long, plaintive neigh. It is the little Dauphin's horse, calling sadly from his empty manger.

And the king? Where is *monseigneur* the king? The king is all alone in a room at the end of the château. Majesties do not like to be seen weeping. As for the queen, that is a different matter. Seated at the little Dauphin's pillow, her lovely face is bathed in tears, and she sobs aloud before them all, as a linen-draper's wife might do.

In his lace-bedecked crib the little Dauphin, whiter than the cushions upon which he lies, is resting now with closed eyes. They think that he sleeps; but no. The little Dauphin is not asleep. He turns to his mother, and seeing that she is weeping, he says to her:

"Madame queen, why do you weep? Is it because you really believe that I am going to die?"

The queen tries to reply. Sobs prevent her from speaking.

"Pray do not weep, madame queen; you forget that I am the Dauphin, and that dauphins cannot die like this."

The queen sobs more bitterly than ever, and the little Dauphin begins to be alarmed.

"I say," he says, "I don't want Death to come and take me and I will find a way to prevent his coming here. Let them send at once forty very strong troopers to stand guard around our bed! Let a hundred big guns watch night and day with matches lighted, under our windows! And woe to Death if it dares approach us!"

To please the royal child the queen makes a sign. In a moment they hear the big guns rumbling through the courtyard; and forty tall troopers, halberds in hand, take their places about the room. They are all old soldiers with gray mustaches. The little Dauphin claps his hands when he sees them. He recognizes one of them and calls him:

"Lorrain! Lorrain!"

The soldier steps forward toward the bed.

"I love you dearly, my old Lorrain. Let me see your big sword. If Death tries to take me you must kill him, won't you?"

"Yes, *monseigneur*," Lorrain replies. And two great tears roll down his bronzed cheeks.

At that moment the chaplain approaches the little Dauphin and talks with him for a long time in a low voice, showing him a crucifix. The little Dauphin listens with an expression of great surprise, then, abruptly interrupting him, he says:

"I understand what you say, *monsieur l'abbé;* but tell me, couldn't my little friend Beppo die in my place, if I gave him a lot of money?"

The chaplain continues to speak in a low voice, and the little Dauphin's expression becomes more and more astonished.

When the chaplain has finished, the little Dauphin replies with a deep sigh:

"All this that you tell me is very sad, *monsieur l'abbé;* but one thing consoles me, and that is that up yonder, in the paradise of the stars, I shall still be the Dauphin. I know that the good Lord is my cousin, and that He cannot fail to treat me according to my rank."

Then he adds, turning to his mother:

"Let them bring me my richest clothes, my doublet of white ermine, and my velvet slippers! I wish to make myself handsome for the angels, and to enter paradise in the costume of a Dauphin."

A third time the chaplain leans toward the little Dauphin and talks to him for a long time in a low voice. In the midst of his harangue, the royal child angrily interrupts:

"Why, then, to be Dauphin is to be nothing at all!"

And, refusing to listen to anything more, the little Dauphin turns toward the wall and weeps bitterly.

Assignment 7

I sometimes begin a drawing with no preconceived problem to solve, with only the desire to use pencil on paper and make lines, tones, and shapes with no conscious aim; but as my mind takes in what is so produced a point arrives where some idea becomes conscious and crystallizes, and then a control and ordering begins to take place.

HENRY MOORE
from "Notes on Sculpture"

1. Read the chapter up to this point.
2. In your journal do *one* of the following:
   a. Write a full-page study of "The Death of the Dauphin." Cover each of the five "Points to Consider" given on page 266.
   b. Explain how each of the terms listed at the start of this chapter applies to "The Death of the Dauphin."
   c. Explain the meaning of the title of the Frost poem, " 'Out, Out—'." Then turn one of the scenes from the poem into a scene for a short story. Use dialogue if you wish.

Assignment 8

As your study of "The Death of the Dauphin" shows, everything that happens in a story happens in a scene. The more concrete, the more real you can make your scene, the better your writing will be. The writer's job is to make each scene fit with the others and to report events with such selectivity and sensory accuracy that the reader will feel it all happened to him.

Here are some basic principles that may help you with scene construction. But you'll need to realize before you start that in writing, as in mathematics, you have to work problems to master principles. Just studying won't get the job done. Allow yourself plenty of practice.

Some Basic Rules for Scene Building

1. *Each scene should have a clear purpose and direction.*
   Beginning scenes will move to a crucial situation quickly. These scenes must get our interest, introduce setting and characters, and pose a puzzle or question. Here the main character's problem is given and the reader learns about those traits that will govern all his decisions and actions.
   Middle scenes will develop plot, heighten suspense, and hold off the outcome. The very first attempt at solving his problem must show the chief actor displaying his basic nature and character traits.
   Final scenes will begin when the chief actor makes his last decision. Then we move quickly to a resolution of plot. If the story is sound, the final decision should reflect the chief actor's ability or inability to solve problems. His problems must always be met by solutions consistent with his character.
2. *Each scene should have a dramatic quality.* This may be produced by tension, friction, foreboding, or conflict.
3. *Each scene should be written as honest reporting of sense impression.* Avoid mere cleverness, unreality, and trick surprises. What produced the experience for you? How were your senses involved? Take your reader by the same route.

4. *Plan scenes for significance.* Each scene should contribute to your theme. Don't use scene as filler. Ask: Is it necessary? If not, take it out.
5. *Present scenes as concrete sensory reports.* To build believability, use reliable factual material.
6. *Your final scene should provide a significant appraisal of life.*
7. *Use direct dialogue to present character and to gain interest. Use indirect dialogue to summarize and supply information.*

1. Read the basic rules above.
2. In your journal do *one* of the following:
   a. Explain how "Some Basic Rules for Scene Building" do or do not apply to the story "The Death of the Dauphin."
   b. Write a part (beginning, middle, end) of a short story. Do as much as time allows—certainly a full page—but don't violate your story just to finish the section you started.
   c. Write a scene of direct dialogue. Try to give your characters a natural tone, one that fits their occupation and experience. If time permits, present the same scene without the use of dialogue. Try to make your reader know "the people and the places and how the weather was."

Assignment 9

Pattern in fiction often refers to stories that are developed by formula. Great stories may seldom be written this way, for their inner nature and urgency require them to find a unique statement. Still at the beginning, you are wise not to be too condescending about the pattern or formula story; such stories may strengthen your own sense of structure. By observing pattern stories and by using them for a time as models, you will learn what you must avoid if your story is to have freshness, and at the same time you will discover some ways to turn them into story.

The best way to understand the pattern story is to read a few and then to try your own hand at writing one. In the process you'll come to understand the truth of the expression, "It's easy to watch men mow."

Here are a few basic story patterns:

1. *Purpose-Accomplishment Pattern*. The hero accomplishes his purpose by means of a weapon. Pearl Buck's "The Old Demon" uses this pattern. Other purpose-accomplishment stories have the chief actor accomplish his purpose by means of ingenuity, courage, or some other quality. In all such stories the means by which the chief actor will ultimately solve his problem must be made clear early in the story. This may be done by foreshadowing or by identifying a key physical object. In the case of "The Old Demon" the river is the weapon by which the chief actor's purpose is to be accomplished, and it is introduced at the very start of the story. In weapon stories the goal is usually a physical one as opposed to more subjective goals in other types of stories. But whether the goal is objective (physical) or subjective (value), the reader must early be pointed toward the object or quality that will in the end provide the story solution.

Stories of this general type move from crisis to crisis until bad reaches its ultimate worst. At that point the chief actor is finally able to use that weapon or quality that he possesses —and about which the reader has long known—to achieve his story goal.

2. *Biter-Bit Pattern*. In this pattern the one who would harm his fellow man (the biter or villain) is himself the one to be harmed (bitten). This pattern is expertly managed by Ben Ames Williams in his story "They Grind Exceeding Small."

3. *Purpose-Abandonment Pattern*. In this kind of story the chief actor has his mind made up right from the story's start. He knows what he wants, and he rigidly pursues his goal throughout crisis after crisis. Only in the last crisis, when his goal is within clear grasp, does he discover a better, higher, or new purpose. At that point the story shifts, and events point toward the realization of the new and better goal. An example of this form is "The Blanket" by Floyd Dell (see page 288).

4. *The Decision Story*. In this pattern the chief actor has a

choice to make, but seemingly can't make it. He sees the different goals and is drawn toward each at different times. The reader becomes involved in seeing him pulled by his choices and suffers with him until he makes his final character-revealing decision at the story's end.

The decision story is a variation of the purpose-abandonment form and, like it, is concerned with inner conflict and a struggle to realize values. Both the values and the inner struggle must, of course, be externalized by the narrator and presented dramatically in the story. The difference between the decision pattern and the purpose-abandonment pattern is that in the decision story the chief actor can't make up his mind until the very end of the story, at which point he makes a final, revealing choice; in the purpose-abandonment story the actor makes his choice at the very start. He is not pulled two ways but follows his fixed goal up to the very end, when he shifts to what has been revealed at the last moment as a greater good.

Another way of giving story predictable structure is to center it on eternal themes. For example, there is the character who seeks to avoid his fate and in the end finds that his own flight has taken him to it; examples are *Oedipus Rex* and "Appointment in Samarra."

Another familiar theme is that of tragic reversal. In this form pride leads to a foolish act, and that act leads to the character's downfall (*King Lear*).

If you start looking, you will find that much that you read falls within a pattern and is strengthened by it, but if the pattern itself dominates character and events without regard to their inner nature and necessity, then pattern is destructive, artificial, and to be avoided.

1. Read the discussion of pattern for this assignment.
2. In your journal do *one* of the following:
   a. Consider "Cinderella" and other story types. List the types that come to mind and stories that fit the patterns you have indicated. Write an opening and closing paragraph suited to one of these patterns or types.
   b. Make a full-page journal entry in which you explain

how a particular story (give author and title) fits a particular pattern. Spend only one short paragraph in summarizing the story itself.

c. Construct the frame or outline for a pattern story. Then write one or more of its key scenes.

5|4

FROM PART TO WHOLE

Now our objective is to put story parts together in an intelligent and satisfying way. Perhaps we can best realize our goal by writing rather than depending on abstract discussion. As Robert Gay said,

> Good writing is the product as much of a cultivated taste as of a cultivated intelligence; and we can educate taste only by tasting, not by talking about it. Ten volumes on the flavors of different kinds and grades of tea might not help the tea taster as much as ten minutes' tasting of teas.
>
> ROBERT M. GAY
> from *Reading and Writing*

Here is part of a story. Read it thoughtfully and see if you can identify the parts and the reason for the author's putting them together in just this way.

THE FATHER

BJÖRNSTJERNE BJÖRNSON

The man whose story is here to be told was the wealthiest and most influential person in his parish; his name was Thord Overaas. He appeared in the priest's study one day, tall and earnest.

"I have gotten a son," said he, "and I wish to present him for baptism."

"What shall his name be?"

"Finn—after my father."

"And the sponsors?"

They were mentioned, and proved to be the best men and women of Thord's relations in the parish.

"Is there anything else?" inquired the priest, and looked up.

The peasant hesitated a little.

"I should like very much to have him baptized by himself," said he, finally.

"That is to say on a weekday?"

"Next Saturday, at twelve o'clock, noon."

"Is there anything else?" inquired the priest.

"There is nothing else"; and the peasant twirled his cap, as though he were about to go.

Then the priest rose. "There is yet this, however," said he, and walking toward Thord, he took him by the hand and looked gravely into his eyes: "God grant that the child may become a blessing to you!"

One day sixteen years later, Thord stood once more in the priest's study.

"Really, you carry your age astonishingly well, Thord," said the priest; for he saw no change whatever in the man.

"That is because I have no troubles," replied Thord.

To this the priest said nothing, but after a while he asked: "What is your pleasure this evening?"

"I have come this evening about that son of mine who is to be confirmed tomorrow."

"He is a bright boy."

"I did not wish to pay the priest until I heard what number the boy would have when he takes his place in church tomorrow."

"He will stand number one."

"So I have heard; and here are ten dollars for the priest."

"Is there anything else I can do for you?" inquired the priest, fixing his eyes on Thord.

"There is nothing else."

Thord went out.

Eight years more rolled by, and then one day a

noise was heard outside of the priest's study, for many men were approaching, and at their head was Thord, who entered first.

The priest looked up and recognized him.

"You come well attended this evening, Thord," said he.

"I am here to request that the bans may be published for my son; he is about to marry Karen Storliden, daughter of Gudmund, who stands here beside me."

"Why, that is the richest girl in the parish."

"So they say," replied the peasant, stroking back his hair with one hand.

The priest sat a while as if in deep thought, then entered the names in his book, without making any comments, and the men wrote their signatures underneath. Thord laid three dollars on the table.

"One is all I am to have," said the priest.

"I know that very well; but he is my only child, I want to do it handsomely."

The priest took the money.

"This is now the third time, Thord, that you have come here on your son's account."

"But now I am through with him," said Thord, and folding up his pocketbook, he said farewell and walked away.

The men slowly followed him.

Assignment 10

1. Read the chapter up to this point.
2. In your journal do *one* of the following:
   a. Write the rest of the story.
   b. Summarize what is to happen in the rest of the story and write its ending in full.
   c. Write a full-page journal entry in which you explain the construction of the first half of the story "The Father." Be specific. Identify the chief actor and what you know of his character. Explain the role of the son and the priest. State one or more possible themes the

writer might be trying to develop. Suggest events that might produce character change within the story. What is a central symbol in the story? Are there any worries, or must the ending be presented before we realize their existence?

Assignment 11

A plot is a thousand times more unsettling than an argument, which may be answered. It is not a pattern imposed; it is inward emotion acted out. It is arbitrary, indeed, but not artificial. It is possibly so odd that it might be called a vision, but it is organic to its material: it is a working vision, then.

EUDORA WELTY
from "Must the Novelist Crusade?"

What follows here is the ending of "The Father," which you started in the earlier part of the chapter. Read it and see what the writer has accomplished and how he has accomplished it.

A fortnight later, the father and son were rowing across the lake, one calm, still day, to Storliden to make arrangements for the wedding.

"This thwart is not secure," said the son, and stood up to straighten the seat on which he was sitting.

At the same moment the board he was standing on slipped from under him; he threw out his arms, uttered a shriek, and fell overboard.

"Take hold of the oar!" shouted the father, springing to his feet and holding out the oar.

But when the son had made a couple of efforts he grew stiff.

"Wait a moment!" cried the father, and began to row toward his son. Then the son rolled over on his back, gave his father one long look, and sank.

Thord could scarcely believe it; he held the boat

still, and stared at the spot where his son had gone down, as though he must surely come to the surface again. There rose some bubbles, then some more, and finally one large one that burst; and the lake lay there as smooth and bright as a mirror again.

For three days and three nights people saw the father rowing round and round the spot, without taking either food or sleep; he was dragging the lake for the body of his son. And toward morning of the third day he found it, and carried it in his arms up over the hills to his farm.

It might have been about a year from that day, when the priest, late one autumn evening, heard someone in the passage outside of the door, carefully trying to find the latch. The priest opened the door, and in walked a tall, thin man, with bowed form and white hair. The priest looked long at him before he recognized him. It was Thord.

"Are you out walking so late?" said the priest, and stood still in front of him.

"Ah, yes! It is late," said Thord, and took a seat.

The priest sat down also, as though waiting. A long, long silence followed. At last Thord said:

"I have something with me that I should like to give to the poor; I want it to be invested as a legacy in my son's name."

He rose, laid some money on the table, and sat down again. The priest counted it.

"It is a great deal of money," said he.

"It is half the price of my farm. I sold it today."

The priest sat in silence. At last he asked, but gently:

"What do you propose to do now, Thord?"

"Something better."

They sat for a while, Thord with downcast eyes, the priest with his eyes fixed on Thord. Presently the priest said, slowly and softly:

"I think your son has at last brought you a true blessing."

"Yes, I think so myself," said Thord, looking up, while two big tears coursed slowly down his cheeks.

1. Read the two excerpts for this assignment.
2. In your journal do *one* of the following:
   a. The ending of "The Father" makes use of the previous scenes. In a full-page journal entry explain how all the key parts have been brought into a coherent unit.
   b. One way of moving from part to whole is to begin rereading a story that you know and like. Then at some convenient point stop, and without looking further at the finished story write the rest of it out in your own words. When you have completed your version, compare it with the original.
   c. Outline a coherent and unified story that makes use of the theme used in "The Father." If time permits, write the opening and closing paragraphs of this projected story.

Assignment 12

You writers, choose a subject that is within your powers, and ponder long what your shoulders can and cannot bear. He who makes every effort to select his theme aright will be at no loss for choice of words or lucid arrangement. Unless I am mistaken, the force and charm of arrangement will be found in this: to say at once what ought at once to be said, deferring many points, and waiving them for the moment.

HORACE
from *The Art of Poetry*

But whatever your theme, you still have your story to write. Writing speed varies greatly with individuals, and as we all know, there are good days and bad. Still, you can make far too much fuss about writing a story. For a beginner, it is quite as important to have a story done and fully written as it is to have it perfected. Learning to finish is an indispensable skill, and you'll need to develop it along with your other writing techniques. The historian Samuel Eliot Morison makes an interesting comment on this subject, and though he is talking about scholars and the writing of history, what he says applies to much else—including short-story writing.

A few hints as to the craft may be useful to budding historians. First and foremost, *get writing!* Young scholars generally wish to secure the last fact before writing anything, like General McClellan refusing to advance (as people said) until the last mule was shod. It is a terrible strain, isn't it, to sit down at a desk with your notes all neatly docketed, and begin to write? . . . Half the pleas I have heard from graduate students for more time or another grant-in-aid are mere excuses to postpone the painful drudgery of writing.

There is the "indispensablest beauty in knowing how to get done," said Carlyle. In every research there comes a point, which you should recognize like a call of conscience, when you must get down to writing. And when you once are writing, go on writing as long as you can; there will be plenty of time later to shove in the footnotes or return to the library for extra information. Above all, *start* writing. Nothing is more pathetic than the "gonna" historian, who from graduate school on is always "gonna" write a magnum opus but never completes his research on the subject, and dies without anything to show for a lifetime's work.

SAMUEL ELIOT MORISON
from By Land and By Sea

Here is a comment by William Saroyan. His story-a-day is a tour de force you need not feel obliged to duplicate, but it may put your own writing problems—real or imagined—in helpful perspective:

With neither a sense of loneliness nor of *withness*, the short stories in my first book were written at the rate of one, two, or three a day for a period of thirty-three days in a small room overlooking the street, in a second-floor flat at number 348 Carl Street in San Francisco, in January, 1934.

They were meant to be a demonstration.

First, the writer, at that time unpublished and sick of it, wanted to find out from editors and publishers what happens when a new writer comes along who can write a great many kinds of short stories. Is he published, or not?

The writer was without money, and in all truth without character, too, in that he wanted no part of any achievement outside of writing. He didn't want to be a writer, either, for the simple reason that he *was* a writer; he had been a writer the better part of his life.

What he wanted was to be published.

During the thirty-three days of writing, about thirty-nine short stories were written and dispatched daily to the editors of *Story* magazine, since they had finally (around Christmas) accepted one story.

The writer informed the editors that he was going to write a new short story every day for a month.

The month of January is a good time to take off on such a program. It is the first of the year, and if all goes well, the year could turn out to be a good year at last.

The writer wanted also to demonstrate that there is probably no end to the kind of stories one writer may write; that the form is inexhaustible.

WILLIAM SAROYAN
from *Saturday Review*

1. Read the material for this assignment.
2. In your journal do *one* of the following:
   a. Write your own stories' first paragraphs.
   b. Write as much of your own short story as time permits.
   c. Pick your own story model and set about writing a full imitation of it. Do as much as time permits. Try to catch the tone of the original. (See Unit 1, "Learn from Models," for a review of this technique.)

5|5

TELL YOUR TALE EFFECTIVELY

Have you ever had the experience of trying to tell another person a joke or relate an event that interested you only to discover he wasn't listening, missed the point, didn't think it was funny, or just couldn't see what you thought was so great? It's a deflating experience in everyday life, but when it happens to your fiction, it's fatal. You have lost your reader. There is no going back and explaining again. In a story each line counts only if it is strong enough to support reader interest.

How can narrative disaster be avoided? Actually, there is no formula for narrative success, but there are useful guide lines that will keep most stories right-side up and between the fences all the way home. These guide lines are simply the "Major Rules of Rhetoric," and as such apply to essays and letters, fact and fiction; they are the rules that govern the effective use of words. Learn the rules. Then when you want to tell a story, set the gauge to fiction and imaginatively adjust for individual story differences. The point in fiction is to make your stories come true, but that only happens when your story takes on a life of its own in the imagination of your reader. Here are the rules that will help it happen.

The Major Rules of Rhetoric

1. Interest your reader.
   a) Aim at imaginative penetration of subject.
      (1) Go beyond the obvious.
      (2) Seek to see into the soul of your topic.
   b) Select significant detail.

      (1) Fix your reader's attention on the point you are going to make.

      (2) Master the narrative hook—i.e., transition between paragraphs.

  c) Engage the senses.

  d) Show, don't tell.

  e) Keep it crisp; keep it clear.

      (1) Avoid the high-flown and verbose; omit the glittering generality.

      (2) Use the concrete and particular word.

  f) Have a point and make a point in sentence, paragraph, and story.

2. Continue to interest your reader.

  a) Avoid the trite in expression and idea (cut stereotyped phrases, jargon, deadwood, redundancy, clichés, circuitous expressions, the passive voice).

  b) Enrich by metaphor and allusion.

  c) Use sentence variety for interest; use contrast of idea for emphasis. Adapt the rules to story by allowing for variety in character, conversation, and scene; emphasis may be achieved by showing a marked difference between what is expected and what is received.

  d) Control tone by diction.

      (1) What do you wish to imply?

      (2) Aim at accuracy in connotation; consider the emotional tone of every word.

  e) Link paragraphs; interlock sentences.

  f) Use your own voice. Write so that when it's read, it sounds like you.

3. Continue to continue to interest your reader.

  a) Edit and revise.

      (1) Sharpen your language and order.

      (2) Make corrections and additions.

  b) Revise and edit.

      (1) Polish (delete irrelevancies; check paragraphing).

      (2) Put the paper in final form.

So much for rules, but rules are deceptive; rules suggest ends achieved when in fact they only point to goals desired. For example, it's quick and easy to say "Number 1: Interest your reader. Rule 1e: Keep it crisp; keep it clear." But the problem is whether you can do either or both. Of course you can—at least to some degree, but only through self-awareness and practice can you learn to do it better. Recite the rules, think about them, but most of all, apply them.

Here is a brief essay that shows you how to make a point and how to use some of the rules. See if you can identify which ones it illustrates. In all you read, watch the rules at work. See if you can find ways to make them serve you and your own stories.

Once upon a time I had occasion to buy so uninteresting a thing as a silver soup-ladle. The salesman at the silversmith's was obliging and for my inspection brought forth quite an array of ladles. But my purse was flaccid, anemic, and I must pick and choose with all the discrimination in the world. I wanted to make a brave showing with my gift— to get a great deal for my money. I went through a world of soup-ladles—ladles with gilded bowls, with embossed handles, with chased arabesques, but there were none to my taste. "Or perhaps," says the salesman, "you would care to look at something like this," and he brought out a ladle that was as plain and as unadorned as the unclouded sky—and about as beautiful. Of all the others this was the most to my liking. But the price! ah, that anemic purse; and I must put it from me! It was nearly double the cost of any of the rest. And when I asked why, the salesman said:

"You see, in this highly ornamental ware the flaws of the material don't show, and you can cover up a blow-hole or the like by wreaths and beading. But this plain ware has got to be the very best. Every defect is apparent."

And there, if you please, is a conclusive comment upon the whole business—a final basis of comparison of all things whether commercial or artistic; the bare dignity of the unadorned that may stand before the world all unashamed, panoplied rather than clothed in consciousness of perfection. We of this latter day, we painters and poets and writers—artists—must labor with all the wits of us, all the strength of us, and with all that we have of ingenuity and perseverance to attain simplicity. But it has not always been so. At the very earliest, men—forgotten, ordinary men—were born with an easy, unblurred vision that today we would hail as marvelous genius. Suppose, for instance, the New Testament was all unwritten and one of us were called upon to tell the world that Christ was born, to tell of how we had seen Him, that this was the Messiah. How the adjectives would marshal upon the page, how the exclamatory phrases would cry out, how we would elaborate and elaborate, and how our rhetoric would flare and blazen till—so we should imagine—the ear would ring and the very eye would be dazzled; and even then we would believe that our words were all so few and feeble. It is beyond words, we should vociferate. So it would be. That is very true—words of ours. Can you not see how we should dramatize it? We would make a point of the transcendent stillness of the hour, of the deep blue of the Judean midnight, of the liplapping of Galilee, the murmur of Jordan, the peacefulness of sleeping Jerusalem. Then the stars, the descent of the angel, the shepherds—all the accessories. And our narrative would be as commensurate with the subject as the flippant smartness of a "bright" reporter in the Sistine chapel. We would be striving to cover up our innate incompetence, our impotence to do justice to the mighty theme by elaborateness of design and arabesque intricacy of rhetoric.

But on the other hand—listen:

"The days were accomplished that she should be delivered. And she brought forth her first-born son, and wrapped him in swaddling clothes, and laid him in a manger; because there was no room for them in the inn."

FRANK NORRIS
"Simplicity in Art"

Assignment 13

1. Read the chapter up to this point.
2. In your journal do *one* of the following:
   a. With the rules in mind, revise a previous journal entry.
   b. Write a brief analysis of the rules that are illustrated in the essay "Simplicity in Art."
   c. From memory, write a Bible story. Then compare your version with the story as told in the Bible.

Assignment 14

The story "The Blanket," which follows, offers its own illustration of the rules. As you read this assignment, try to identify some of the key points at which the rules work.

"The Blanket" by Floyd Dell is a story with a universal theme. What themes are going unused in the life around you? You may find a sense of pleasure and community by joining those benefactors of humanity who from the start of time have interested, amused, and informed their listeners by being themselves, tellers of tales. Now is your chance, but first read the story.

THE BLANKET

FLOYD DELL

Petey hadn't really believed that Dad would be doing it—sending Granddad away. "Away" was what they were calling it. Not until now could he believe it of Dad.

But here was the blanket that Dad had that day bought for him, and in the morning he'd be going away. And this was the last evening they'd be having together. Dad was off seeing that girl he was to marry. He'd not be back till late, and they could sit up and talk.

It was a fine September night, with a silver moon riding high over the gully. When they'd washed up the supper dishes they went out on the shanty porch, the old man and the bit of a boy, taking their chairs. "I'll get me fiddle," said the old man, "and play ye some of the old tunes." But instead of the fiddle he brought out the blanket. It was a big, double blanket, red, with black cross stripes.

"Now, isn't that a fine blanket!" said the old man, smoothing it over his knees. "And isn't your father a kind man to be giving the old fellow a blanket like that to go away with? It cost something, it did—look at the wool of it! And warm it will be these cold winter nights to come. There'll be few blankets there the equal of this one!"

It was like Granddad to be saying that. He was trying to make it easier. He'd pretended all along it was he that was wanting to go away to the great brick building—the government place, where he'd be with so many other old fellows having the best of everything. . . . But Petey hadn't believed Dad would really do it, until this night when he brought home the blanket.

"Oh, yes, it's a fine blanket," said Petey, and got up and went into the shanty. He wasn't the kind to cry, and, besides, he was too old for that, being eleven. He'd just come in to fetch Granddad's fiddle.

The blanket slid to the floor as the old man took the fiddle and stood up. It was the last night they'd be having together. There wasn't any need to say, "Play all the old tunes." Granddad tuned up for a minute, and then said, "This is one you'll like to remember."

The silver moon was high overhead, and there was a gentle breeze playing down the gully. He'd never be hearing Granddad play like this again. It was as well Dad was moving into that new house, away from here. He'd not want, Petey wouldn't, to sit here on the old porch of fine evenings, with Granddad gone.

The tune changed. "Here's something gayer." Petey sat and stared out over the gully. Dad would marry that girl. Yes, that girl who'd kissed him and slobbered over him, saying she'd try to be a good mother to him, and all. . . . His chair creaked as he involuntarily gave his body a painful twist.

The tune stopped suddenly, and Granddad said: "It's a poor tune, except to be dancing to." And then: "It's a fine girl your father's going to marry. He'll be feeling young again, with a pretty wife like that. And what would an old fellow like me be doing around their house, getting in the way, an old nuisance, what with my talk of aches and pains! And then there'll be babies coming, and I'd not want to be there to hear them crying at all hours. It's best that I take myself off, like I'm doing. One more tune or two, and then we'll be going to bed to get some sleep against the morning, when I'll pack up my fine blanket and take my leave. Listen to this, will you? It's a bit sad, but a fine tune for a night like this."

They didn't hear the two people coming down the gully path, Dad and the pretty girl with the hard, bright face like a china doll's. But they heard her laugh, right by the porch, and the tune stopped on a wrong, high, startled note. Dad didn't say anything, but the girl came forward and spoke to Granddad prettily: "I'll not be seeing you leave in the morning, so I came over to say good-by."

"It's kind of you," said Granddad, with his eyes cast down; and then, seeing the blanket at his feet, he stooped to pick it up. "And will you look at this," he said in embarrassment, "the fine blanket my son has given me to go away with!"

"Yes," she said, "it's a fine blanket." She felt of the wool, and repeated in surprise, "A fine blanket —I'll say it is!" She turned to Dad, and said to him coldly, "It cost something, that."

He cleared his throat, and said defensively, "I wanted him to have the best. . . ."

The girl stood there, still intent on the blanket. "It's double, too," she said reproachfully to Dad.

"Yes," said Granddad, "it's double—a fine blanket for an old fellow to be going away with."

The boy went abruptly into the shanty. He was looking for something. He could hear that girl reproaching Dad, and Dad becoming angry in his slow way. And now she was suddenly going away in a huff. . . . As Petey came out, she turned and called back, "All the same, he doesn't need a double blanket!" And she ran up the gully path.

Dad was looking after her uncertainly.

"Oh, she's right," said the boy coldly. "Here, Dad"—and he held out a pair of scissors. "Cut the blanket in two."

Both of them stared at the boy, startled. "Cut it in two, I tell you, Dad!" he cried out. "And keep the other half!"

"That's not a bad idea," said Granddad gently. "I don't need so much of a blanket."

"Yes," said the boy harshly, "a single blanket's enough for an old man when he's sent away. We'll save the other half, Dad; it will come in handy later."

"Now, what do you mean by that?" asked Dad.

"I mean," said the boy slowly, "that I'll give it to you, Dad—when you're old and I'm sending you —away."

There was a silence, and then Dad went over to Granddad and stood before him, not speaking. But Granddad understood, for he put out a hand and laid it on Dad's shoulder. Petey was watching them. And he heard Granddad whisper, "It's all right, son —I knew you didn't mean it. . . ." And then Petey cried.

But it didn't matter—because they were all three crying together.

1. Read the material for this assignment.
2. In your journal do *one* of the following:
   a. Write an analysis of "The Blanket" in which you show how the author let the rules help him tell his tale.
   b. Write another version of "The Blanket." You may change the characters, the blanket, anything but the theme.
   c. Find your own story and start to tell it.

Assignment 15

I think the best writing is often done by persons who are snatching the time from something else—something that is either burning them up, as religion, or love, or politics, or that is boring them to tears, as prison, or a brokerage house, or an advertising firm.

from *An E. B. White Reader*
edited by W. W. Watt and R. W. Bradford

The war was terrible and brutal, and there were many atrocities. Also, I think the fact that I wrote these stories in prison had a great influence on their mood. I wrote *Legends* and *Realities*—my publisher changed the title to *The Leper and Other Stories* because he thought it would sell better. I wrote *Legends* during my first imprisonment, from 1956 to 1961. I was in solitary confinement for 20 months, it was very cold, and I wrote with gloves on my hands, on toilet paper. I didn't get writing paper for two years.

MILOVAN DJILAS
quoted in "A Literary Conversation
with Milovan Djilas"
by Thomas J. Butler

Our final story for study is one written by a student. Through this story you may be encouraged to look about you and find in the events of everyday life the material of fiction.

If there is any final advice, perhaps it's this: observe, reflect, write.

THE SILERS

ERIC BEST

The Silers' house was just off the narrow frost-scarred road that crept downhill under an arch of maple trees. At the dip where it started up again to lose itself in the darkness of the pine woods beyond, it met their graveled and grass-tufted driveway. He went to see them almost every day, and if he missed one, he tried to go twice another time. He was seldom formally invited but he felt they wanted him to come as often as he wished, for the number of cokes they kept in the corner of the kitchen never dwindled. Perhaps it was strange that a small boy of nine should so enjoy a couple five times his age, but Mr. Siler liked little league baseball and (although Mrs. Siler read books he couldn't understand) the conversation, albeit over his head at times, was steady enough to prevent the prolonged silence that so often hangs between two generations.

Jamie's parents let him go as often as he wished, provided the lawn was mowed and his room was tidy. He resented the various chores, not because he felt his responsibilities were unfairly put upon him, but because summer work seems like drudgery for a small boy. The drone of the lawnmower would fill the hot stillness of the summer afternoon until he would finally finish, and then, pulling his bicycle from the barn, he would coast down the dark shaded road to pedal up the Silers' driveway and announce he had finished the lawn, a fact they already knew from the silence. Then he would get a coke from the small kitchen and spend five minutes hunting for a can opener that always seemed to be hung in a different place. Mr. Siler would usually come to find it for him, and they would walk outside to the terrace to relax together, Mr.

Siler with his beer and Jamie with his coke.

He didn't always understand the Silers, and perhaps it was this that fascinated him the most. Mr. Siler, short and slight, knew all about Babe Ruth and knew who had the best spitball in the National League when Lefty Gomez was in his prime. But his knowledge extended to and beyond *The New York Times* crossword puzzles, which he completed faithfully, and Jamie had the feeling that there was far more in his mind than he let out to him. When they refloored the living room together, Mr. Siler bent far fewer nails, something Jamie attributed first to his age, then to his philosophy of life. Jamie had no idea what exactly someone's philosophy of life was, but he sensed that when people sat alone and looked serious, more went through their minds than variations on a curveball. He saw Mr. Siler like that often, a curl of steely smoke licking up around his two fingers from the cigarette constantly pinched between them, and he wondered what made his face lose its smile.

When his thoughts of Mr. Siler turned to his seriousness, he inevitably began to think of Mrs. Siler. His mother had told him she was sick, but it was a sickness everyone seemed to be afraid of and so never discussed. Because it had a funny name that he couldn't remember he seldom thought about it, but on hot days when she lay quietly in front of the fan he couldn't ignore her obvious misery. The longer she was forced to stay on the couch, the less uncomfortable he became about her incapacity, and he began to invent little things to do to amuse her, trying to disrupt the boredom he knew he would feel if he were in the same position. She read great thick books about things people think about, and occasionally the kind of mysteries his sister read. He would sit across the room trying to read one of her books (an occupation that demanded more patience of him than he could usually muster during the afternoon), and watch her, her eyes distorted by the thick lenses of her glasses, as she balanced the book on her stomach and slowly turned the pages. From time to time she laid the book on its back to reach for a cigarette and light it. As the summers went by, it took her longer and longer to pick the cigarettes up, take one out, and snap her lighter with enough force to ignite it. So he began to light them for her, and found himself pleased not only by the excuse he had found for doing something forbidden, but also by the knowledge that she was more comfortable if she did not have to do it herself.

He understood the way the Silers treated him— like a guest whose familiarity was such that he no longer needed to be treated as one. He did as he was told, but usually tried to do things before that became necessary. He talked to them about anything that interested him, usually what occupied his time when he wasn't with them. When he was nine and first knew them, his major concern was baseball, but as he grew older and started going out with girls and being with many other people, he felt that what he told them interested them more. Their interest grew, he thought, not because they hadn't been interested before, but because the older he became, the more he recounted experiences that they could recall from their own childhoods. For Mrs. Siler, anyway, any departure from the routine that her life had become relieved her boredom greatly, and he enjoyed telling her what he had been doing. She would lay her book down on her stomach and demand that he sit and tell her all he had done over the weekend he had spent away. And so he would recount all the things that had seemed strange or amusing to him, hoping they might seem the same to her and that she would enjoy hearing them. She usually did, and she used to amuse him with her reactions to some of the situations he had managed to get in. Her reactions used to make him wonder what she had done as a girl. The only contact he had had with the younger years of either of them came from the wedding pictures that hung on the wall. Hers made her appear gay and even frivolous, her face framed by a floppy white hat, her mouth in a wide smile that he could never really remember seeing on her face. Mr. Siler's picture had the same creative effect— creative because it was the picture of another man —not only a man who bore the characteristics of youth, but a man whose immediate association with it and its thoughtful carelessness seemed greater than any other force within him. The Mr. Siler Jamie had come to know somehow betrayed the fact that the little picture was the picture of him as he *had been*—someone passed, perhaps even someone destroyed—but in any case, someone who no longer existed. Jamie had suddenly found the explanation for Mr. Siler's seriousness. For the seriousness was not so much the presence of something, as it was the absence of the happiness that Jamie as a little boy sensed should somehow appear in everyone. And as usual, the consideration of Mr. Siler's seriousness brought him back again to thoughts of Mrs. Siler.

Mrs. Siler's sickness no longer needed a name. Jamie grew into the realization that its progress was even more frighteningly steady than he had first suspected. The halting steps he could remember her taking had become more of an accomplishment and less of a habit, and as her incapacity increased, her ability to accept it lessened. Her complaints had once struck him as irritating and often unnecessary, but he found his objection sprung from his feelings for Mr. Siler. Jamie had enough male instinct to resent seeing Mr. Siler inevitably do as Mrs. Siler wished, for he felt somehow he was jeopardizing his dignity. He had seen irritation on Mr. Siler's face more than once when he was forced to put aside his paper to get her a glass of water or another pack of cigarettes that she could undoubtedly do without, and he wished that somehow she could know it was unfair to constantly demand things of him. But Mr. Siler's compliance was usually so amiable that no doubt she never suspected how he might feel.

Yet sometimes Jamie himself was not so sure how Mr. Siler felt about the constant needs of his wife. He had built her a makeshift birdfeeder that hung in view from her couch, and never let it empty—he knew enough about New England to know that probably the most interesting visitor to it would be a sparrow, but he wanted to entertain her in any way he could. Despite his own amusements (which were little more than crossword puzzles, gardening, and radio baseball games), Mr. Siler was constantly within call of his wife, and would run to her, when, in the last summer of her illness, her bell told him that she had discovered something else she needed. His devotion almost approached the point of servitude, yet Jamie never remembered a remark that betrayed any feelings of resentment.

Jamie's thoughts drifted to the last summer they came—it was the last summer, because after she was gone there was no need to seek the coolness of the New England woods. She was quieter that summer, less complaining anyway, perhaps because the pain in her legs destroyed whatever desire she might have had to talk. The birds interested her more then than he remembered their having done before, and the flowers Jamie's mother periodically brought from their garden made her much happier than he thought flowers usually made people. She read even more than she had previously, and it was unusual for him to see her without a book in her lap. Jamie was sad that summer, not because he sensed it was the last, but because he never heard her say anything appreciative to her husband. That she knew all Mr. Siler did for her he was sure, but he could not help wishing she would tell him all that it meant to her. Perhaps she did tell him— Jamies hoped so, for later that year when he heard she had died, he hoped not too much had been left unsaid.

1. Read the material in this assignment.
2. In your journal do *one* of the following:
   a. Rewrite a previous journal entry.
   b. Write an outline or summary of the story by Eric Best. Then consider what he did to give the events reality. Be specific. If time permits, outline or summarize a relationship with adults from your own childhood; consider the story potential of that relationship.
   c. Start a story based on a childhood experience.

5 | Review

By now you may have discovered that fifteen journal entries are not enough to make you a skilled writer of short fiction, but at the same time, you should be encouraged with the progress you have made, for throughout the entire book you have worked to improve as both reader and writer. Now, if the work has been done, if you have read the chapters and written the assignments, your reward is a heightened awareness of what goes on in a sentence, in a paragraph, and in a story.

But remember, assignments are only guideposts; the journey is yours. By now you have gained considerable skill in finding your own way, and you have been exposed to the journal habit long enough to make it your own. Now, write every day! You will find no better review exercise. In the words of Epictetus, "If you wish to be a writer, write."

Review Assignment

As a start on this final, open-ended, lifetime project, do any one or all three of these assignments in your journal:

a. Shape your own writing by keeping a daily anthology of thoughts and passages taken from your reading. These selections may serve as models for imitation or emulation. Give complete source information for each selection. Each quotation should present a statement that you personally find interesting. Also, be on the lookout for and include in your journal any comments about writing that you find useful or stimulating.

b. Write a long short story that represents you at your intellectual and literary best.

c. Write a full-page journal entry every day for two weeks. Make each of the entries an original passage that is either serious or humorous in tone.

I can't remember who said it, but I don't think you can escape that very tired old maxim, "If you want to be a writer, write." It's no good escaping to a sanctuary in Cornwall or Cape Cod; it's no good planning and daydreaming; the thing to do is write. Only the heat of discipline and effort will let the person know whether he should or should not go on wanting to be a writer. And only such discipline and effort will produce a writer of real merit. The second thing I think a writer must do is to involve himself in the stream of life, take part, do a job—too many youngsters feel that a job is beneath the dignity of a writer. Perhaps the time does come, when the writer has accumulated enough resources, that he should go off and write exclusively. But to write about life one must know something about it, and the demands of a job, working with and for a variety of persons, is an important way to develop this knowledge.

MAURICE EDELMAN
quoted in *Counterpoint*
by Roy Newquist

Look sharply after your thoughts. They come unlooked for, like a new bird seen on your trees, and, if you turn to your usual task, disappear; and you shall never find that perception again; never, I say —but perhaps years, ages, and I know not what events and worlds may lie between you and its return!

RALPH WALDO EMERSON

Index

of Authors and Titles

Very brief excerpts are indicated by an asterisk (*) preceding their page numbers.

A 1
B 2
C 3
D 4
E 5
F 6
G 7
H 8
I 9
J 0